Hotel and Catering Supervision

General Editor

Dr. Edwin Kerr
*Chief Officer, Council for National
Academic Awards*

Subject Editor

D. Ashen
*Head of Department of
Hotel and Catering Studies
Plymouth College of Further Education*

Hotel and Catering Supervision

KEN GALE
BA (Hons.), Cert.Ed.
Lecturer, Plymouth College of Further Education

PETER ODGERS
FHCIMA, DMS, Cert.Ed.
Senior Lecturer, Westminster College

PITMAN PUBLISHING
128 Long Acre, London WC2E 9AN

© Macdonald & Evans Ltd 1984

First published 1984
Reprinted 1987

British Library Cataloguing in Publication Data
Gale, Ken
  Hotel and catering supervision.
  1. Food service management—Great Britain
  2. Hotel management—Great Britain
  I. Title II. Odgers, Peter
  647'.95'068   TX911.3.M27

ISBN 0 273 02816 2

Photoset in Times by
Northern Phototypesetting Co, Bolton
Produced by Longman Group (FE) Ltd
Printed in Hong Kong

Preface

The concept of hotel and catering supervision has changed in recent years owing to the growth of the industry, increases and changes in the amount of legislation regarding employment, continued recognition by government and financial institutions and improvements in technology. Managers and supervisors in the industry therefore have to be trained and educated to meet these developments.

In the last few years human and economic aspects of the industry have become an integral part of all courses offered to both craft and management students, first through HCIMA and National Diploma courses and in more recent years through TEC (now BTEC) Diplomas and Higher Diplomas. Craft students are now also able to study for BTEC Certificates in Food Production and Service or Accommodation Operations either to supplement or in place of City and Guilds courses.

Following the modular structure of BTEC courses this book has been written to cover the five core units—communication, human relations, supervisory studies, personnel practice and procedures and commercial and economic aspects of the industry—for BTEC Certificates, Diplomas and the bridging span of Higher BTEC Diplomas. In addition, the book will also cover the business and supervisory studies, the industry and management aspects of the HCIMA examinations Parts A and B, including the greater input of supervisory studies now required by the recently restructured syllabus for Part A.

Consideration has been made in the writing of the book to accommodate the new BTEC programmes to be introduced in 1985 as well as topics not contained in either BTEC or HCIMA syllabuses which the authors feel are important for a supervisor or manager to understand in order to carry out their duties effectively.

Finally the authors would like to dedicate this book to their wives, Linda and Joanna, by way of thanks for their encouragement and tolerance during its writing. Special thanks must of course go to Joanna Odgers for her painstaking efforts in typing the script.

1984   KG
PO

Contents

CHAPTER ONE

The Development of the Hotel and Catering Industry

CHAPTER OBJECTIVES

After studying the chapter you should be able to:
* understand the needs that created the industry;
* understand the development of the industry.

THE INDUSTRY DEFINED

Before we examine the history and development of the hotel and catering industry, we must establish some form of definition which covers its
wide scope. To establish such a definition it may be best to examine
other definitions. The Hotel Proprietors Act 1956, section 1, defines a
hotel as "an establishment held out by the proprietor as offering food,
drink and if so required sleeping accommodation, without special contract, to any traveller presenting himself who appears able and willing to
pay a reasonable sum for the services and facilities provided, and who is
in a fit state to be received". As far as a definition is concerned for the industry it may be far removed from reality; however the key words "to
any traveller" does lead us to a definition of a traveller – "any person on
a journey from one place to another, however short or long". This
implies that a hotel must provide accommodation, food and drink to
any person who is away from home.

As we are all well aware, in order to live, it is necessary to sleep,
eat and drink; this we all do in our own houses. However from time to
time it may be necessary to spend some time away from our homes;
hence the need for places for travellers to sleep, eat and drink. The more
people travel, the more they are away from home and therefore the
greater the demand for accommodation and places of refreshment.
Different people have different needs with regard to sleeping, eating,
and drinking, this being examined more fully in Chapter Eighteen.
These needs have to be catered for and consequently the industry has
provided them.

People spend time away from home for the following reasons: to
work or for other business purposes; to go to school or college; to go
shopping; for leisure or recreational purposes; and to go into hospital or
prison. In all these situations they will require either accommodation or

food and drink, or both. It is therefore reasonable to assume that the provision of these needs has created an industry, with a common aim to supply accommodation, food and drink where and when required.

The hotel and catering industry as it is described today only found its title in the 1940s with the passing of The Catering Wages Act in 1943 and the Standard Industrial Classification 1948. The 1948 classification included:

(a) hotels and other residential establishments;
(b) restaurants, snack bars, etc;
(c) public houses;
(d) industrial and staff canteens.

It is interesting to note that institutional catering was not included, this being the provision of accommodation and food in hospitals, educational establishments, the armed forces and other institutions, i.e. in general in non-profit making establishments.

Various other classifications such as the Standard Industrial Classification 1958 and the Board of Trade Enquiry 1964 included catering in institutional establishments if it was operated by outside contractors. However the Economic Development Committee 1966 included all aspects of institutional catering. It is with this classification that the industry may be best described, although there have been some subsequent alternative classifications by the Standard Industrial Classification 1968 and the Hotel and Catering Industrial Training Board in 1968.

HISTORY OF THE HOTEL AND CATERING INDUSTRY

We have established that people need accommodation, food and drink whilst away from their home, either through necessity or for recreational purposes. As transport and social needs have developed from ancient civilisation through to modern times so the industry has responded to meet those needs.

Early travel

From early civilisation to the mid-sixteenth century the only form of transport available was either on foot or horse-back, although wagons were used by merchants to transport their wares. The Romans built roads between the main cities and towns of the time, along which posting houses known as *stabuli* were set up to provide lodging, food and drink. All towns at this time had ale houses which only provided drink. When the Romans left and up until the end of the eleventh century, these roads, posting houses and ale houses were left to decay or were destroyed. The only travel during this period was of an essential nature by messengers and merchants who were accommodated in monasteries and abbeys. Royalty and other dignitaries were accommodated in the nearest castle or manor and their entourage in local houses.

At the end of the eleventh century pilgrimages increased people's travel and broadened their horizons, even though most of the accommodation was still provided by religious houses. Catering on a large scale was provided in the castles and manor houses for noblemen, travellers and tenants alike, although there was segregation between the classes. It is said that Richard II provided, at his own expense, meals for some 10,000 people every day. By the fourteenth century the inn was well established in London and other large towns, with ale houses and taverns in smaller towns. Such buildings were often only sheds, although purpose-built stone buildings had begun to appear, in which food was provided for travellers, together with a free bed. Legislation was brought in to control the number of establishments, the prices they charged and the contents of foodstuffs and wine.

Towards the end of the sixteenth century travel increased more rapidly through merchants using wagons as a form of transport and the use of the horse-drawn carriage for the nobility. To cater for this need a network of posting houses of Tudor design was constructed. These posting houses provided changes of horses, accommodation, food and drink for travellers. Their design was based on a central courtyard with stables surrounding them and rooms above for horsemen. Dignitaries had more luxurious rooms in the main house.

Stage coach travel

As the population grew, and consequently trade with it, the seventeenth century saw the development of stage coach travel, until there was a stage coach network radiating from London to all points of the compass. Demand grew for inns and competition developed between innkeepers as to the service they provided. The inns also changed character; as well as providing for the traveller they were used as social meeting places and by businessmen to carry out their transactions.

The latter part of the seventeenth century also saw the development of coffee houses, firstly in Oxford and then in London. These coffee houses gained in popularity due to the fact that they did not discriminate between sex or class, they offered cakes and pastries and also provided a social meeting place. At the same time, the spa towns of Bath, Buxton, Tunbridge Wells and Epsom developed as holiday resorts for the wealthy. This was due to stage coaches making travel quicker and more comfortable.

Stage coach travel became even more popular throughout the seventeenth and eighteenth centuries, and this popularity led to improvements in roads and the building of inns along all routes. By the nineteenth century travel by stage coach was much faster due to regular horse changes, and the setting up of the mail service had resulted in an ever-expanding network of roads. The industrial revolution increased demands for trade, and with this increase in trade people became more wealthy and wanted to travel. To cope with this demand more inland resorts such as Malvern and Cheltenham developed for health reasons, also providing leisure and recreation facilities.

The changes in demand created by the industrial revolution helped improve standards within the industry and developed a commercial market that bridged the gap between the classes. Hotels originated in Paris and Switzerland in the latter half of the eighteenth century. The first hotels as such in the UK were built in the late eighteenth and early nineteenth centuries in London and Edinburgh and offered luxurious accommodation and service to their customers.

Seaside resorts became fashionable during this period for both medical and recreational purposes. Eastbourne, Brighton, Bognor Regis and Torquay became holiday resorts at this time, with hotels being built to accommodate the more wealthy classes. Boarding or lodging houses were built for the middle classes, who were expanding rapidly as a social group because of the wealth created by the industrial revolution.

As London grew as a centre for commerce and business the demand for coffee houses grew. This demand became more specialised as the professions used them more and more, and led to private clubs being established in which the different professions could meet and do business. With the development of coffee houses and the increase in the sale of more substantial food in them, the inns and taverns were gradually transformed into selling alcoholic liquor only. Legislation was subsequently introduced to control these premises due to increased drunkenness and alcoholism.

Railway travel

The railway had a revolutionary affect on travel simply because it was quicker, cheaper and more comfortable. The first commercial railway was built in 1830 and by the end of the century a whole network had been built up throughout the country. The affect it had on the hotel and catering industry was to reduce the demand for inns as travellers changed from road to rail, the inns becoming either local ale houses or private dwellings. Hostels were built on railway termini, not only at the London mainline stations but also in the provinces, accommodating many more people than previously in a more ostentatious style. Seaside resorts grew, firstly in the south of England at Bournemouth and Torquay, followed by the emergence of Blackpool and Southport in the north. These resorts and others closer to London became popular for day trips by the working classes as well as for longer holidays by the middle classes.

Steamship travel

The late nineteenth century also saw the development of the steamship, which stimulated the building of luxury hotels in major European cities in order to accommodate the wealthy travellers. By now London was the centre of wealth in the world and was visited by foreign travellers who demanded more luxurious amenities and more intense services. To cope with this demand the Savoy Hotel was opened by D'Oyly Carte in 1889 and managed by Cesar Ritz, to be followed by the Hotel Cecil in 1896, Claridges in 1898 and the Carlton in 1899. Whilst these hotels were built to meet the demand created by European visitors, the wealthy classes in this country became regular patrons of the hotels, due to the continental cuisine and service offered which had hitherto not been known. The term "restaurant" came into use at this time, replacing "dining rooms" or "dining halls". Those who used private clubs for accommodation and refreshment now transferred their allegiance to the new hotels and restaurants, one influence on this being that clubs tended to be bastions of male society, whereas the hotel or restaurant accepted women. The shops, cafes and commercial restaurants became popular places to eat out for the less-wealthy classes at this time. The first Lyons teashop opened in 1894.

Motor car travel

The twentieth century saw the emergence of the motor car; by 1914 there were over 130,000 on the road. Motor cars gave an independence of travel to their owners and thus competed with the railways. Because of this the roadside inn returned to popularity, and guest-houses and hotels were opened in more remote tourist resorts to cater for the independent traveller who did not have to rely on the set tracks of the railway as a direct result of motor travel. Trust Houses were founded in 1903, setting up throughout the country.

First World War

The industry suffered a great setback during the First World War, due to hotels being commandeered for soldiers' billets and hospitals, the imposition of food rationing, government controls on fuel, and manpower being diverted to the war effort. Industrial catering started in the munitions factories with the object of providing the workforce with adequate nourishment. However such catering for the worker lost its impetus after the war and almost faded out until the late 1930s.

The social and economic changes of the 1920s and 1930s

After the First World War there was a short period of prosperity created by the postwar boom, during which the industry continued to develop. This development was moderated to a certain extent by temperance campaigns and Bills introduced by Parliament, and there was an air of discontent as the working classes wanted better standards of living and employment rights. This led to the General Strike in 1926 and was followed by the great economic depression making the early 1930s a difficult time for the industry due to its reliance on economic prosperity.

Developments took place in motor cars, motor coaches and air travel in the mid and late 1930s as the country began to recover from the economic depression. Employees were given better working conditions, which included the provision of meals at work, more pay and holidays with pay. These developments enabled the industry to recover quickly and it expanded in all areas. Air travel, including regular air services to Europe and, later, the USA, increased the demand for luxury hotel accommodation and resulted in the Dorchester, Grosvenor House, Mayfair, Cumberland, Strand Palace and Park Lane hotels opening between 1927 and 1932. The ocean liner *Queen Mary* was launched in this period, providing a high level of luxury for overseas travellers and the US tourist market.

Mass production of motor cars reduced their costs and made them available to a greater cross-section of the population, thus increasing travel and holidays and in doing so creating more hotels and catering establishments. The use of motor coaches became more widespread for touring holidays for the working classes, who now had more money and holidays with pay. The working classes also put a demand on the industry to supply recreation and holidays to suit their needs, which resulted in holiday camps being opened at seaside resorts by Billy Butlin in the late 1930s.

Second World War

The Second World War had a similar effect on the industry as the First, with premises being commandeered, food supply restrictions and manpower being recruited. The effect on industrial catering was, however, beneficial, with government legislation requiring factory owners to provide meals for staff and communal restaurants being used to ensure that the population had one hot meal per day. There were over 25,000 industrial and staff canteens in use by the end of the War.

The effects of the Second World War

The War had taken its toll on the nation, and the country had to build for the future. However technology had advanced, one of the good things to come out of the War being the development of the jet engine and air travel. From 1945 to 1950 the country consolidated itself, having learnt from the War. As for as the catering industry was concerned, industrial catering was now well established and a spin-off from this was the setting of the school meals service. The welfare service too was being established, free medical care for all, which in turn involved the development of hospital catering.

The setting up of the British Tourist and Holidays Board in 1947 and the British Travel and Holidays Association in 1950, to promote the UK as an overseas tourist market, contributed to the organisation of the Festival of Britain in 1951 which generated massive business for the hotel industry. This period also saw the industry as we know it today establishing and organising itself with regard to education, training and promoting itself.

THE DEVELOPMENTS OF THE 1950s, 1960s AND 1970s

With the industry now established this period saw the emergence of the large-scale hotel and restaurant companies such as Grand Metropolitan and Fortes, together with the continued growth of Trust Houses. The government and commerce generally realised the potential of the tourist market and its contribution to the economic well-being of the country. Because of this, finance was made available and various organisations set up to promote the country in the late 1960s, e.g. the Hotel Development Scheme in 1968 and the tourist boards.

Air travel
In 1957 transatlantic air travel exceeded sea travel for the first time, due to the creation of tourist class air fares a few years earlier. The following year, 1958, saw the introduction of the first jet service from London to New York; by this time there were more than a million overseas visitors coming to the UK each year. The first jumbo jet come into operation in 1970. This increase in air travel put new demands on the industry, and hotels opened at London's Heathrow Airport in 1960, catering specifically for the short-stay guest and introducing new systems into hotel operation to cope with the vast numbers of people checking in and out. The Hilton Hotel opened in London in 1963 and several other US companies started to develop their interests here. Heathrow Airport became the centre of airline catering for the world, producing over a million meals per day for in-flight catering services. This method of catering, using prepacked foods and microwave ovens, developed a whole new technology in foods and equipment available for all areas of the industry, leading to the fast food services available today.

Motorway travel

The demand for fast travel and the continued development of the car led to the motorway network which was opened with the M1 in the late 1960s. Just as in Roman times the road network led to *stabuli* being opened, so the motorway led to the development of motels where motorists can park their cars close to their rooms for a one-night stop. Motorway services also expanded to cope with the vast numbers of people seeking refreshment and developed new systems and equipment to cope with such demands. The development of the motorway inevitably saw a decline in the use of the railway and a subsequent decrease in the use of railway catering services.

Hovercraft and ferry services

The development of continental travel with more people taking cars on to the Continent, has created a similar effect to that of the motorway in the provision of refreshments on cross-Channel ferries, hovercrafts and at the ferry ports.

CONCLUSION – THE FOOD AND DRINK INDUSTRY TODAY

Today there is an increased accent on leisure and the multicultural world we live in, while the commercial sector of the industry in this country has developed into a whole range of different types of establishment providing food and drink.

The provision of food now satisfies a wide range of gastronomic, economic, ethnic and convenience needs or tastes. Restaurants or similarly-titled establishments tend to be national in the type of product they sell to provide for our multinational range of tastes. The increase in foreigners living or holidaying in this country and, likewise, the British travelling overseas has increased the demand for and acceptance of our and their cuisines. With this increase in acceptance so the price has dropped, so that it is now possible to eat in a cheap French restaurant — something that always used to be regarded as expensive in this country. A wide variety of choice is also available, including the choice of being adventurous or of eating a standard product in a nationally-owned chain of restaurants. The modern restaurant world has given us both standardisation and individuality in food and because of our increased culture we accept both.

The provision of drinks in establishments has been a part of our social history, although it tends to be more dependent on trends than the provision of food, reflecting the essential nature of eating as opposed to the social nature of drinking. The ale house still exists, but the late 1960s and 1970s saw the development of wine bars and in the late 1970s and early 1980s cocktail bars emerged. More recently some public houses have changed to become family entertainment centres incorporating wine and cocktails amongst their facilities. Some traditional ale houses are now reintroducing brewing on the premises which represents a complete circle in their development since the eighteenth century. Whilst ownership of public houses is now more restricted to the breweries, what competition there is is fierce and has forced them to change and re-change their image. To a certain extent their custom has been equally fickle, being dictated by the economic climate and the disposable income that the customers have.

SELF-ASSESSMENT QUESTIONS

1. Explain the needs for the industry.
2. List reasons why people stay away from home.
3. Explain the types of accommodation that were available for travellers before this century.
4. Explain why holiday resorts developed.
5. Explain the influence the coffee shop had on the industry.
6. Explain the effect the World Wars had on the industry.
7. Explain the long term effect that the General Strike and economic depression had on the industry.
8. Explain the demands that the jet aeroplane put on the hotel industry.
9. List reasons for the expansion of restaurants and public houses in recent times.

CHAPTER TWO

Communication Techniques

```
CHAPTER OBJECTIVES
After studying this chapter you should be able to:
* define communication;
* distinguish between the various forms of communication;
* explain the function of communication within an
  organisation;
* explain the process of communication.
```

INTRODUCTION

In day-to-day, face-to-face contact between individuals it is usually possible, with care, to work out whether communication is taking place between two individuals. Certain processes and behaviour patterns will occur which will tell us that the "message is getting across", that "the point has been taken". We will hear the "communicator", the person passing on the message, speaking in a familiar language, using various tones and expressions to convey the meaning of the words that he is using. Similarly, the person who is listening will be receiving the message and will demonstrate this by using certain signs and adopting various expressions.

We may not be happy that the "message" has been correctly conveyed — it may not have been taken in the intended fashion — so therefore we may use various means of ensuring that the message has been transmitted as intended. Simple questions may suffice: "Is that clear?" or "Do I need to explain further?" To obtain certainty, more specific questions may be directed: "Repeat the directions to me to ensure that your have have them right."

COMMUNICATION – A DEFINITION

In all this simple face-to-face human exchange of ideas and information we say that communication is taking place. Effective communication is taking place when understanding is achieved — when the message is getting across. Communication, then, is the means by which individuals:

(*a*) pass on information to one another;
(*b*) pass on understanding to one another.

It can be achieved in a variety of ways: through speaking and listening; by writing and reading; and through a whole range of non-verbal expressions which we often use without even thinking about them, e.g. nudging, winking and pointing. In all of these forms it is essential that at least two people are involved, otherwise communication is not taking place.

In addition, communication involves intention. When we communicate we intend to put across a particular message and may be disappointed if we are not successful in this aim. Similarly, when we are in a position to obtain a particular message we normally intend to receive that message. Thus the protester carrying a placard containing a comment or slogan about nuclear arms or the laboratory treatment of animals intends to put across a message. In the same way a young person sitting in a classroom listening to a lecturer describing methods of cost and stock control has an intention to learn. In both of these situations, however, the intention to communicate is not always successful. The CND poster may only be glanced at by a few people and the student in the classroom may not be able to keep his eyes open because his evening bar job is too tiring.

COMMUNICATION SKILLS

It is important therefore to talk about communication skills; the means by which we transmit and receive information and ideas more effectively. It is necessary to improve our communication skills because not only is it necessary that understanding is achieved but also, as a result of communication, that action usually takes place. If communication at work is ineffective then the desired action is unlikely to take place; the incorrect interpretation of a meal order means that a customer is likely to be dissatisfied with his meal. Thus efficiency at work will not be achieved unless effective communication takes place.

It is important therefore to concentrate upon communication skills and to ensure that all members of the catering workforce are equipped to communicate effectively with all other members of the workforce with whom they operate. Without this interplay of communication the aim of providing an efficient service to customers will not be achieved. No matter what job we are talking about — hotel manager, chef, housekeeper or kitchen porter — communication has to take place between a variety of people, at a variety of levels and for a variety of purposes.

COMMUNICATION IN THE ORGANISATION

So far we have considered the way in which communication takes place between individuals on a face-to-face basis. We sometimes call this human interaction, where action of some form is occurring between people.

We must now consider the way in which communication takes place within an organisation. We are no longer simply talking about face-to-face , person-to-person communication but the way in which communication takes place amongst large groups of people.

Many small units exist in the catering industry where direct person-to-person communication may take place, but we must consider what happens when information and ideas have to pass through a complex organisation such as a large industrial catering establishment or a chain of luxury hotels. Anyone who has played the party game "Chinese Whispers" will be aware of the problems involved in passing on information of a relatively basic kind to a large number of people. Distortion inevitably occurs, with some often amusing results. However when a communication chain operates in a large catering establishment, when orders are being passed down from a higher authority, great care must be taken to ensure that distortion of the original instructions or directives does *not* take place. Such distortion can often be prevented by writing down the information to be passed along, but often this is not wholly successful in preventing some form of distortion, e.g. the way in which a memorandum is written may sometimes be such that its "tone" or style of writing offends the reader and the desired effect is not achieved. Considerable skill is therefore required in communication to ensure that the intended message is transmitted.

We have briefly considered the kinds of problems that may be encountered as a result of inefficient communications taking place within the organisation. We now need to consider how these problems may be overcome. A chain or series of chains of communication will exist within an organisation and the complexity of the organisation will normally determine the complexity of the chain.

Thus a large luxury hotel with many different departments, sections and functioning parts is likely to have a complicated system or chain of communication which may incorporate a diverse range or different links. These might include daily departmental heads' meetings carried out, perhaps over breakfast, with the purpose of ensuring company policy is being carried through. They may involve the chef de cuisine delegating various duties to the various sous chefs and chefs de partie, or they may involve the head hall-porter telephoning the hotel engineer or outside contractor to say that one of the lifts is faulty. These are three extremely simple examples that represent small items in the overall daily functioning of a large hotel, but if they are not carried out carefully, with due attention and application of the relevant communication skills, then inefficiency is likely to occur.

Therefore our discussion of the way in which communication takes place within the organisation must first of all deal with what is actually involved in communication. We need to examine what is involved in every link in a chain of communication. We will consider then the process of communication.

THE PROCESS OF COMMUNICATION

If one person effectively communicates with another—if messages are transmitted and understanding is achieved—then we say that a process of communication has taken place. We can break down this process into a number of component parts as follows.

The intention of the sender

An intention to communicate on the part of the "sender" has to exist. In other words an individual must have an idea, a set of information, a set of orders or instructions to pass on or convey to another individual or group of individuals. In simple terms the process of communication will not begin unless there is a "message" to send. The meaning of this message will need to be clear, i.e. it will be pointless to formulate a set of instructions to give to operatives if it will not be possible for them to carry them out within the required time or to the required standard. Careful consideration must then be given to the content of the message. We should ask ourselves: "What is it I am trying to say?" "What information do I want to communicate?" "What orders do I want to give?"

The language of communication

Having carefully formulated the "message" and what it will contain, the sender must now consider the most suitable means of getting the message across to his audience.

The means by which a particular message is conveyed needs careful consideration, as different forms have strengths and weaknesses. The language used is therefore important and a variety of different types exist which we may use. In everyday usage we tend to use what we term informal language, where the general tone is relaxed, where certain mannerisms or slang terms might perhaps be permissible and often where many meanings may be taken for granted. The use of this "informal" language tends, however, to be restricted to those individuals who are familiar with its usage. Thus the slang and casual mannerisms of one group may not be fully understood by another and successful communication is less likely to be achieved. (We will see in Chapter Four the way in which informal communication can be beneficial to the organisation of the workplace.)

Formal language can, however, be used in a variety of specific contexts. The type of language used will be more elaborate than the informal type, in the sense that greater and more detailed explanations are likely to be used in order to "get the message across". An example of formal language might be the language used by judges, barristers and solicitors in a court of law. In this situation informal language could not be used because of the danger of misinterpretation and therefore misuse of certain ambiguous statements. Legal language therefore is very specific, using terms which carefully describe certain details and which are less likely to be misconstrued.

Formal language also embraces a whole spectrum of different types of technical language, the use of which is necessary for clear communication to take place in a particular technical field. If a restaurant, for example, specialises in the preparation and presentation of haute cuisine food in the traditional French style, then it will be necessary for the kitchen staff and food service staff to be aware of and be able to use culinary French in order to communicate both with one another and with customers who may be making enquiries about the menu. In this context culinary French is a necessary form of technical language to be used to ensure that dishes are prepared exactly as specified in the traditional style.

The implementation of computer technology in many fields of industry requires that industry must come to terms with the language of computers. The catering industry is no exception to this and, where computer systems are being introduced, staff who are using these systems will need to be able to use the formal language of computer technology. A hotel receptionist will need to be familar with the various codes on her computer terminal so that she may quickly and accurately obtain information that will enable her to tabulate a customer's bill. A catering lecturer will need to be able to interpret the meanings of terms such as N$, REM and DIM if he is to be able to use the most basic program for storing and updating examination questions.

Whenever detailed and complicated tasks have to be carried out where specialist knowledge has to be conveyed with the minimum amount of ambiguity then the use of an appropriate formal language will be necessary to ensure that this is successfully achieved. Thus formal language will be used in the business world, by the legal profession, by those with specialist skills and in areas where a high degree of technical accuracy is necessary.

The medium of communication

When we have formulated the "message" in a given language which is appropriate to the field we are working in, we have to consider the most suitable medium or means by which we can transmit our message. For example, if the message we are referring to is a set of fire drill instructions to be issued to all staff in a hotel, then it is important that we use a medium which is most likely to reach the largest number of staff possible. Direct face-to-face transmission might be considered, but where specific procedures are involved such as the use of fire exits and contacting the fire brigade we have already seen that distortions can occur. Placing a detailed set of instructions on a well-placed notice board would avoid any major distortion of fact or ambiguity of meaning, but notices of this kind often have a tendency to be overlooked. Perhaps a more suitable medium to send the fire drill instructions would therefore be a means of personal memorandum to all members of staff, thus reducing the likelihood of ambiguity and increasing the likelihood of reaching all staff.

The above example illustrates the need to consider carefully the medium or channel through which our message is conveyed. If a wrong choice is made then the careful formulation of the original idea or set of information and the use of a particular kind of language will be wasted. A carefully conceived and sensibly-worded industrial relations policy put together by the management of a large industrial catering company may well be badly received if it is circulated to staff on a photocopied sheet which is poorly printed and contains no personal touch. However, if management call a meeting or a series of meetings with the workforce designed to outline that policy and explain in detail the way in which they expect it to operate then it is more likely to meet with a favourable reception. Consideration of the size of the organisation clearly plays a large part in deciding upon the most effective method of communication. In face-to-face communication, problems of choosing a medium of communication are not normally found. Indeed, in small units of operation such as a small guest house direct face-to-face interaction will probably suffice. However, when we are talking about large-scale organisations we must carefully consider the method, means or medium of communication.

Receiving the message

The previous three stages in the process of communication have mapped out the development of the original idea or set of information on the part of the sender. The second stage in the process entailed making a decision on the most suitable kind of language to be used and the third stage involved a consideration of the most suitable medium through which the message or original idea could be transmitted. The fourth stage in this process changes the initiative from the sender of the message to the receiver of the message.

In simple terms the receiver must be in a position to receive. This will involve listening or reading or, more broadly, being aware that a message is being conveyed. This appears to be a relatively uncomplicated stage in the process of communication; the receiver simply has to be able to listen to the sender, who perhaps is giving out instructions, or perhaps to read a memorandum from head office.

However the receiving of information is a skill which requires effort, concentration and often a great deal of hard work. Even the most conscientious student will realise how difficult it sometimes is to listen to a lecturer after a very long day in the classroom. Similarly, no matter how interested an individual might be in a particular piece of literature, sometimes the activity of reading causes considerable problems. Thus a particularly important communication skill is being able to place yourself in a position to be able to receive information, i.e. to be receptive to the information that is being transmitted. This involves concentrating on the powers of reading, listening and general awareness and placing yourself in a position to be able to receive information; in other words you must have an intention to receive the message.

Interpretation of the message

We saw in the second stage of the communication process the importance of formulating our message in an appropriate language, whether formal or informal, everyday or technical. The fifth stage is a test of how successful the sender has been in sending the message in a suitable language and how well the receiver can apply himself to actually understanding the message in the language it has been sent. Some examples may illustrate this point more clearly.

We will first of all take the case of informal language. If for example two friends are speaking in a local dialect about a job they are carrying out, then the language they are using is informal but restricted to those who know how to use it. They are likely to understand each other's meanings, but an outsider who is not familiar with the local dialect may well find certain words and phrases difficult to understand and therefore may be excluded from fully understanding all that is being exchanged in the conversation.

Similar problems will be met when we are considering formal language. The use of culinary French in the restaurant kitchen, for example, will fulfill a specific function. If the various chefs de partie are not fully familiar with culinary French then certain meanings will be misconstrued and dishes may well be prepared incorrectly.

A hotel receptionist unfamiliar with the language code of the computer terminal at the receptionist desk may well misunderstand certain symbols and miscalculate a customer's bill.

In all three of the above examples the receiver may have the best intentions to receive the message but because of not being completely familiar with the language being used a communication breakdown will occur. With the best will in the world the receiving of information as intended by the sender is often beyond the means of the receiver. It is not sufficient simply to give instructions or orders; it must be possible for that person who is receiving those instructions or orders to understand them and be able to interpret them in the intended manner.

Communication and action

The final stage in the process of communication actually tests out whether or not the process has been successful; to use a simple example the "proof of the pudding lies in the eating." A simple demonstration of whether a message has been understood or not is the action that results from it. If the safety officer of a large luxury hotel gives fire drill instructions to all staff and guests telling them to use fire exits and to muster in the hotel forecourt, and in the emergency all the staff and guests congregate in the hotel foyer causing much confusion and chaos, then clearly a breakdown in the chain of communication has occurred.

The receiver of the information at this final stage will act or respond in a certain kind of way, indicating to the sender of the information that the message has been correctly or incorrectly interpreted and therefore whether the process of communication has been successful or not. There are many ways of establishing whether or not information has been received and understood; some sort of "feedback" usually provides this indication. If the information given out is a set of orders or instructions and they are acted upon in the desired manner then successful communication has been achieved. We often carry out exercises in understanding or comprehension to ensure that communication has been successful. We may ask simple questions such as "Do you understand?" or "Are you sure you follow my reasoning?" If we are not happy with the response—an unconvincing nod or perhaps a muttered "Yes" we may press the individual further. We may ask for a brief demonstration of understanding or suggest a "trial or practice run" to see if the receiver of the information really does understand what has to be done. The whole process of education and training entails these kinds of activities and in the final analysis students will demonstrate their understanding or the ability to learn by partaking in phase tests or examinations.

In order to assess whether or not successful communication has been achieved, understanding is constantly checked. Informally, we constantly require reassurance that other people have obtained our meaning; we request feedback by questioning "Are you with me?", "Do you follow?", "Is that all right?" Similarly, in more formal contexts we require some sort of response that indicates understanding; this may range from students in the classroom completing comprehension exercises in a range of spoken, written, visual, graphical and statistical material to junior management trainees applying months of classroom training in manpower management techniques or quality control to a real-life practical working situation.

CONCLUSION

Constant appraisal is therefore required to assess whether communication has been successfully achieved and constant attention is required to ensure that each stage of the process of communication has been successfully completed.

It is therefore necessary to be alert and aware of all the pitfalls that may befall all of us when we attempt to communicate—giving and receiving instructions; applying suitable telephone techniques; writing memoranda, business letters and notices with careful attention to layout, style and tone; dealing with the general public in a manner that demonstrates confidence, politeness and efficiency; and generally being able to come to terms with each stage in the process of communication and to act according to the demands of each of those stages.

So far we have largely concerned ourselves with the way in which an individual affects the communication process and how the efficiency of that process is dependent upon the behaviour of the individual. We are concerned with human behaviour in the catering industry and therefore we now need to consider in detail the nature of communication as it operates in a variety of working situations within the industry. In the next two chapters we shall examine in detail the way in which the communication process operates within an organisation.

SELF-ASSESSMENT QUESTIONS

1. Write a clear definition of communication.
2. With reference to the organisation of a hotel, explain what you understand by the term "a chain of communication".
3. Distinguish clearly between formal and informal language.
4. Explain the advantages and disadvantages of formal language.
5. Describe the importance of "feedback" to the process of communication.

CHAPTER THREE

Communication and the Formal Organisation

CHAPTER OBJECTIVES

After studying this chapter you should be able to:
* define a formal organisation;
* describe the way in which communication takes place through the formal organisation;
* explain the relationship of the individual and the formal organisation.

INTRODUCTION

We need to examine the nature of formal organisations before we can establish how communication operates within them. We may define an organisation as an organised system within society. Further, we need to ask what is this state of being organised? The word has its origins in biological systems. The human body, for example is made up of a number of organs—the heart, the liver and the spleen—all of which are interdependent and all of which have have specialised functions to carry out to enable the human body to operate. If the human body malfunctions in any way then doctors and physicians need to analyse our bodily organs to find the origins of the malfunction. The functional interdependence of the various specialised bodily organs creates an organic whole, giving us an identifiable structure and a capability to carry out certain tasks or bodily functions.

Just as the human body is organised and made up of inter-related and interdependent functioning parts, so a group of individuals is brought together for a specific purpose, to carry out specific tasks and fulfill certain objectives; in other words to be part of an organisation.

We need now to describe in detail the various factors that are relevant to an understanding of the structure and operation of any formal organisation.

FORMS OF CONTROL

Any organisation will be set up and controlled by an authority. This authority may take many forms: it may be the government or it may be a private body; it may be in the form of an individual or it may be a group of controllers, i.e. what is sometimes known as a business consortium. Whatever form this authority takes it will normally be finally responsible for the running of the organisation and will have a considerable financial interest in its success or failure. So within the organisation there may be individuals or groups with forms of authority or control—the management team for instance—but the final decisions will in some way reflect the wishes of the controlling authority. For example a monthly catering magazine will be run by a team of journalists, editors, feature writers, guest columnists, typesetters and so on. This team will organise and control the contents of the magazine, making decisions about the layout, space given to certain features, coverage given to a trade exhibition and so on. If, however, the magazine begins to lose money or perhaps to print articles that are in some way offensive to the controller, then it is likely that he would exercise his authority over the magazine's editorial team suggesting alternative ways of running the magazine.

Control therefore often takes place in a hierarchical manner and, as we shall see later in our analysis of leadership, it entails delegation, coordination and giving out of responsibilities. Figure 1 should illustrate that, when all is running smoothly in the formal organisation, the need for the intervention of the major controlling influence—the chief executive, the major shareholder or the company director—as in the example above should not be necessary. Therefore the distinction is sometimes made between allocative control, where the final decision e.g. the allocation of more funds for buying new equipment, or appointing a new management team, rests with the controlling authority, and organisational or operational control, where decisions are made within the organisation regarding such things as personnel policy.

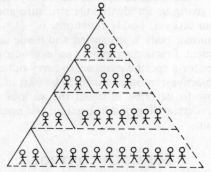

Fig. 1.   *Various levels of operational control.*

For example, a chain of international hotels may well be individually operated and controlled by a relatively independent management who will be responsible for achieving acceptable levels of profitability, for hiring and firing staff and generally maintaining the standards desired. However, should any hotel in this chain be seen to be consistently falling short of the required standards then it is likely that its management team would be made aware of its shortcomings and, if improvements were not made, then the possibility of replacement would presumably be considered.

OFFICIAL RULES

Any formal organisation will incorporate a set of official rules which will be laid down and designed to ensure that the organisation runs smoothly and efficiently. These official rules will describe the guidelines to which all individuals working within the organisation will have to adhere. They will specify a diverse range of acceptable and unacceptable ways of doing things and for the organisation to be effective the rules must be followed by all those who work within the organisation.

Official rules are therefore written down and may be referred to on any occasion should disputes arise regarding correct procedure. Thus, in the same way that any member of society must adhere to the laws of that society, any member of an organisation must abide by the rules of that organisation. Equally, in the same way that the government makes the laws of society, the owners or controlling authority of the organisation will specify the rules of the organisation. To take the comparison one stage further, should an individual break the laws of society, then he will receive an appropriate punishment; in the same way an individual within the organisation who breaks the rules is also open to some form of punishment.

Clearly it is important that the rules which determine the running of the organisation are practical, realistic and up to date. Without these considerations staff will find the rules hard to abide by. For example, rules laid down by a hotel regarding standards of dress amongst staff may well be inappropriate in the light of contemporary fashion and impose an unreasonable restraint on the members of staff concerned. Obviously, considerations of health and hygiene will be of paramount importance in this situation, but much ill-feeling amongst staff can be created if the rules regarding appearance are based upon prejudice rather than reason.

Sensitivity to the rules of an organisation is therefore important, not only on the part of the staff who have to abide by them but also by the employers and management who make and apply them.

THE NATURE OF RULES

The need for a system of rules within an organisation then is undeniable.

We need to establish what form these rules will take and how we may describe them.

Small-scale organisations

The catering industry embraces many small operational units and it is quite likely that in many of these the rules will not be so rigidly defined and adhered to as they might be in a larger organisation. The reason for this is simple. In a small operational unit such as a seaside guest-house or a small family restaurant there is often an informal working atmosphere, an interchange of duties and a relatively relaxed working environment. In such an environment the imposition of strict or inflexible rules may well cause resentment and bitterness amongst the staff. Staff working in such an environment tend to enjoy the relaxed atmosphere and work much more efficiently as a consequence. Quite simply, the working environment has a "personal" touch which may be damaged by management imposing more rigid working guidelines. The whole process of communication is therefore much more likely to operate on a face-to-face basis, with the use of memoranda, notices and official literature being inappropriate. Control by management is likely to be informal instructions being passed on by word of mouth and staff being allowed to work in relaxed conditions rather than having to be constantly aware of time schedules and management supervision.

The informality of this type of control is based upon mutual trust, a sense of responsibility and a close working relationship with management; the need for strict formal controls in the form of rules is less likely to arise. Thus, although official rules will always exist, the statement and expression of these rules will vary between establishments.

Large-scale organisations

We may contrast the informality of the small-scale organisation with the formality of the large-scale organisation. In the latter a need develops for a set of clear, concise official rules and procedures which are written down and leave the minimum of doubt or ambiguity. When the scale of an operation increases it is usually linked with an increase in the number of staff. When this occurs, the relationship between the different levels has to be defined and clearly specified, otherwise overlapping, duplication and ill-feeling may develop.

A division of labour

In a large-scale organisation a division of labour exists whereby all the staff are divided up into certain specialist areas. Thus within a large hotel the kitchen brigade, the reception team and the housekeeping staff will all represent specialist areas. Similarly, within the kitchen brigade itself a form of division of labour exists between sous chefs and the various chefs du partie.

Official rules will operate not only to ensure that these divisions are maintained but also to ensure that they are realistic, that they are up to date and that they do not impose unnecessary restrictions upon the workforce. This division of labour provides a specific set of rules for each department within the organisation, each section and each individual. Thus, as we shall see in a later chapter (see page 101) an individual may be given a job description which will detail exactly his or her area of operation, i.e. a set of rules to guide behaviour. The contrast with the individual employee in the small seaside guest-house who helps with food preparation, waits at the tables and helps with the weekend changeover is very clear. In fact this kind of overlapping of duties in a large operation would probably cause chaos, confusion and inefficiency. A night cleaner employed at a large hotel to clean the grill-room area would probably be responsible for cleaning the floor, the bar, fixtures and furnishings and for wall maintenance. If she then found, for example, that in the bar area all the rubbish and empty bottles had been cleared away, ash trays emptied, the floor of the bar mopped or vacuum cleaned, the woodwork and the brass footrail at the bar polished, she is likely to be somewhat confused as to what exactly her duties are. Clearly, in this situation an overlap of rules between the night cleaning staff and the grill-room bar staff exists which, if allowed to continue, will cause confusion, inefficiency and, possibly, bad feeling between the staff concerned.

Official rules then must be carefully constructed to ensure that such a situation as described above does not occur. In a large organisation rules have to be, by definition, of a technical nature and impersonal. They are technical in that the organisation is designed to operate like a machine which is made up of a number of interconnected functioning parts, each having a specific task to carry out. The rules describe the way in which this takes place. They are impersonal because they are designed to apply to all or any individuals who may work in the organisation, irrespective of their individuality or personality. The rules describe the job to be carried out and therefore tend to be more concerned with the goals of the organisation than the goals of the individual. We shall see later, however, that a consideration of the needs of the individual is also important if the organisation is to operate effectively.

THE INDIVIDUAL AND THE FORMAL ORGANISATION

We have so far considered forms of control within the formal organisation, the role played by official rules and the way in which these operate within different organisations. No organisation can function without individuals and we therefore need to examine the individual in the specific context of the formal organisation. In this context we will examine what the formal organisation demands from the individual rather than vice versa. This will provide us with a further insight into the way in which communication occurs within a formal organisation.

The personnel officer of a large luxury hotel, the staff supervisor of an industrial catering operation or the proprietor of a small village public house will each have an "idea" of the kind of individual they require to carry out a particular job. With the formal organisation it will be necessary to specify and make clear what the requirements of the individual are rather than simply to have an idea of the kind of individual that may be wanted.

We have seen that the formal organisation has certain rules which provide guidelines for behaviour within it. Individuals must therefore be selected so that they can fit into these guidelines quite comfortably. In the same way that a given job can be defined in terms of duties, responsibilities and procedures, so can individual requirements be defined to fit a particular job. It will be necessary that an individual possesses some or all of the following to enable him to carry out a particular job:

(a) qualifications;
(b) experience;
(c) relevant skills.

We will examine each of these in turn to demonstrate their relevance to the formal organisation.

Qualifications

It will be necessary for qualifications to fit a particular job. In the vast majority of cases if an individual is either over-qualified or under-qualified for a particular job he will not be as successful at that job as the individual who possesses the appropriate qualifications. Cases do exist of poorly-qualified individuals making excellent hotel managers and university graduates in English literature making excellent kitchen porters, but these are exceptional cases rather than the normal or average case.

The qualifications an individual possesses must be seen to "fit" a particular job. A given qualification denotes a level of expertise in a certain area which may be used as a means of increasing an individual's suitability for a particular job in the formal organisation. Therefore, we would normally expect that a junior hotel receptionist would be in possession of the City and Guilds 709 certificate before taking up a particular position. Similarly, a management trainee taken on by a group of industrial caterers would be expected to have successfully completed the BTEC ordinary, and possibly higher diploma courses.

Qualifications do not necessarily indicate all aspects of an individual's intellectual capacity and overall capabilities, but they do provide a yardstick which enables us to place the individual at the appropriate level within the formal organisation. We can say, quite simply, that an individual, by possessing certain diplomas and certificates, is qualified to take up a position in the formal organisation.

The achievement and possession of some qualifications may also provide us with an indication of the character of the person who possesses them. A general catering student, for example, applying for a post as a commis waiter at a large luxury hotel, and who, in addition to his City and Guilds 706/1/2 certificates, also possesses some BTEC units which he has studied for in addition to his basic studies, may well be viewed in a favourable light by the panel who are interviewing him. Possession of such additional qualifications indicates keenness, enthusiasm and conscientiousness. In addition it probably demonstrates that the student is willing to work hard, take on extra responsibility and will be a valuable acquisition for the food service team. His possession of BTEC certificates will also contribute to his ability to communicate more effectively with other staff members at different levels and in different departments within the organisation of the hotel. The successful completion of a human relations or personnel practices unit, for example, will increase his practical knowledge of the value of incentive schemes in different managerial approaches which otherwise may have been unknown to him. Such knowledge may well provide him with a promotional stepping-stone when he has gained sufficient experience in his own particular field.

The above example should demonstrate the value of qualifications both to the individual who possesses them and to the organisation he works in. Ideally, a qualification should symbolise a level of attainment and ability and provide an indication of the suitability of an individual to carry out a particular task.

Experience

The previous section emphasises that qualifications can provide an indication of an individual's abilities. However, until that individual has the opportunity to put into practice what he learned in theory in the classroom and the demonstration kitchen in an actual working situation, it may be argued that he is inexperienced.

Experience therefore is something which develops with time and after application to tasks in a variety of appropriate situations. We therefore talk of "relevant experience", i.e. experience which has been gained which is appropriate to the particular task the individual may be involved in or the position he may be applying for within the organisation.

Hotel management represents an area where experience is essential. It will be necessary that the general manager of a hotel be experienced in aspects of the establishment he is engaged in running and organising. Such a range and depth of experience will aid in such diverse areas as budgeting for the summer season, working out staff rotas, ordering food supplies and so on. Many managers will possess qualifications which will not only be relevant to the various positions they take up but also will often represent high academic attainment. However, unless these qualifications can be applied in the wide range of practical real-life situations he will meet in the actual day-to-day running of the hotel then he will be unlikely to succeed.

As we shall see in later sections, experience not only makes an invaluable contribution to the ability of a manager but it also plays a large part in the communication process which takes place in any catering establishment and which is essential for its successful operation. Experience of human relations will improve the ability of any individual in the workplace to communicate more effectively. Put in simple terms, contact with, and understanding of, a wide range of individuals will enable more effective communication to occur as the need arises in the future. Communication skills can be improved.

Possession of relevant skills
We can see from the previous section that the possession of communication skills is of extreme importance in any working situation where interplay and liaison between individual workers is necessary. The catering industry is characterised by a wide range of such relationships which can occur on a variety of levels.

The employer–employee relationship
The catering industry is made up of a large number of small owner-operated establishments, the exclusive restaurant, the seaside guesthouse and the small family hotel being good illustrations. Attention to communication skills in these working situations will be essential; casual comments or misunderstood meanings can produce tension between the employer and the employee and result in inefficiency.

Management and other staff levels
In a large-scale organisation the day-to-day running of the operation will be given over to a manager. If the manager does not possess adequate or appropriate communication skills then he will fail in one important area of his duties, management and manpower resource. He will, if successful, act as an effective mediator between the needs of the employer or owner, who is expecting a suitable financial return on his

investment, and the employee, who is expecting a working wage which fairly reflects the effort he expends in carrying out certain tasks.

Staff—customer relations

It has been said that if we can talk about the catering industry having a product, then that product will be the satisfied customer. If the customer leaves a catering establishment dissatisfied then he is unlikely either to return to it or to recommend it to his friends. Part of his satisfaction will stem from the nature of communication between the customer and the catering staff. A necessary skill which a hotel receptionist or a waitress will therefore need to possess is that of being able to communicate with the customer in such a way that a friendly, polite and efficient service is provided.

So far in this section we have emphasised the importance of one particular skill within the formal organisation of any catering establishment, that of communicating effectively at a variety of different levels. A complex organisation will require a communications network to link together the various elements that comprise it. In addition, this complex organisation will, as we saw earlier in this chapter, have a division of labour made up of staff possessing a wide range of specialised skills. If anyone in these skill areas is defective or functioning incorrectly then the whole organisation will consequently suffer—a chain is only as strong as its weakest link.

The need for the possession of specialist skills will be of greater importance where the large-scale formal organisation is concerned because tasks will be broken down into specific areas with little or no overlap between them. A smaller, less formal organisation, may allow for an overlap of skills to occur so that flexibility may be achieved.

In this section we have described some of the important features an individual must possess if he is to fit effectively into the formal organisation. We have seen the necessity for possessing qualifications, relevant experience and certain specific skills. In Chapter Five we shall see that, in addition, the character of the individual also has to be considered in terms of such things as his personality, his temperament, his attitude to work and to those he works with.

CONCLUSION

We have seen in this chapter that communication in the formal organisation is defined by specific rules and standards and follows specific channels. The formal organisation is that part of the establishment which is designed to carry out specific functions and achieve the objectives of the establishment. We have seen that it is more likely to be in evidence in a large-scale organisation because of the greater need for rules and standards to govern the behaviour of the workforce. A small-scale organisation will be seen to be less formal in its make-up because of the greater degree of flexibility made possible by the smaller number of individuals employed within. In the next chapter, however, we shall see that in a large-scale organisation informal communication also takes place and in many respects has a very important role to play in the effective running of the organisation as a whole.

SELF-ASSESSMENT QUESTIONS

1. Distinguish between allocative and operational control.
2. Explain the function of official rules.
3. Define the division of labour.
4. Explain the relationship between the possession of certain qualifications and the ability to do a particular job.

CHAPTER FOUR

Communication and the Informal Organisation

CHAPTER OBJECTIVES

After studying this chapter you should be able to:
* define an informal organisation;
* describe the way in which communication takes place through the informal organisation;
* explain the factors that influence the development of an informal organisation.

INTRODUCTION

At this stage we need to point out that no organisation can exist independently of its surrounding environment. It is a simple exercise to point out that all companies, whether they are catering establishments or other industrial firms, form a part of a wide social structure. Any catering establishment will need to have close contact with its environment as a means of surviving. This may occur on a number of levels. For example, the success of a hotel in a given tourist area will, to a certain degree, depend upon the support it obtains from local transport systems in providing its customers with a means of moving about the local area, from local services such as water, electricity and sewage disposal, or from the local Jobcentre in providing a source of part-time staff during the peak season. All this support is a necessary part of what is known as the infrastructure of the tourist industry. Without this support tourist establishments—hotels, cafes, restaurants and so on—would find survival very difficult.

The above example should therefore serve to illustrate the links that exist between any organisation and the environment in which it is placed. We sometimes refer to the context in which the organisation operates. As this context varies, so the nature of the organisation will vary also. The informal organisation of a given catering establishment will therefore be a reflection of the context in which it operates. We need to explain further the nature of this connection.

THE INFORMAL ORGANISATION AND ITS CONTEXT

We need first of all to explain in more detail the exact nature of this context. A context is a setting. It is the social, political, economic and geographical environment in which the establishment is situated; in more simple terms it is the community in which the establishment exists. In other words, then, the character of the community will play a large part in the formation and character of the informal organisation and the communication that takes place within it.

Two examples of different contexts or community settings may serve to illustrate the above point.

Example 1

A medium-sized hotel, situated in an old and well-established seaside village is likely to have developed, over a period of time, links with the local community. This community will most probably centre around traditional industries, such as agriculture or fishing, and a developing tourist industry. Contacts with local traders and suppliers are likely to have existed for some time and staff, both full-time and part-time will be resident in the local area. Within this hotel, over the course of time, an informal organisation will develop. It will be based upon the existence of long-serving and established staff, sympathetic management and a mutual understanding of goals and objectives. The staff, being drawn from the same community, will have much in common; they will probably live near each other, use the same shops, drink in the same pub and may even be relatives. The degree of understanding between them may be such that sophisticated or detailed explanations will not be necessary; many meanings will be taken for granted and many tasks will be carried out "on the nod". They will speak in a common language or dialect, share the same jokes and will have social contacts that extend beyond the work environment.

In this setting the need for management to impose a formal means of communication will not be great; the informal links that exist within the workforce will facilitate the communications process. Management will simply have to "tune in" to it and adapt it to fulfill their needs. The work environment in this hotel will be an extension of the wider environment, i.e. it will be part of the context, the community itself.

Example 2

A similar-sized hotel, but placed in a different setting, might be organised in a very different way. It might be situated on the suburban fringe of a fast-growing city, perhaps near an airport or large rail terminal. The speed of growth of this urban area will mean that the people who live in it will be relative newcomers to the area who will have had little opportunity to establish many contacts or friends in the area. Growing urban areas of this kind often attract families from all over the country, perhaps in search of new jobs or promotional transfers.

Thus, although the staff of the hotel may commute considerable distances to and from work each day, or even if they reside in the immediate area of the hotel, they are unlikely to have done so for any great length of time. The effect of this on the working situation in the hotel is that, because of the lack of tradition and because of their relative newness to the area, many of the staff of the hotel will not know each other, will be unaware of each other's backgrounds and will be generally unaccustomed to each other's different ways of life. This will not necessarily mean that they will be unable to work together or even establish friendly contacts with one another, but it does mean that management will have to be more concerned with creating a formal organisation so that working relations can develop and the establishment run efficiently. The staff will not have so much in common, coming from a wide range of social backgrounds, and therefore meanings will have to be spelt out to ensure that duties, for example, are correctly carried out. Unlike the hotel in the older, more established community, little can be taken for granted or assumed to be understood and therefore management will be required to develop a more formal organisation.

Over time, if labour turnover is low and management maintains a perceptive supervisory role, it may be the case that effective informal practices develop replacing some of the formal organisational procedures. Until this occurs, though, the formal organisation will be required to ensure that levels of efficiency are maintained.

We shall see in Chapter Seven the way in which effective informal communications can lead to the development of identifiable informal groups which can make a profitable contribution to the overall operation of the establishment.

We now need to consider in detail the way in which informal communication takes place, the various channels it may follow and its relationship to more formal patterns of communication as outlined in Chapter Three.

COMMUNICATION PROCEDURES

Any efficient organisation will depend upon the operation of carefully thought out and designed communication procedures. These enable orders and instructions to be passed on and carried out, they allow for the delegation of responsibilities, and above all they co-ordinate and bring together the various working elements of the organisation into a cohesive structure. We are now really talking about the design of the formal organisation, which will specify the way in which communication procedures will be carried out. For example, the organisation charts in Chapter Seven show the way in which communication is designed to take place within the establishment. Authority, for example, will be delegated from the general manager of a hotel, through the food and beverage manager, the chef de cuisine, the sous chef and the various chefs de partie, to the commis chefs, kitchen porters and apprentices. This type of formal organisation is sometimes known as *line* management, where communication follows a line, i.e. there is a chain of communication, a chain of command.

A problem with line management

The above example may be used to illustrate the fact that line management is sometimes not the best means of communication and delegation of authority through the organisation. Informal procedures are often more effective.

The existence of more than one boss can often damage the working atmosphere, making the workforce feel confused or resentful or unaware of exactly to whom they are answerable. Line management, for example, where authority is delegated through a number of individuals, each responsible for a share of the job, may produce a feeling at the lower end of the hierarchy that there are too many bosses. The commis chef may feel that he is answerable to a chef de partie, a sous chef *and* a chef de cuisine. This should not happen if the formal organisation is running smoothly, but can often occur in times of pressure, during food service for example, when instructions may be given out of line. This situation may lead to the commis chef being confused about his position and possibly resentful of the restraints and pressures that the "organisation" is imposing on him.

Closer informal contacts between individual members of the workforce may reduce the chance of the above situation occurring. This may be achieved on a group basis, whereby a more participative structure within the kitchen brigade is created informally, allowing some sharing of decision-making and task allocation and thus reducing the feeling of "too many bosses". Alternatively, closer informal contact on an individual basis might be encouraged as a means of reducing the tension that might exist in this situation. This could be achieved through participation in social club activities, a less obvious management role on the part of the chefs, or weekly staff meetings where any tensions that might have developed can be defused.

Informal communication procedures take a number of forms and the role of management is clearly important in relation to the success or failure of these procedures. Management therefore needs to be aware of the existence of the informal organisation and the way in which communication can take place within it. In this way such communication may be implemented to benefit the organisation as a whole.

The continuous lines in Fig. 2 show the formal communication links that connect the various members of the organisation together. The dotted lines represent the informal communication links that may exist between members of the organisation. As can be seen, it is possible to superimpose one set of communication links on another. The lines denoting the informal communication links show the contacts that can exist between individuals within the organisation, irrespective of their position in the formal hierarchy and not necessarily following the pattern described by line management. This kind of chart traces the actual interaction—literally the action between—that takes place within the organisation. The compilation and appraisal of such a chart will enable management to be aware of the important contacts that are being made within the establishment, in addition to those laid down by the formal organisation.

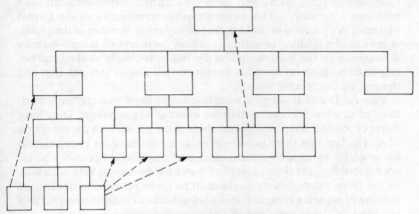

Fig. 2.   *An informal organisation chart.*

The study of sociometry is also relevant in enabling us to understand the makings of the informal organisation. J. L. Moreno attempted to trace the patterns of relationships that existed between individuals in an organisation but that were not necessarily defined by line management or personnel policy. Basing his study upon the feelings of individuals towards others in the organisation, he compiled what he called a sociogram. This described contacts between individuals based on feelings of attraction, repulsion and indifference. From his observations Moreno was able to establish who was liked and disliked within the organisation, who the most respected individuals in a group might be and what individuals would best comprise a working team.

Analysis of the sociogram in Fig. 3 will tell us a considerable amount about the informal organisation and the communication links that exist within it.

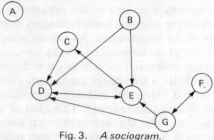

Fig. 3.   A sociogram.

Application of the sociogram to a hotel reception team

It will be noticed first of all that individual A in Fig. 3 is clearly isolated, presumably disliked by other members of the working group (in this case the reception team) who show no informal communication links with him whatsoever. This pattern evolves irrespective of the formal nature of A's position or, indeed, that of any other member of the group. A may hold a position of authority within the reception team—he may for example be the head receptionist—but he is clearly unliked and not respected because no informal interaction links exist between him and the rest of the reception staff.

Persons D and E—senior receptionists perhaps—clearly hold positions of some importance within the informal organisation. They have direct or indirect links with all members of the group, with the exception of A. The fact that these two are popular members of the group should be noted by perceptive management and they should possibly be incorporated into the development of a more efficient working situation. In the given example they might each be given responsibilities for the running of separate reception shifts because they command respect and are liked by other members of the reception team.

Analysis of the diagram will further demonstrate the nature of the communication process. It will be noticed that not all interaction between members is two-way, i.e. some arrows show a communication flow in only one direction. It will be noticed that the most common one-way flow is toward D and E, indicating that they are in a position to receive information and contact with other group members. The two-way flow indicated *between* D and E also indicates that they like one another, can work with one another and can communicate with one another. This may further support the placing of these two individuals in positions of responsibility in different reception shifts. In addition to having contacts with the majority of the reception staff, they also interact with one another, indicating that they would be able to liaise effectively and thus ensure the smooth transition from one reception shift to another. This co-operation will be essential to ensure the effective and efficient running of the reception team.

Finally we must consider what might be a problem area in our example—the lack of informal contact between the head receptionist and the remainder of the reception staff. This may be a problem for line management or for the hotel proprietor, particularly if the formal links that exist between the head receptionist and the other senior receptionists show signs of strain. Swift action on the part of management, e.g. setting up a work-study group or arranging regular informal meetings for all reception staff to attend, may prevent a serious personnel problem from occurring.

The sociogram can therefore provide management with an important portrayal of the behaviour of working groups on an informal level, enabling it to encourage those groups that benefit the overall running of the operation and to discourage those that may otherwise damage efficiency. The whole progress of charting informal organisation is one which, if carried out responsibly and perceptively, can provide management with a clearer picture of their area of supervision and responsibility.

THE GRAPEVINE

The term "grapevine" is often used to describe the communication that takes place through the informal organisation. It is a term usually denoting forms of oral communication between members of the workforce, but there is no reason why it should not from time to time cover written communication as well.

The term originated during the American Civil War to describe the communication system operating at the time, telegraph wires being temporarily strung from tree to tree like a grapevine to transmit the required messages. This temporary method of communication often suffered from distortion and crackle, and messages were sometimes misinterpreted by those who heard them and passed them on. Needless to say, rumours of doubtful accuracy were often in circulation as a result.

The grapevine is the most common form of communication that takes place in the informal organisation. It is the means by which information, instructions, ideas, etc., are transmitted through the workforce by informal means. Man seems to possess a natural inclination to communicate in some way or another, and, simply because he is placed within a formal organisation during his working day, does not mean that he will stop communicating in the way that is natural to him; it would be a very sterile, unimaginative and indeed uncharacteristic workforce that was not motivated to discuss aspects of their work between themselves.

Management must therefore recognise the existence of the grapevine and that it is an inevitable feature of communication within the informal organisation. It may be used to advantage by the perceptive manager or supervisor as a means of effectively communicating information, as a means of monitoring feedback from the workforce and of generally developing links with the informal organisation. Management that is too reliant upon the rigid codes and messages of the communication process through the formal organisation is overlooking the usefulness of the grapevine, which can transmit messages very quickly and in a language that the workforce understands.

The fact that the grapevine is a particularly rapid means of communication must not be overlooked by management. However, it must be pointed out that the grapevine has one built in disadvantage, as the original example of the grapevine at the beginning of the section showed. It can be an inaccurate means of transmitting information. Verbal messages can often be distorted, exaggerations may occur, falsehoods perpetrated and unfounded rumours generated. Rumours can be conveyed through the grapevine which are usually based upon unreliable and unchecked sources of information.

From a postive point of view, however, the grapevine provides a channel of communication for the informal organisation which, if carefully dealt with and considered by management, can provide a valuable contribution to the process of communication through the organisation as a whole.

We next need to consider in more detail the way in which this contribution is made to the organisation. We saw earlier in the chapter that it was not possible to divorce or isolate the working environment from wider social influences; in other words it is important to place an individual's work into a broader context. Without this it is possible that the individual may feel that the work is in some way artificial and bears no real relation to the real world for him. Entering the workplace, the worker constantly has to adapt to rules, regulations, work schedules, etc., which are quite alien to him and perhaps have little meaning. This has the increasing effect of lowering his productivity and level of job satisfaction to such an extent that he may leave the job. It has in fact been shown in a study by Elton Mayo and George Lombard that high labour turnover is closely linked with low job satisfaction and more importantly, that low labour turnover is associated with the existence of an informal organisation between the various groups of workers within the firm. This is a clear demonstration of the role that communication has to play in the informal organisation.

THE DEVELOPMENT OF INFORMAL ORGANISATIONS

We will now examine the various forms or types of informal organisation and the way in which they can develop within a company. This will vary according to their relationship with the formal organisation.

Social contact

If the constraints and pressures of the working situation are not too great, then it is likely that informal, often random and temporary, social contacts may be made. During tea-breaks and lunch-times, on the journey to and from work, or during a quiet period of the working day it will be possible for individual workers to generate social contacts. This may begin as purely casual contacts, discussing events of worldly interest—a television programme or a news item for example—but may develop over time into longer-lasting more permanent social contacts. The establishment of social contacts on this individual basis is often the beginning of a wider framework of social realtionships within the firm. In short, they may represent the beginning of the informal organisation.

The work environment

Social contacts will only occur within the formal organisation if the work environment allows it. Clearly, if the pressures and constraints imposed by the work environment are too great, then informal social contact will be kept to a minimum. It is unlikely that the individual will experience complete social isolation within the work environment, but it is quite easy to imagine a working situation where social contacts are few and far between. Studies of the work environment, particularly those of Mayo, Maslow, Herzberg, etc., show that for efficient working conditions to exist, attention must be given to the needs of the workforce. As we shall see in a later chapter (see page 79), it is an important management role to ensure that employer needs, such as reaching certain productivity levels, are achieved whilst at the same time maintaining a work environment that satisfies certain employee needs such as a level of social contact amongst fellow workers.

The process of adaptation

The needs of the formal organisation require that individual workers have to adapt in some way to fulfill these needs. The role of management is to ensure that this process of adaptation is achieved with the least possible effect on the formal organisation and on the individuals working within it. The perpetuation of the informal organisation is a means by which this may be achieved. We have already seen that the existence of an effective informal organisation can reduce labour turnover. In other words when the informal organisation is such that individuals feel a sense of belonging to it they are less likely to experience job dissatisfaction, less likely to take random days off and less likely to want to leave the company.

Our discussion of informal groups has shown the way in which a "society of the firm" can develop within an organisation. This term is used to describe the sense of belonging, mentioned above, that the informal organisation can sometimes create. It will be a working situation in which the workforce will share common aims with which they will be able to identify. Again the management role is crucial here in ensuring that the identification of the workforce with the "society of the firm" does not in any way damage their identification with the aims of the company itself.

Trade unions, throughout history, have developed from this form of informal organisation, usually as a form of collective adaptation or a response to what they see as being the unfairness of a given set of working relations. Increasingly, as trade unions are seen to represent the needs of the workforce in many areas of the catering industry, it is essential that management develops a relationship with the unions such that satisfaction of these employee needs does not conflict with those needs of the employers.

The development of a "society of the firm" within establishments in the catering industry may not occur as readily as in other industries because of the transitional nature of much catering work.

Customer relations and an unstable workforce
Customer satisfaction is the goal of any successful catering estabishment. This has to be achieved for a variety of customers, from the casual customer in a pub to the full-board customer staying at a seaside hotel for a six-week vacation. The responsibility for creating customer satisfaction across this broad range is of course that of the staff. If staff relations are poor then it is more than likely that staff–customer relations will also be lacking in some respect. And if customers are unhappy with the service they receive they tend not to return to the establishment.

The contribution of the informal organisation to good staff–customer relations therefore cannot be undervalued. Management will experience difficulties in running an establishment where the nature of the work is seasonal, where many of the staff are part-time or casual and where the level of commitment to the firm may not be so high as where staff turnover is less and where employment is on a more permanent basis. In a seasonal establishment, for example, the employment of a core of non-transitional and permanent staff may be essential to ensure that continuity in the informal organisation is maintained from one season to the next. In addition, treating part-time staff with care and respect and making positive efforts to integrate them within the organisation will have the effect of reducing any resentment or casual attitudes amongst the staff and may in turn lead to a regular turnover of semi-permanent rather than temporary part-time staff. This in turn is likely to lead to increased customer satisfaction, in that they will recognise similar faces from year to year, develop a friendly rapport and generally feel part of a community during their stay in the hotel or guesthouse.

By paying attention to the informal organisation, management may be able to develop a stable workforce which in turn will lead to increased productivity and overall efficiency.

Worker participation schemes

Although not common in the catering industry, worker participation schemes represent a system of working where, potentially, close links between the formal and informal organisation are created. Clearly, many forms of participation exist in any working situation and without a minimum level of participation the organisation would not function at all. Worker participation therefore refers to the involvement of the workforce, not simply in carrying out their assigned day-to-day tasks, but also in taking responsibility and becoming involved in the decision-making process. Increased participation tends to create increased commitment to the objectives of the firm, and if a situation exists where, if not all, at least a large percentage of the workforce participates at all levels, then a high degree of commitment will also exist. In the extreme, worker participation not only involves the day-to-day running of the firm but also some form of financial investment and profit-sharing.

When we discuss various forms of leadership in Chapter Eight we shall see that the success of worker participation schemes is very much dependent upon the type of worker involved and the attitude of management toward participation.

CONCLUSION

This chapter has demonstrated the importance of the informal organisation and the communication network that exists because of it. Communication will invariably take place in a variety of informal ways, no matter how loosely organised the system of communication may seem. It may be in the form of random contact between members of an unstable workforce or it may be a sophisticated system of communication integrating the informal and formal organisations as part of a worker participation scheme.

Management will be unable to suppress communication that takes place through informal channels, and progressive management is likely to implement, adapt and integrate such communication in order to benefit the working of the organisation as a whole.

SELF-ASSESMENT QUESTIONS

1. What is the relationship between the informal organisation and its context?
2. What does a sociogram tell us about the informal organisation?

3. List the advantages and disadvantages of the grapevine as a form
of communication.

4. Explain how customer satisfaction may be affected by workforce
instability.

5. Define the "society of the firm".

CHAPTER FIVE

The Role of the Individual

CHAPTER OBJECTIVES

After studying this chapter you should be able to:
* identify the various factors that contribute to behavioural differences between individuals;
* distinguish clearly between the various factors;
* explain the way in which the intellectual capacity of an individual is made up;
* explain the way in which the formation of attitudes takes place.

INTRODUCTION

Analysis of human relations in the workplace, and particularly within the context of the hotel and catering industry, requires first of all our appraisal of the features which contribute to the differences that exist between individuals. If we can establish the criteria which enable us to understand where these differences lie, then this should provide us with a basis for a clearer understanding of what is involved in the broad range of human relations in the workplace. We may classify the various factors which influence the behaviour of individuals in the following way:

(a) personality;
(b) intelligence;
(c) attitudes.

We will see that these factors are not mutually exclusive, i.e. they overlap in a number of ways, but our understanding of the composition of individual differences will be improved by examining each of the factors in turn.

PERSONALITY

The factor that we term personality is perhaps the most difficult to measure and to define clearly. However it is arguably the most important factor to be considered in attempting to understand the make-up of the individual.

Personality is the key to understanding the individual, the person. If

we can understand the personality of an individual then we have un-
locked the door to a more complete understanding of that individual.
Personality then is that aspect of the individual which we need to
scrutinise carefully in order that we may be aware of what is involved in
human relations.

The most straightforward approach to an understanding of
personality is in terms of what we may call personality traits. A
personality trait is a recognisable behaviour pattern which indicates elements, or possibly the whole, of an individual's personality. Behaviour
of a certain kind should provide us with evidence of personality.
Further, a given personality will be recognisable in terms of certain
personality traits. Thus we may talk of an individual as displaying a
certain personality, for example, *extroversion*, and we will be able to
recognise this personality because of certain characteristics or
personality traits which it embodies, e.g. exaggerated expressions and
movements, confidence, gregariousness, aggressive language, wearing
of bright clothing, etc. In addition, our understanding of this particular
type of personality will be further enhanced if we make a comparative
analysis, and look at the characteristics or personality traits that make
up the personality of *introversion*. These characteristics may include
shyness, withdrawal from human contact, nervousness, quiet speech,
wearing of nondescript clothes, etc.

In the context of the catering industry we may give an illustration of
the way in which these characteristics may be affected by attitudes to
dress. Catering staff invariably in the course of their duties come into
contact with the general public. Consequently many employers require
that staff wear uniforms, both in industry and institutions. The effect of
this regulation on staff may vary according to the different personality
traits involved. An extrovert member of staff, for example, may feel
restricted, as he may use an individual or unusual style of dress as a
means of self expression. It is likely that the uniform he is required to
wear may act to suppress some of his extrovert characteristics. An
employer may find this effect as being desirable because it can bring
members of staff "into line", encouraging them to conform to the requirements of work.

The effect of uniform may also be seen in relation to the more introverted character. It may give him a feeling of greater confidence and
status, helping him to recognise his position as a member of a team
rather than as an isolated individual. To the eyes of the outsider all
members of the team have an equal status as determined by the
uniform.

By further examination it can then be seen that a spectrum of
characteristics for any related personality may be drawn up. In this way
we are able to contrast extrovert characteristics with introvert

characteristics in different situations, thereby improving our overall understanding.

We may contrast other personality characteristics in this way; a person who displays the characteristics of *emotional instability*, for example, may best be understood by first of all drawing up a list of all the characteristics or traits which we would recognise in such a personality. Emotions such as sadness, happiness, love, hate, anger, fear, etc., manifest themselves in various forms of expression such as crying, laughter, aggressiveness, etc. The ability to control our demonstration of these feelings is a measure of our emotional stability. Clearly, an emotionally unstable person who is unable to control his or her emotions will be to some degree socially insecure and may find coping with a particular job difficult.

An example may help to illustrate this point. Let us examine the same job from the perspective of two different establishments. A receptionist in a medium-sized hotel will be expected to cope with several different tasks at the same time. These may include dealing with a complete booking on the telephone whilst simultaneously a resident guest may wish to settle his account in a hurry in order to catch a train. Meanwhile the head waiter is waiting for the menu to be typed for lunch, the cocktail barman wants his float from the safe in order to open up the bar and the house telephone is ringing.

In contrast, the receptionist in a large hotel usually carries out only one main function per shift. In addition, in a large establishment there are more staff who may be moved in if a particular section is under pressure. The most pressure a receptionist in this situation is likely to experience is either from a large queue of people checking in or out of the hotel or, perhaps, from enquiries. She is more able to concentrate and therefore to cope with the specific job in hand.

These two contrasting situations clearly show the need for being aware of an individual's emotional stability. The less emotionally stable an individual might be, the less able he is likely to be to cope under pressure. As we shall see in a later section (see page 113), awareness of this factor is particularly important where job selection is concerned.

The difference between emotional stability and instability is again a question of degree, and a recognition of this difference and the effect it may have on a job situation, as described above, is particularly important in the catering industry. In addition, placement of individuals with radically opposed personality traits of any kind in close working proximity may lead to clashes of personality, social tension and, ultimately, job inefficiency.

At this stage we should note that, in general, individuals cannot be strictly categorised as simply displaying one personality. Although we may refer to a particular person as being an extrovert, or to another as emotionally unstable, generally we use the terms to describe *elements* of an individual's personality. Thus we may say that any one individual may possess a number of personality traits, the combined effect of which build up a picture of that individual's personality.

We can see then that the various personality traits are simply the discernible characteristics of an individual's personality; these traits will vary from individual to individual and from time to time. The question of individual personality thus remains a topic for debate, and we have to answer such questions as "Where does personality originate?" and "What environmental factors influence its formulation?" The significance of these questions may be seen in the light of the following example.

Some people may argue that the children of hoteliers or publicans are "born naturals" to the trade, that it is almost an inherited family tradition, and that their children take to the business as naturally as a duck takes to water. However, others may argue that, as their families probably live on the premises, the children have been brought up in the hotel or pub environment. By helping their parents and listening to the way various situations are handled, they therefore have the opportunity to pick up knowledge and skills from a very early age.

The debate as to the origin and relative influence of inherited characteristics and environmentally-determined characteristics is a long and sometimes heated one. For our purposes we may reasonably conclude that personality comprises a number of inherited features that are moulded by personal experience in the variety of social environments we find ourselves in.

INTELLIGENCE

Intelligence, like personality, contributes to the differences that exist between individuals, i.e. different individuals possess different levels of intelligence.

Again, as with personality, there is a widely-held view that intelligence is an inherited part of our mental make-up and that its development is largely dependent on the environmental conditions to which an individual is exposed. Thus if it were possible to take a group of individuals who had inherited identical levels of intelligence and to chart the development of their intelligence through totally different environments, their intelligence at the end of a given period of time would differ according to their differing environmental exposure.

In order to understand the concept of intelligence and the way in which it operates we need to analyse the various elements that comprise our intelligence or intellectual capacity. As Fig. 4 illustrates, intellectual capacity may be broken down into at least six component elements. A

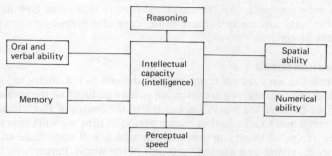

Fig. 4 *The six elements of intellectual capacity.*

fuller understanding of intelligence therefore will be achieved if we briefly analyse each of these elements in turn.

Reasoning

This can be defined as the intellectual ability to reach conclusions after having systematically argued or thought through a number of stages, building upon relevant information and eliminating irrelevant information. The power of reasoning also incorporates what we sometimes term a "logical approach"; we might also refer to someone who possesses the power of reasoning as having a "rational mind". We may illustrate the use of the powers of reasoning in the following way.

Hoteliers in seasonal operations often have to consider a variety of elements in deciding when to open and close for the season. Some decisions may be made on the basis of historical or statistical information, i.e. evidence relating to opening and closing at a particular time in previous seasons. However, in addition to this, current or forthcoming events and constraints may also require consideration. For example, the question could be asked "Shall we open for Easter?" An analysis of previous years when the hotel was opened at Easter shows perhaps that it is inadvisable because of relatively low takings and the difficulty of appointing casual staff. Against this, however, it is noticed that Easter falls very late this year and an unusually warm spring is predicted in the long-range weather forecast. A reasoned judgment will be made on the basis of all these factors, perhaps in this case influencing the seasonal hotelier to open for Easter on this occasion. The importance of the effective use of powers of reasoning can be similarly applied to the closing of the operation at the end of the season. Whether to close in September or October may be influenced by the prospect of good or bad weather, how busy the hotel was last year, or the fact that the only reason it was busy last year was *because* of the unusually good weather.

The above example should illustrate that the application of the powers of reasoning to problems in the practical world is both a general and a universal necessity. The example further illustrates how its use will affect the success or fortune in the case of a hotel operation or a business in general.

Perceptual speed

Perception in very simple terms may be defined as the ability to "see". However the "seeing" we are referring to here includes all the means by which we observe the world, i.e. our use of the senses of sight, hearing, taste, smell and touch, so that over a period of time we will observe an infinite range of events or phenomena which will contribute to our experience, giving us a kind of "picture" of the world. Perception, however, also entails some degree of understanding; our ability to perceive something in a complete sense will require us to refer back to past experience of some similar or related event.

From this position we evolve the idea of *perceptual speed*, i.e. the ability to "see" things quickly. For example we may *hear* a particular bird-call, say a nightingale, and from past experience of hearing a similar bird-call perceive that the noise we are now hearing is in fact a nightingale. How quickly we carry out this process may be referred to as perceptual speed.

The quick reactions that perceptual speed may produce can be beneficial for catering operations in terms of savings in time, money, labour and ingredients. For example, in the event of a fire in a kitchen, sharp reactions can save damage or reduce injury. Whilst this may be considered in terms of the siting of fire-fighting equipment (power of reasoning) it is still the quick and correct application of such equipment in an emergency which makes it effective. A more specific example might be the production of Hollandaise sauce. It is known that it will curdle if the butter is added too quickly; however, speed of reaction in realising that this is occurring may well result in the sauce being saved by quickly adding the curdled sauce to a teaspoon of boiling water in a clean saucepan and gradually whisking it in.

Once again from a practical point of view, in industry, where the use of sophisticated technology such as automated systems and computerisation is becoming commonplace, or more broadly in life in general, the ability to perceive things quickly and learn is essential. In fact a manager or personnel officer in the process of recruiting staff may well decide that such a capability is a necessity in order to carry out a particular job.

Memory

We are constantly putting into practice our ability to recall events, ideas, facts, theories, faces, names and information. The intellectual ability to carry this out we call memory. We may say that anyone who can recall such information quickly and completely has a "good memory", and if they cannot then they have a "bad memory".

From the point of view of the practical application of the powers of memory, there is a need to train our memory to store information which we regard as relevant to the carrying out of particular tasks. It will be of no use for a chef to possess the practical ability or skills to carry out a task such as baking a cake or preparing a complicated menu unless he can actually memorise and recall these tasks during food preparation. Clearly our minds often find it difficult to distinguish between useful and useless information, so quite often we may not remember what we used to remember at a particular time or place. For practical purposes we therefore use what we might call, in various forms, an aide memoire, i.e. a means of helping our memory; the forgetful chef previously mentioned may well use a recipe book as his aide memoire.

Memory is thus a limited capacity. We cannot hope to memorise all the information we come into contact with in our lives. The value of memory lies in our being able to recall information which is useful or beneficial to us in certain circumstances.

Oral-verbal ability

The process of communication has been dealt with in some depth in Chapter Two, where the value of oral and verbal skills has clearly been demonstrated. We are concerned here with oral/verbal skills in relation to the differences between individuals. We may begin by saying that there is a direct relationship between an individual's general ability to communicate facts, ideas and information and his verbal and oral ability.

It is first of all important to distinguish between the two. Verbal skills are those skills related to the use of words, whereas oral skills relate more specifically to the use of words in speech. Our use of words, either in a written or spoken form, demonstrates our ability to communicate to others our knowledge in the form of ideas, information and skills. Oral and verbal communication is thus a reflection of an ability to articulate our knowledge to other people.

Within the catering industry, effective use of oral and verbal skills is absolutely essential for the effective running of any operation. Not only is the demonstration of these abilities essential, but also our ability to be able to distinguish as to when one form should be used in preference to another. For example, should the hotel manager simply telephone to apologise to a justifiably dissatisfied guest or should he make the effort of writing a letter of apology?

In the catering industry success can, in many respects, be measured in terms of satisfied customers, and one means of achieving this is by means of the oral and verbal skills of the members of the industry who are in direct contact with the public; as already demonstrated by the previous example, it is an essential aspect of dealing with customer complaints. In addition, the promotion of further sales may be achieved by means of a skilful use of oral or verbal skills. For example, a potential customer who requires catering facilities for a wedding or some other special function may be unaware of other services that are available in this area. Thus an ability to give information persuasively about these other services, such as bedroom hire, use of toastmaster, provision of a discotheque or dance band, or perhaps preparing the wedding cake, may bring much additional business.

It is clearly important that verbal and oral abilities are used to help the customer feel satisfied, but we will also see in the later sections on motivation and leadership (see pages 54 and 79) how important they are for effective staff relations.

Numerical skills

Numerical skills will be required in important areas such as accountancy, tabulation and budgeting. Although in many operations much of this work is being computerised, there nevertheless remains considerable importance attached to numerical skills.

Numerical skills are simply the ability to use numbers, to carry out complex calculations and apply these calculations to everyday life. Numerical skills are obviously important in a specialised area such as hotel accountancy, but we can also see their importance in other fields. Simple examples of this occur in bar work where a barman or barmaid may have to calculate accurately the costs of large rounds of differently-priced drinks, work out change and so on. Costing and control also require a high degree of numerical skills, the individual with the responsibility in this area having to calculate suitable profit margins, consumption rates, market prices and so on.

Spatial ability

This may not appear to be as important as being able to calculate a bill correctly or convert food quantities into metric equivalents, but there are many areas within catering—marketing, for example (see below)—where spatial ability is a postive attribute.

Spatial ability is the means by which an individual is able to visualise the use of space. This ability is most readily apparent in such professions as graphic design, architecture, and technical illustration, where there is a necessity to place objects in functional relationships to one another, while at the same time ensuring that the end-product is in some way pleasing to the eye as well as being simply functional. In the catering industry spatial ability is of particular importance in the area of design; a new hotel kitchen, or on a grander scale, a new hotel and catering department building in a college would require the application of spatial skills. Such ventures require, at the planning stage, the ability to "see" the way in which various kitchens, food service areas and classrooms should be designed and placed in relation to one another to ensure maximum functional efficiency combined with some degree of aesthetic consideration.

On a smaller scale we may also see the value of spatial ability when we consider something as important as marketing, e.g. being able to design a poster advertising a trade exhibition or helping to compile an attractive brochure advertising a large country hotel. Both of these exercises will in many respects be essential to the success of the venture and therefore the value of possessing spatial ability cannot be over-emphasised.

In concluding this section on intelligence and its contribution to individual differences, we can see that the whole area of intellectual capacity is a complex one. It is not sufficient for us to state merely that one individual "is more intelligent" than another; we have to analyse the whole area of intelligence in depth in order to understand how one individual differs from another and how the different abilities we possess can be applied.

ATTITUDE

The attitude of an individual is a clear demonstration of the kind of person he or she is. In simple terms, when we talk about someone possessing a particular "attitude" we mean that he has a particular outlook on life; he sees the world in a specific way. This outlook is to a large extent predetermined by the environment in which he has been brought up, the influence to which he has been exposed, in short the whole spectrum of his learning experiences. Those attitudes that an individual expresses will be a reflection of his background in terms of his home, his school, his friends, his work, the newspaper he reads and so on. This range of learning about the world, sometimes known as socialisation, moulds the individual into a particular form so that his expression and opinions are representative of this learning.

Clearly, all individuals are exposed to different environmental influences, no matter how small, so that all our attitudes to life will be different in some way or another. People from similar backgrounds may express different attitudes, so the whole question of different attitudes is, along with our consideration of personality and intelligence, of central importance to the study of individual differences.

The origin of attitudes
This can be traced back to the earliest days of an individual's life within

the family he is born into. There is no evidence to show that we are actually born with certain attitudes, so therefore we must look to social influences which might regulate the development of different attitudes.

The family then is a source of attitude learning; perhaps the most important one, because the early years of an individual's life are usually spent with the family and are therefore the most formative. Thus the earliest attitudes a child expresses will usually approximate quite closely to those of his parents.

In later years other influences continue to affect the formation of attitudes in a child's mind—the child goes to school, listens to teachers, meets new friends, watches television, and so on. Gradually, over a period of time, attitudes will become formed and, it has been argued, the more formed these attitudes become in an individual's mind the less likely they are to change to any great degree in later life.

We can represent the formation of attitudes over a period of time as in Fig. 5. Note that politicians, religious leaders, public personalities, etc., will exert an influence, usually through the mass media, on an individual's attitudes throughout his life.

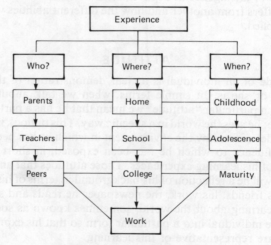

Fig. 5.   *The formation of attitudes.*

The change of emphasis from simply talking about "attitudes" to talking about "formed attitudes" is intentional because of the growing, relatively unchanging, nature of attitudes. Individuals are all open to influence and are therefore susceptible to change, but the likelihood of this occurring in later life seems to become reduced, so differences in attitudes are therefore of primary importance in relation to differences between individuals.

Attitudes found within the catering industry

A range of attitudes can be found amongst those who work in the catering industry. Some of these attitudes may be expressed in a subject not necessarily connected with catering, e.g. euthanasia or abortion, while others might refer directly to catering work and the feelings that individuals might have towards it.

Motivation

One of the most important levels of analysis concerns motivation. We will see in Chapter Six that the motivation of workers is of the first order of importance to the effective running of the catering industry. In fact, motivation largely relates to an individual worker's attitude toward work. We say that if a worker, for whatever reason, is not motivated to work then he has a negative attitude towards work. If on the other hand he appears to be enthusiastic and highly motivated we say that he has a positive attitude towards work. We will see that one of the roles of a good manager or an effective leader is to engender a positive attitude toward work amongst the workforce. Indeed, the manager himself must possess this positive attitude otherwise he is unlikely to motivate the workforce into achieving the goals of the organisation.

Many factors affect an individual's attitude towards work and it will be the responsibility of the company and its management to implement the means of improving and maintaining a favourable attitude. This objective may be complicated by different workers and groups of workers being motivated by various factors. Nevertheless we may list some of the factors which might affect an individual's attitude towards work.

(a) Wages, pay increments, promotional scale.
(b) Conditions in the workplace.
(c) The demands of the job (effort, schedules, etc.)
(d) Fringe benefits.
(e) Management–worker relations, e.g. confidence, respect.
(f) Staff relationships (informal group contact).
(g) Respect for technical skills at higher levels.
(h) Effective communication links, e.g. contact with the administration.
(i) Job security.
(j) Identification with company objectives.

The above factors, and possibly others, may have to be taken into consideration when the attitude of workers towards their work is assessed. It may be possible to correlate the attitude of the worker to morale, i.e. his feeling of well-being within the work situation, by arguing that if the worker indicates a positive attitude towards work then the morale of that particular individual is high. Conversely, if many of the above factors are not taken into consideration the attitudes of the worker may be negative and thus his morale may well be low.

All the above considerations apply particularly in the catering industry where considerable emphasis is placed upon team-work in the effective running and organisation of a given operation. If members of a team possess a negative attitude towards work the efficiency of the whole team, and consequently the whole operation, will suffer. Analysis of specific aspects of hotel and catering operations and management brings us to the second perspective from which attitudes in the industry need to viewed.

Staff–customer relations

We need to consider next the way in which attitudes affect the relationship between staff and the customer. First of all the attitude of the staff, as discussed above, will need to be such that the operation is running smoothly, with morale at an acceptable level. However catering for the needs of customers is of primary importance in the hotel and catering industry and therefore we also need to be aware of the different kinds of customer attitude that might be encountered.

Customers at any given establishment will come from a variety of racial, ethnic, political and social backgrounds, either from one country or from a cross-section of different countries. These differing backgrounds will be reflected in a range of different attitudes and these attitudes may well be shown in the behaviour patterns of individual customers or guests. Hotel staff will need to pay particular attention, say, to the attitudes of a person from a deeply religious background, e.g. a Moslem during the month of Ramadan due, in this case, to the unusual hours at which meals have to be eaten.

In general, then, we can say that catering staff may be required to accept a range of different attitudes amongst guests despite the fact that these attitudes may be very different to those of the staff and in some cases may even offend certain members of staff.

CONCLUSION

The preceding analysis should now provide us with a picture of the way in which individuals may differ. We can move from the self-evident physical differences that exist between every person to a more subtle analysis of the intellectual capacity of an individual and the balance between, say, a person's spatial and numerical ability.

The factors of personality, intelligence and attitude are the most recognisable means by which we can distinguish rationally between individuals, apart from their superficial physical appearance. This kind of analysis is absolutely essential, in that it allows us to develop an understanding of the role of the individual in the workplace, to find out "what makes him tick". An understanding of the individual and the differences between individuals should lead us naturally on to the next area of analysis, that of the factors that contribute to individual motivation.

SELF-ASSESSMENT QUESTIONS

1. Define a personality trait.
2. List four characteristics of introversion.
3. List four characteristics of extroversion.
4. What are the main elements that make up the intellectual capacity of the individual?
5. Where might the formation of attitudes take place before an individual starts work?
6. Outline some of the factors that might influence an individual's attitude toward work.

CHAPTER SIX

Individual Motivation

CHAPTER OBJECTIVES

After studying this chapter you should be able to:
* distinguish between a number of different theories of human motivation;
* describe the basic principles of these theories of human motivation;
* explain the relevance of these theories to an understanding of the catering workplace.

INTRODUCTION

In the last chapter we examined the factors that contribute to the differences between individuals. In this chapter we shall be examining the factors which affect the motivation of individuals, i.e. those factors which motivate human action. The justification for this kind of approach is simple. On a practical level we might be curious as to how a piece of machinery functions, i.e. how it works. Perhaps, more importantly, when it is broken we might be anxious to determine why it is not working so that we can get it working again as quickly as possible. Similarly, our curiosity may be roused as to the "functioning" of individuals, i.e. what makes us work.

Immediately we can recognise certain basic physical functions that operate without motivation. Breathing takes place without us noticing it and our hair grows whether we like it or not, although we might be consciously motivated to influence our bodily functions; for example, growing our hair requires no motivation but going to the hairdressers to have it cut or styled does.

We are interested, then, not in the physiological functions that operate without motivation, but in conscious behaviour. It is generally agreed that motivation is related to the needs of the individual; that if the individual feels the need for something then he will be motivated to fulfill that need. An analysis of human needs should therefore enable us to understand the factors that motivate human behaviour, i.e. that cause action. More specifically, this analysis should provide us with an insight into the way in which motivation operates within the context of the hotel and catering industry.

NEEDS OF INDIVIDUALS

As was seen in Chapter Five, many factors contribute to the differences between individuals. Similarly, the needs of individuals are equally diverse. We therefore need to classify these needs in some way so that we can see more clearly the way in which they affect the motivation of individuals. Various ways of classifying needs have been attempted, but the simplest method is in terms of *primary* and *secondary needs*.

Primary needs

These are sometimes referred to as innate or physiological needs, i.e. those needs that are necessary for human survival and the preservation of the species. Primary needs are those which if not satisfied would cause severe suffering and eventually death. We may include in this category the need for air, food and drink, sleep, sex, warmth and bodily elimination. These needs do not vary from society to society; without exception, they are necessary for humanity to survive. They may differ by degree, however; the diet in one society may be radically different form that of another, but this does not alter the fact that in both cases nutritionally satisfactory diets are necessary for survival.

Secondary needs

These are less easy to classify as they are affected by the social situation in which the individual is found. We define this category of needs as "acquired" social and psychological needs that have evolved over a period of time. We may include amongst our social needs the need for love and affection, companionship, social status and esteem. Psychological needs could include the need for self-expression, self-respect and confidence. Both kinds of secondary need will vary with the individual and consequently will be difficult to enumerate and classify with certainty.

Our discussion of management techniques at a later stage (see page 60) will bring into focus the fact that the relationship between a primary need and motivation is self-evident, in that most individuals when in need of food or warmth are motivated to act so as to satisfy those needs. It is not easy, however, to pin down what a given individual's social or psychological needs might be and, therefore, the way in which he may be motivated to act. The individual mentioned on page 42, with a dominant, extrovert personality, may be motivated towards fulfilling the need for companionship, attention and group contact. On the other hand, the individual with the more introverted personality may well be motivated towards fulfilling the need for silence, peace and solitude.

The action that management takes can thus affect the secondary needs of any given workforce, and it may well be that if careful attention is not given to the factors which motivate the workforce then such things as productivity and efficiency may be affected. Management should therefore be fully aware of the effects any proposed action may have on the secondary needs of individual workers. If these secondary needs can be recognised then management can attempt to motivate individual workers to fulfill them.

We have said then that needs may be classified into two general categories, primary or innate needs and secondary or acquired needs. In addition we have also stated that needs in all their different forms are limited to motivation; man is motivated to fulfill his needs. We next need to ask in what way does the relationship between motivation and needs operate? Having established what these needs are, an examination of some theories of motivation may enable use to answer this question.

THEORIES OF MOTIVATION

It is generally recognised that needs arise at different stages, and that the needs of an individual are not consistent or in, many cases, predictable. Agreement exists however that man, having satisfied a given need, tends to seek out other needs for satisfaction. Accordingly, between individuals in different social settings a priority of needs exists. The need for a colour television in the UK in the 1980s is common amongst most sectors of society; however 10 or 15 years previously this need would have been less evident. Similarly, many families, having become used to the convenience of a motor car, create elaborate justifications for the need for a *second* family car.

Maslow's theory of motivation

A. H. Maslow proposed a *theory of human motivation*, called Maslow's hierarchy of needs, which argued that needs could be placed within a hierarchical framework according to their priority. He listed these needs as follows:

(a) basic physiological needs — level 1;
(b) safety and security — level 2;
(c) belonging and social activity — level 3;
(d) esteem and status — level 4;
(e) self-realisation and fulfilment — level 5.

The basic principle of Maslow's theory of motivation is that each level of needs dominates another (see Fig. 6); until a basic need has been satisfied, man is unlikely to pursue other needs.

Thus we can see that in primitive or poverty-stricken societies, where life is carried out at a subsistence level and survival is threatened, it is unlikely that the members of that society will look far beyond the basic needs. Life will continually be a matter of satisfying the basic physiological needs. However in societies where technology is advanced and industrial productivity and relative economic stability

Fig. 6. *Maslow's hierarchy of needs.*

has been achieved, the satisfaction of basic physiological needs is no longer a major preoccupation. In a society such as the UK the need for food, water and warmth are rarely needs that dominate our life — we take them for granted. In general, personal incomes are at such a level that we can afford to satisfy our basic needs in a relatively effortless fashion. Having realised this, and wanting this state of affairs to continue, we attempt to make *safe* and *secure* our relative comfort. We achieve this in many ways; by storing food, by taking out life assurance, by joining a pension fund or a trade union, and so on.

In many respects, then, the satisfaction of the safety and security needs (level 2) establishes, consolidates and maintains the satisfaction of the basic, physiological needs (level 1). For example the need for a pension scheme (a level 2 need) is linked to a need for food and warmth (level 1 needs) during retirement when no earned income will be received.

Lower and higher-order needs
On this basis then, we may bracket together level 2 and level 1 needs as *lower-order needs*. These needs are finite and on the whole are satisfied in purely *economic* terms. By this we mean that once an individual has earned sufficient income to satisfy his lower-order needs and has established a steady income at this level he will then search out other needs. Maslow classifies these as *higher-order needs*; they include the needs for a sense of belonging and social activity, for esteem, prestige and status and for self-realisation and fulfilment.

Maslow's theory applied to the catering industry
At this stage we may assess the relevance of Maslow's theory to the catering industry by dividing up the workforce broadly into four

categories and applying the needs, modelled to each category in turn. We will examine the assertion that if you pay an individual enough (thus satisfying his lower-order needs) this will be sufficient to bring about the motivation to work. Rather than conclude in each case as to whether Maslow's theory applies or not, we will leave each example to be further discussed and examined by the student.

The itinerant workforce
This is a largely casual or seasonal body of workers, not necessarily permanent residents in their chosen area of work. Quite often their basic needs are satisfied in terms of being provided with food or accommodation at their place of work. Their relative impermanence often means that their wages are spent on entertainment, recreation and the satisfaction of short-term goals. The student might like to consider what factors exist to further motivate this category of worker.

Part-time or secondary employment
A large portion of the catering workforce is made up of employees who are working on a part-time basis or who are using employment in the catering industry as secondary employment, subsidiary to other employment elsewhere. This type of worker is often motivated to work:

(a) because of a lack of interest in outside or domestic life, i.e. taking up part-time employment to alleviate boredom;

(b) to satisfy the desire to obtain such things as luxury goods for the home—a new car perhaps or to save money to help pay for the family holiday.

The student may like to consider whether, in this case, the motivation exists to satisfy the needs beyond the lower-order ones.

Supervisory and management grades
This group of workers exists throughout the industry and operates in establishments at many levels. Their work is very time consuming and entails considerable responsibility, requiring the ability to co-ordinate staff functions, delegate responsibility, etc. Remuneration for this kind of work is substantial and in many cases fringe benefits such as company cars, expense accounts and free or cheap holidays often exist. In this example the student might like to decide whether financial satisfaction is the main motivating factor or might the need for recognition, status, promotion and a developed career structure also be considered?

Owner-operators
It is estimated that approximately 90 per cent of catering establishments are small units and consequently it is likely that these will be organised

and run by the owners themselves, employing a small number of versatile staff. Obviously a motivation will exist in this case to ensure that the operation makes a profit; what other needs will such owner-operators need to satisfy in this type of example?

The above classification of the catering workforce is both limited and broad. We have for example excluded much of the industrial labour force from our consideration. Our discussion is not intended to be exhaustive; we have simply put forward some examples so that the inquiring reader may discuss and test out for himself the relevance of Maslow's need's model to the catering industry.

Herzberg's theory of motivation

The next important theory of motivation in the workplace that we need to study is that formulated by Herzberg in the USA in the 1960s. Herzberg examined not only the motivational factors that Maslow had considered but also what he termed the maintenance factors. His basic contention was that if worker dissatisfaction existed through adverse job conditions, the improvement of these conditions would not be motivational in itself. Rather, in the eyes of the workforce these improvements of factors simply maintain what is necessary for suitable working conditions. Their absence from the work has a dissatisfying or negative effect on the workforce. Hence these factors have also been known as hygiene factors in that they support the mental health of the workforce.

Herzberg found, similarly to Maslow, that motivational factors, i.e. those factors which in their various forms lead to job satisfaction, also exist. Some of the motivational factors that Herzberg found in his studies were:

(a) achievement and recognition;
(b) areas of responsibility;
(c) promotional prospects.

Such factors as personnel policies and even fringe benefits were considered by the workers studied to be only maintenance factors, necessary for general job satisfaction rather than being motivators in themselves.

Motivation and maintenance factors

From Herzberg's analysis, a motivation maintenance model can be constructed whereby the factors which "motivate" can be contrasted with those that "maintain".

(a) Motivation factors have an intrinsic quality, i.e. they relate to the content of the job itself. Such factors might be the actual routine of carrying out the job, obtaining recognition for work carried out and having responsibility for job-related areas.

(*b*) Maintenance factors, in contrast, have an extrinsic quality, i.e. they relate to the context of the job—the setting or environment within which it takes place. In this category we can list such factors as company policy, actual working conditions, interpersonal relations and the way in which administration operates.

Maslow and Herzberg compared

Before moving on we can briefly compare the models of Maslow and Herzberg. The first point to be made is that Maslow's findings tend to relate to motivation in the general sense, i.e. they are not directed specifically towards an industrial or commercial setting. Herzberg's study, however, relates specifically to an examination of individual motivation in the workplace and cannot be realistically applied outside the workplace, as can the model of Maslow. Herzberg's analysis is particularly relevant in the modern industrial context where technology is highly advanced and socio-economic status is generally at a relatively comfortable level. Herzberg would argue that Maslow's lower-order needs for such things as safety and security are in fact maintenance factors, and that only the higher order needs for such things as status, esteem and recognition are motivational factors. So, where the workforce in any given society or situation has achieved a reasonably high level of social and economic status, the application of Herzberg's motivational–maintenance model is more appropriate than Maslow's need-priority model, where motivation is not really applicable to the lower-order needs.

McGregor's theory X and theory Y

A landmark in the study of human relations in the workplace was the publication of Douglas McGregor's highly influential book *The Human Side of Enterprise* in 1960, which brought into currency the now famous theory X and theory Y. In this work McGregor distinguished between two basic approaches or attitudes toward human relations; on the one hand theory X outlined the autocratic or authoritarian approach to individuals in the workplace, while theory Y outlined the supportive or participative approach. In order to understand McGregor's contribution to the field of human relations in the workplace, and more particularly to the study of motivation we will examine these two theories in some detail.

Theory X

This theory relates to a particular managerial approach. At a later stage (see page 79) we shall examine various types of leadership and managerial techniques, and an understanding of McGregor's work will in turn clarify this area.

McGregor's theory X is very much in line with what is known as the authoritarian or autocratic view of management, that management knows best, that orders are issued and should be followed unquestioningly by all who work within the organisation. This management theory is very much dependent upon the principle of power; by virtue of his position a manager can exert influence and authority over workers within the organisation.

The basic principles underlying theory X is that man has an inherent dislike for work and will avoid it wherever possible. Therefore individuals in the workplace need to be coerced, controlled, directed and in some cases possibly punished in order to achieve organisational goals. The theory continues by suggesting that individuals are on the whole unambitious—they wish to avoid responsibility and expect and desire direction and security from above. This in simple terms can be termed "donkey, carrot and stick" motivation; in order to move the donkey, a carrot attached to a stick is suspended at a point just beyond the reach of the donkey's nose, the assumption being that the animal will be stupid enough to pursue the carrot despite the fact that, for the duration of the journey at least, the carrot will remain at a fixed distance from him. The donkey does not want to move, but the inducement of the carrot is a persuading force, bringing about obedience. Support for this kind of theory provides justification for autocratic forms of management.

The following examples will serve to illustrate the effect that this kind of attitude may have in certain situations.

In the hotel and catering industry working hours are often not specified as it is commonly regarded that the employee is free to go home when a job has been completed. This has both advantages and disadvantages and can lead to minor disputes when management or staff who have customer contact also have to cope with staff who are waiting to close the kitchen. Several examples of this situation form different viewpoints which can be considered or discussed.

(a) A restaurant which closes at 11 p.m. may well try and rush customers through a meal in order to get rid of them as quickly as possible because the waiting staff know they cannot leave before the customer. This, however, gives a bad impression to the customer.

(b) A hotel dining room which serves the hotel's residents may well have last orders for meals at a certain time. A late arrival may therefore receive an adverse reaction from the kitchen staff who are cleaning down; they do not have to face the customer, who may well have already paid for the meal.

(c) A kitchen porter may well not be so efficient or thorough if he knows that when he finishes he may leave work.

Kitchens are notorious for their poor working conditions, heat, etc. However in the majority of establishments which have had extractor fans, etc., installed the equipment may be taken for granted, not used properly or, in some cases, not even switched on because it makes too much noise.

The quality of food served to staff may well be below that served to the customers. This will obviously affect staff morale and their attitudes to the establishment and its image.

(a) Whilst employers may not be able to consider giving the staff prime cuts of meat, etc., the food should be considered as important. The constant use of left-overs or of certain types of food may well have demoralising effect.

(b) Another consideration is that some staff may be allowed to eat off the menu or even in the restaurant, which may lead to resentment from other less favoured personnel. Against this it may well be a motivating factor in the status of some positions.

Theory Y

This theory may also be aligned with a particular managerial approach, which at this stage we may term the participative or democratic form of leadership. From its title it can be guessed that this form of leadership encourages participation in terms of responsibility and involvement at all levels of the organisational structure. This management approach has a *supportive function*, so that instead of applying pressure to achieve goals, as in the autocratic style of management, it creates a framework of support for the management team by delegating responsibility and allowing democratic processes to work.

McGregor's theory Y can be assumed to follow from this type of managerial approach. In contrast to theory X, theory Y states that individuals expend physical or mental effort at work as naturally as they do when at play. In addition, it argues that external controls are not the only means by which effort and application to a given role may be brought about. In this theory McGregor points out that individuals within the workplace may actually identify with the objectives and goals of an organisation and become committed to them. They may recognise the importance or value of these goals and rewards and thus may exercise self-control and self-direction in order to seek out responsibilities related to the job.

In more general terms theory Y argues that potential intellectual capacity in society is not full utilised and that individual capacity, in terms of imagination, creativity and ingenuity, is widely, not narrowly, distributed through the population.

From McGregor's analysis it becomes evident that the adoption of theory X or theory Y by management will have considerable effects upon the behaviour, performance, attitude and general well-being of the workforce. As we have seen, there exists a correlation between an autocratic management and theory X and between a participative form of management and theory Y. This can have dramatic consequences in terms of the workforce because, as McGregor points out, people tend to behave in the manner expected of them, either living "up" or "down" to the expectations of their superiors. Thus, for example, an employee working under an autocratic manager who is implementing McGregor's theory X is likely to behave in a manner expected of him, even though he may possess organisational skills and be able to take certain responsibilities. We could say that this individual was "living down" to management's expectations of him, such that there is obviously a wastage of talent and ability. This is pointed out by M. J. Boella in relation to the catering industry when he states: "In this industry unfortunately some managers expect the worst from all their subordinates and by making this apparent they inevitably get the worst results."

Our examination of the theories of motivation derived by Maslow, Herzberg and McGregor all illustrate the importance of a clearly-worked out managerial technique. Satisfactory standards, adequate levels of productivity and organisational efficiency cannot be achieved without careful attention being paid to management techniques and the personnel policy adopted. The value of the work carried out in this field therefore cannot be underestimated, and management must be aware of the implications of these theories and others in order to enable their organisations to function successfully.

Taylor and Mayo
In concluding this chapter we ought to refer to the work of F. W. Taylor and Elton Mayo carried out in the USA in the early part of the present century. Taylor is regarded by many as being an original thinker in relation to the human side of industry; indeed his major work *The Principles of Scientific Management* clearly emphasises the relationship between individuals in an industrial situation and their productive efficiency. The influence of his work created changes in the attitudes and roles of management, which in turn led to improvements in human relations in all areas of business, commerce and industry. Taylor carried out his researches at a time when interest in human relations in industry had increased because of the First World War. He attempted to provide a solution for what he saw as the "human problem" that affected industrial production. He argued that efficiency could be improved if the problems in industrial human relations could be dealt with.

Where Taylor emphasised the problems of human relations in industry, Mayo, a sociologist, was keen to assess the development and positive contribution of human relations in the industrial field. Mayo argued that if any industry has an organisation which is made up of individuals in different roles, all carrying out different duties, then this will be essentially a *social* system. He therefore argued that an understanding of this social system, and the individuals who are a part of it, is absolutely necessary for the smooth running of any industrial organisation.

CONCLUSION

We have briefly assessed some of the more important contributions to the study of individual motivation within the work environment. Our understanding of the catering industry and its successful operation will only be complete when we can apply the findings of this and other research to the various situations to be found throughout the catering industry.

SELF-ASSESSMENT QUESTIONS

1. Distinguish between primary and secondary individual needs.
2. Explain the relationship between motivation and needs.
3. List the needs placed in Maslow's hierarchical framework.
4. Distinguish between McGregor's theory X and theory Y.
5. Give an example to show when the fulfilment of a primary need is subordinated by the fulfilment of a secondary need.

CHAPTER SEVEN

The Role of Groups

```
CHAPTER OBJECTIVES
After studying this chapter you should be able to:
* distinguish between the role of formal and informal groups
  as they operate within the catering industry;
* explain the relationship these groups have with the
  organisation within which they exist;
* describe the different roles that groups have to play.
```

INTRODUCTION

So far our study of human relations in the workplace has concentrated upon the various aspects of the individual and his position within an organisation. We have examined in some detail the factors which contribute to the making of individual differences and we have analysed the factors that affect the motivation of individuals. We now need to broaden our analysis to incorporate an examination of the way in which groups operate within the context of business organisations in the hotel and catering industry.

In simple terms, groups of individuals are usually formed and recognised by certain objectives; the reason for forming a particular group is to carry out this objective, however loosely defined it may be. Thus we may say that the roles of various groups may be defined in terms of these objectives. The formation of a pressure group, e.g. CND is to bring about changes, to exert pressure. The formation of a charity such as the Save the Children Fund is to help people, in this case children, who are unable for whatever reason to look after themselves.

Similarly, within industry groups are formed to carry out certain functions. Within any given organisation there will be a number of different groups existing, each having a role to carry out and all contributing to the general aim of the organisation as a whole. It will be seen that the complexity of group relations in any industry will vary according to such factors as the size of the organisation, the functions of various groups, the types of group and many other factors.

Our analysis of groups may first be simplified by classifying them into two distinct categories. We call these categories formal and informal groups and we will discuss each in turn.

FORMAL GROUPS

The organisation of a given catering operation will define the structure and size of the formal groups that exist within it. In addition, the number of formal groups will be clearly defined in a similar way (see Fig. 7). Thus an analysis of formal groups and the various organisations they operate within will be examined in terms of a number of factors.

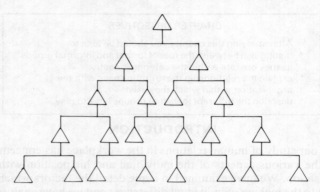

Fig. 7.   *Hierarchical structure of formal groups.*

The size of the operation, its location and whether the operation is seasonal or not will be predominant factors. Therefore our understanding of formal groups will be preceded by an analysis of the type of operation in question. We must also consider the role of the organisation's objectives and personnel policy in the system of communication that links the various groups together.

We will begin our analysis of formal groups therefore by considering a number of different types of hotel operation, bearing in mind that each example will only be representative of a range of many subtypes which may exist.

Large scale luxury hotel

The general characteristics of such an operation (see Fig. 8) are:

(a) delegation of responsibility throughout;
(b) a chain of command;
(c) a chain of communication;
(d) impression of inflexibility throughout;
(e) specific job descriptions for all members of the workforce.

It must also be remembered that hotels of this type are usually 24-hour operations, open seven days a week. Consequently all departments operate 16 and sometimes 24 hours a day. For this system to operate efficiently a hierarchy within the departments must be organised on a shift basis.

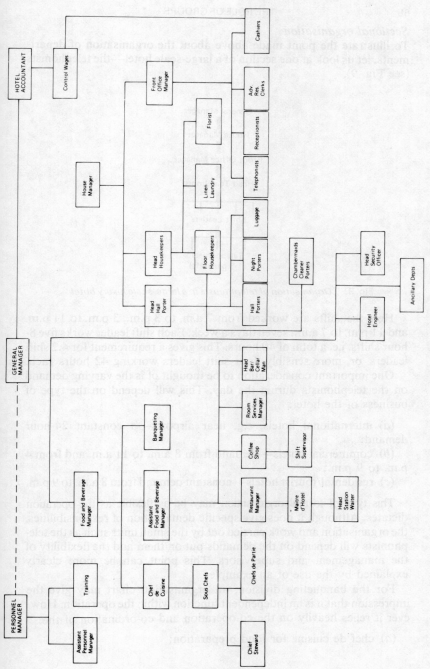

Fig. 8.   Formal groups in a large-scale luxury-type hotel.

Sectional organisation

To illustrate the point made above about the organisation of departments, let us look at one section of a large-scale hotel—the telephonists (see Fig. 9).

Fig. 9.   *Organisation of telephonists in a large-scale luxury hotel.*

Here the shifts are worked from 7 a.m. to 3 p.m., 3 p.m. to 11 p.m. and 11 p.m. to 7 a.m., seven days a week. Each shift leader works five 8-hour shifts, i.e. a total of 40 hours. This gives a requirement for 4.2 shift leaders, or, more sensibly, four shift leaders working 42 hours each.

One important consideration to be thought of is the varying demand on the telephonists during the day. This will depend on the type of business of the hotel:

(*a*) international hotels, e.g. near airports—a constant 24-hour demand;

(*b*) commercial hotels—demand from 8 a.m. to 11 a.m. and from 4 p.m. to 9 p.m.;

(*c*) residental/tourist hotels—constant demand from 8 a.m. to 9 p.m.

This type of formal organisation may be as flexible as the operation dictates. Although it does give specific demarcation of responsibilities, the organisation and work carried out by the small units such as the telephonists will depend on the demands put on them and the flexibility of the management and supervisors. This point can be more clearly explained by the use of an example.

For the banqueting division, an organisation chart may give the impression that it is an independent function within the operation. However it relies heavily on the co-operation and co-ordination of the:

(*a*) chef de cuisine for food preparation;

(b) chief steward for equipment/cleaning;
(c) restaurant manager for staffing;
(d) housekeeper for linen/table arrangements;
(e) head bar/cellarman for sale of liquor;
(f) security officer;
(g) head porter for movement of furniture/equipment.

The banqueting manager may therefore be regarded as the co-ordinator of other departments, services and staff, whilst actually having no or very few direct personnel in his department.

This may also be said of hotels dealing with tours/conferences/party travel at inclusive prices, where accommodation and food-based departments have to be co-ordinated. Flexibility may therefore be more necessary on the part of management/departmental heads/supervisors (shift leaders) rather than on the part of operatives.

The personnel manager and accountant are more independent, acting on company policy from head office and providing direct services and controls to all the departments that operate on a much more formal basis.

Medium-sized hotel

By this we mean a hotel of about 50–100 rooms, whose formal structure is as typified in Fig. 10.

Different demands will be put on such hotels, depending on their location, market, type and star rating (2, 3 or 4 stars). These demands will obviously dictate their organisation. All departments will operate for 8–10 hours per day, with the exception of reception, which will normally work 12–14 hours per day, and porters, who will work a 24-hour day. Most staff will work a 5–6 day week. Use will also be made in most departments of part-time staff to cover peak periods. Some establishments may even rely on general assistants to cover such peak periods or time off.

It will often be found that chambermaids will work a 6-hour day while bar/food/kitchen staff may have to work split shifts.

In several departments we would expect to find flexibility in the attitude of staff towards job descriptions, and a similar degree of co-operation and co-ordination between heads of departments.

Sectional organisation

In a larger operation the front office personnel will have specific duties, e.g. advance reservation, telephonist, etc. However the receptionist on duty in a medium-sized hotel can also expect her functions to cover:

(a) advance reservations;
(b) reception;

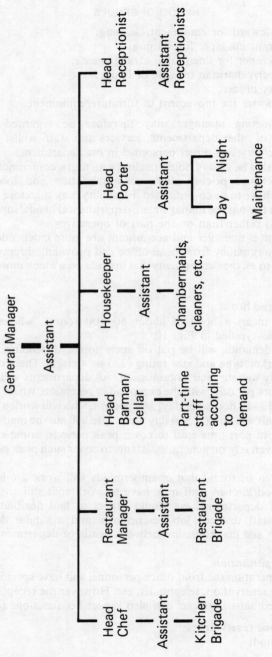

Fig. 10. Formal groups in a medium-sized hotel.

(c) billing and cashiering;
(d) information;
(e) telephonist;
(f) control aspects;
(g) secretarial services;
(h) social functions.

Similarly, kitchen personnel in larger operations are expected to be responsible for specific aspects of food preparation, e.g. sauce, fish, pastry, larder, roast/grill, vegetables, the breakdown obviously being dictated by the scale, size and type of the operation. However in medium-size operations chefs also are expected to be "all-rounders", capable of performing at least two or more functions, e.g.:

(a) sauce/grill/roast/fish/soup;
(b) breakfast and vegetables;
(c) larder;
(d) pastry.

This may well be dictated by the hotels' buying policy with regard to using prepared or convenience foods.

Small hotel

By this we mean a hotel run by the proprietor and his wife and employing two or three general assistants.

Various constraints on formal group organisation will exist within this type of operation, as previously mentioned, and its organisation structure (see Fig. 11) will be largely dictated by the skills of the proprietors in terms of their ability to meet the demands of food preparation and service.

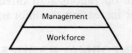

Fig. 11. *Organisation structure in a small hotel.*

The relationship between management and staff will clearly be very close, much closer than in a large operation. Therefore informal relations will play an important part in the successful running of the operation and will define much of the working situation.

Flexibility in terms of attitude, shifts, overtime, etc., will be required on the part of the management and the staff and, clearly, very broad job descriptions will have to be drawn up. A hotel operation of this kind tends to run by routine and the organisation of individuals rather than of groups. Thus although certain formalities are recognised, much of the success of the operation is dependent upon good informal relations between the different individuals working in the hotel.

Daily routine
This is the sort of routine that two general assistants might have to work in such an organisation.

   (*a*) 8 a.m.—serve morning teas.
   (*b*) 8.30 a.m.—serve breakfast.
   (*c*) 9.30 a.m.—wash up after breakfast.
   (*d*) 10 a.m.—lay up clean dining room for dinner.
   (*e*) 11 a.m.—make beds and clean rooms/corridors, etc.
   (*f*) 1 p.m.—finish work.
   (*g*) 6.30 p.m.—serve dinner.
   (*h*) 8 p.m.—wash up after dinner.
   (*i*) 8.30 p.m.—lay up dining room for breakfast.
   (*j*) 9 p.m.—finish work.

The ease with which this schedule may be carried out is often created by the fact that two general assistants might know each other well, thus being linked on an informal as well as on a formal basis. This often means that they will be able to operate quite naturally as part of a team. In addition, management, whilst acting in an accepted managerial capacity, will also be expected to carry out certain routine functions within the operation such as cook, receptionist, bar-person, maintenance, buyer, etc. When the social function is added to this list of possible tasks, i.e. informally chatting with guests in the lounge or bar, it can be seen that the role of the manager in a small-scale operation is a complex one.

Finally, in such small operations staff often live and eat with the proprietors, thus further increasing the informality of operations.

INFORMAL GROUPS

We have seen how important formal groups are to the successful functioning and overall efficiency of a number of different types of hotel operation. They will be integrated into the organisational structure, will be defined by personnel policy and will be administered by management.

However, within any organisation it will be found that the formation of informal groups also takes place. We can define these groups as those that are originally formed, not within the context of personnel policy or management objectives, but those that arise spontaneously to fulfill a need not necessarily met by any formal group. The importance of informal groups can be seen when we consider the fact that no formal system can foresee every eventuality or predict sudden changes of events.

The benefit of informal groups thus lies in the fact that they blend with formal groups that exist within the organisation, forming a cohesive working unit. By examining the functions of informal groups we will also bring to light their dysfunctions, i.e. the unwanted or unintended consequences of their existence.

Informal communication
It is necessary at this stage to make reference to Chapter Four, which deals with the informal organisation and the way in which communication takes place within it.

We need only say here, in addition, that although the existence of informal groups is closely linked to the informal organisation, informal communication often occurs within the organisation on a one-to-one basis as well as a group basis.

Perpetuation of cultural values
A second important function of informal groups is the part they play in the perpetuation of cultural values. We have already seen the importance of a culture in terms of individual differences and group identity.

Culture is an important aspect of all our lives; we cannot therefore expect the workforce of any given company to simply abandon their cultural values and beliefs when entering their place of work. Informal groups provide a means by which individual workers can continue to have a social or cultural identity whilst at the same time performing their specific function as a member of a formal working group. This will be particularly true in the hotel and catering industry, where the workforce is often drawn from a wide range of cultural backgrounds. It would be folly on the part of management to attempt to ignore these cultural affiliations; indeed progressive management is likely to encourage the formation of informal groups that perpetuate cultural values in order to create satisfaction throughout the workforce.

However this function also has its disadvantages. It could be that, by allowing the perpetuation of cultural values through these informal groups, possible segregation between cultural groups could occur, perhaps causing conflict in certain areas. In addition it is possible that this allowed perpetuation of cultural values on the part of the informal groups could cause resistance to change on the part of the workforce. For example, this could occur when the informal group maintains that past methods have been effective, so why change now. This attitude may well be damaging if the change which is being suggested is intended to bring about an improvement in working conditions or productivity.

Management must therefore ensure that it is in tune with the traditions and values of informal groups when intending to bring about change of any kind to the system.

Social needs and satisfactions

A third important function of informal groups is the way in which they provide for the *special needs and satisfactions* of the individual in the workplace. This is particularly important when the organisation is large, formal and impersonal, when it is to be expected that specialisation and a fairly strict division of labour exist. In this situation the worker is likely to feel a lack of personal identity, that he is merely a number, a small cog in a rather large machine and that he has very little status within the work environment.

This possible feeling of isolation, lack of meaning and power can have the effect of alienating or estranging the individual from his place of work. In turn this will have the effect of reducing productive output and overall efficiency. Clearly then the importance of informal groups in this area should not be under-emphasised; management cannot afford to discourage the formation of informal groups. When an individual can think about meeting friends and discussing sport or politics or sharing a joke with them during a tea-break or when having meals, he will be thinking little about what he finds disagreeable in his work. Management should therefore consider carefully the means by which this informal group function may be fostered. The formation of sports or social clubs may be encouraged, or perhaps inter-departmental soccer or table-tennis competitions organised.

No-one today would deny the need for tea-breaks at strategic times worker satisfaction and efficiency is achieved.

There is, of course, a danger in the formation of informal groups, in that it is possible for individuals to lose sight of company objectives if those of the informal group become dominant. In other words a "conflict of roles" may occur, where perhaps the role of staff social secretary impedes the efficiency of head receptionist. It is obvious that everything that benefits the employee is not necessarily beneficial to the employer. No-one today would deny the need for tea-breaks at strategic times during the day; they provide a welcome diversion from work and enable employees to relax and talk with friends. However disputes may occur regarding the length of these tea-breaks, management considering that if they are too long they will have a damaging effect upon service or production.

It can be seen then that this is an important area and one which requires careful analysis by management so that a balance between worker satisfaction and efficiency is achieved.

Social control in the workplace

Finally we must consider informal groups as they operate as agencies for social control in the workplace. We have already seen that control is exerted over the individuals in a workplace by virtue of the formal system. Thus if an individual is constantly late for work, for example, he may be penalised by a wage reduction; similarly, if certain deadlines are not met then pre-arranged bonuses will not be paid. These forms of social control operate as part of the formal structure; they will be defined by the personnel policy and workers will be contractually obliged to conform to them.

Social control also exists through the operation of informal groups. There will be pressure to conform by virtue of what are known as norms, i.e. the socially accepted way of doing things, and workers will be very conscious of what is seen to be the right or wrong thing to do in a given situation. This may be apparent in relatively minor things such as mode of dress, patterns of speech, leisure habits or, more significantly, in relation to the work itself. In some cases, for example, incentives are linked to group activity and if any member of that group is not seen to be making an adequate contribution, then there will pressure upon him to conform.

We sometimes find that these norms are so strong that non-adherence to them may bring about rejection or social ostracism—what has come to be known as "sending someone to Coventry". This entails ignoring and not communicating with the individual who has violated the accepted mode of behaviour until that person decides to conform.

Summary

To conclude this discussion of the role of formal and informal groups as they operate in the hotel and catering industry, we may make the following remarks.

(a) Firstly, it seems self-evident that in any organisation where human interaction takes place, some form of informal group formation will develop.

(b) Secondly, therefore, management will need to recognise the existence of these informal groups and perhaps integrate them with existing personnel policy.

(c) Thirdly, management must be particularly aware not only of the advantages that informal groups bring to organisations but also the possible disadvantages, some of which we have mentioned above.

(d) Finally, it must be seen that the informal group structure, whilst being related to and integrated with the formal group structure, must nevertheless always be subordinate to it.

The formal group structure will always be most important within the organisation and the various informal groups that evolve can be described as having a complementary or supportive role.

FACTORS AFFECTING THE GROWTH OF GROUPS

We continue with a discussion of some general points which relate to the role of groups within the catering industry. There are a variety of factors which affect the growth of both formal and informal groups and some of these require analysis.

Organisational flexibility

The efficiency of groups functioning within a given operation is affected by the degree of flexibility the organisation has. If, for example, the organisation is fairly rigid then we say that constraints are imposed upon the groups working within it. This may be measured in terms of efficiency; for example, if a production schedule is drawn up which places undue strain upon the workforce, then the effectiveness and efficiency of the group in question will be affected.

Autonomy

Another form of organisational constraint relates to the degree of autonomy or independence that a given group—a department or section—might have. A rigid system which allows for little autonomy and limited decision-making ability may well create tension at a number of levels. On the other hand, excessive flexibility may well encourage a high degree of autonomy, perhaps reducing effective communication and increasing the risk of inter-departmental isolation so that overall efficiency suffers.

Arising from this point, we should also briefly mention the need to define *the relationships between groups* and thus monitor such things as areas of responsibility, channels of communication, relative status, etc, to ensure that each group functions effectively according to predetermined goals.

The effects of change

The effective functioning of groups must also be seen in the context of change, whether this be social, economic or technological. Any organisation must be capable of adapting to a changing environment so that if change of any form occurs then the organisation and the groups within it may respond accordingly. Clearly, if a particular organisation becomes outmoded, perhaps in terms of methods of preparation or equipment used, then constraints are going to be imposed on the efficiency of that organisation and the working relations within it. A further example to illustrate this point is where, if a change occurs in the economy of scale within which a given operation functions, the organisation will also have to change otherwise undue constraints may be imposed upon the groups operating within that organisation.

THE SUPPORTIVE FUNCTIONS OF INFORMAL GROUPS

We have seen in these discussions the close relationship that exists between the organisation and the efficiency of the operation. This efficiency can be greatly enhanced if informal groups develop and operate to support the predominant formal group structure. Two important and closely related ways in which informal groups may achieve this supportive function are as follows.

The society of the firm

A phrase which is sometimes used to describe the sense of belonging to a company that individuals may feel is the society of the firm. A simple explanation of this phrase would be in terms of the attitudes of the individuals who work for the firm; they see themselves not simply as workers carrying out certain defined "nine-to-five" functions, for which they receive a pay-packet at the end of the week, but more as belonging to the company. They enjoy companionship in the workplace, achieve some degree of job satisfaction, feel they have a certain status and enjoy a position of mutual respect within the hierarchy of the company.

This notion of the society of the firm will only come about if the creation of informal groups occurs in a balanced positive manner. In addition, management will have to possess a progressive attitude toward such a development so that it may be encouraged and allowed to make a positive contribution to the standards within the company.

Coalition of interests

Closely linked to the notion of the society of the firm is what might be termed a *coalition of interests*. We may describe this as where the interests of individuals and groups within one company or operation are brought together in an attempt to achieve a mutually acceptable common goal. This will be very difficult to bring about in practical terms because so often the interests of different sections of the workforce or of management may differ widely. However a coalition of interests is something that management may strive to achieve in their own areas of operation. Some of the means by which this may be brought about are as follows.

(*a*) Incentive schemes may perhaps be organised on a group basis, where all members of the group work together to achieve a common goal, e.g. the front office team.

(b) Participative decision-making allows all members of staff to feel as if they are contributing to the progress of the company and brings them into contact with the running of the actual operation.

(c) Encouraging alignment with the firm's objectives may be difficult to achieve without some degree of concession or compromise by both employers and employees.

(d) Introducing direct worker participation schemes in the form of company shares or worker ownership by degrees involves all staff in achieving economic profitability.

(e) The creation of friendly competition between units of the same firm in terms of productivity levels on the one hand and social events, e.g. department hockey matches, on the other.

In all these attempts to bring about a coalition of interests or create a society of the firm, care must be taken on the part of management not to create a claustrophobic environment whereby staff feel trapped by their work environment and the demands it might place upon them. Ideally, all staff will feel that their efforts, either via the formal group structure or the informal group structure, will collectively be contributing to the overall success of the firm.

CONCLUSION

We must conclude from the foregoing discussion that we cannot afford to generalise about the role of groups in the catering industry. We have seen that the role of groups in the industry is very much context bound, i.e. we have to examine situations individually to obtain a picture of the most efficient group relationships. Our analysis shows that what is necessary for the success of any operation is a harmonious working relationship between the informal and formal group structures which will contribute to an overall cohesive working unit. In addition the value of intelligent leadership will, of necessity, be involved. In the next chapter we will examine the various factors connected with leadership.

SELF-ASSESSMENT QUESTIONS

1. Describe a formal group.
2. Describe an informal group.
3. Draw up an organisation chart for a medium-sized hotel (50 to 100 rooms).
4. What is the more common name given to the process of informal communication that takes place in a large-scale organisation?
5. Describe why the perpetuation of cultural values might be important in a working situation.
6. What is the term "social ostracism" more commonly known as?
7. Explain the phrase "the society of the firm".

Leadership

INTRODUCTION

So far we have examined the factors which affect individual and group behaviour in the context of the hotel and catering industry. We have studied various theories which have been proposed to explain what motivates individuals and, further, we have attempted to assess the roles of the different types of group that may be found in industry and the effect these may have on the success or failure of a given operation. From our examination it should therefore have become clear that the workplace in all its different forms presents a very lively human situation. It is constantly changing according to influences, both internal and external, and varies according to individual and group behaviour. In this constantly changing environment various controlling elements are necessary in order to channel the energies into a cohesive, productive working unit.

It is fair to say that, without some form of leadership, a large amount of human activity is directionless and confused. In the context of the workplace this will clearly lead to inefficiency, time wasting, lost production, etc. We have discussed the importance of organisation to any given operation and the way in which it relates to formal and informal group behaviour. No organisation, however, will function without some form of leadership; indeed leadership is necessary to create an organisation that is suitable in any given working situation.

LEADERSHIP AND MANAGEMENT

It is first of all important to make a clear distinction between leadership and management. Generally speaking, we would expect a good manager to possess powers of leadership, but the two do not necessarily go hand in hand. By definition, a successful leader by some means gets people to follow him, but there is no guarantee that he will be leading these people in the right direction. Thus an individual may have strong leadership qualities but he may encourage people to follow him in directions which are not necessarily in accordance with the aims of the organisation. He could therefore be termed a bad manager.

On the other hand a manager may be particularly proficient in drawing up personnel policies, objective planning and work-study programmes, but not have the qualities to implement them nor to motivate the individuals in the workforce to follow him.

These examples are, on the whole, extremes. Generally speaking, management will also possess qualities of leadership. Therefore our analysis of the factors which contribute to the quality of leadership and to the various types of leadership that might be found in different situations can be regarded as essential to our understanding of organisational management.

The importance of leadership

The role and value of leadership in the catering industry cannot be underestimated. In the same way that it is essential to provide a good service and constantly to update and renew equipment and methods, it is equally important to provide the industry with a steady stream of intelligent and highly motivated leaders. In general it is true to say that good leaders help to develop good employees, and an operation with good employees is likely to be an efficient operation, able to compete successfully in its own particular field.

Our approach to the study of leadership, then, will follow two main paths. Firstly, we will analyse the factors that are generally held to be the most important in contributing to successful organisational leadership. Secondly, we will outline and discuss the various types of leadership and their applicability and appropriateness to particular industrial and commercial settings.

FACTORS CONTRIBUTING TO EFFECTIVE LEADERSHIP

Before we discuss these factors we ought to look back to Chapter Six, which deals with individual differences. It will be seen that an understanding of this chapter will have some bearing on the present analysis.

Intelligence

It is generally agreed that the most successful leaders are in possession of higher-than-average levels of *intelligence*; this is, then, clearly an important factor to be considered.

When we considered the factors that contributed to the intellectual capacity of an individual we noted such things as powers of reasoning, perceptual speed, memory, numerical ability, etc. It can be clearly seen that possession of these elements at a relatively high level will be an advantage as far as leadership is concerned. For example, a hotel manager, when preparing his annual budgeting schedule will require, amongst other things:

(a) Powers of reasoning so that he can calculate or predict the necessary stocks to obtain, the likely number of guests to cater for, the numbers of staff required, etc.

(b) In addition he will also have to calculate the accounts for the budgeting schedule, thus requiring numerical ability.

(c) In a more general sense the manager will also need to possess oral ability, i.e. an ability to communicate his knowledge, skills and experience to his staff in order to motivate them to carry out various activities.

(d) He will also need a powerful memory which will enable him to memorise as much useful information as possible without having to refer to records in a time of pressure.

(e) He will need spatial ability in relation to such things as staff deployment, utilisation of space and other resources, etc.

(f) He will also need perceptual speed when "sizing up" the pros and cons of a given situation when there is very little time for careful contemplation. This might arise when dealing with the kind of crisis that sometimes occurs during food service, when time for thinking is reduced to a minimum and a quick decision has to be made.

From the above points it should therefore be evident that the successful leaders within an organisation will possess an intellectual capacity which will be larger than the average employee he will be in control of.

Experience

Intelligence alone will be insufficient as an element contributing to the quality of leadership; indeed it is possible for an individual to possess a high level of intelligence but be unable to channel this into constructive or purposeful activity. Child prodigies, for example, who are very intelligent for their age, may only be able to direct this in limited areas of application. Experience is a quality which contributes heavily to successful leadership. A manager with a breadth of experience and a wide range of interests and activities is therefore more likely to be able to cope with and be familiar with the kind of situations that may arise in the work situation.

Experience is not simply exposure over a long period to events, people and situations; it is *learning* from them and being able to apply this knowledge in future, similar situations. The leader who possesses a breadth of experience is usually also a person who has developed a reasonably high level of maturity and emotional stability. As we observed earlier (see page 43), possession of this personality trait is particularly important in any environment where constant human contact takes place under some degree of pressure, where deadlines have to be kept and standards maintained.

Human relations attitude

This factor naturally evolves from experience. Our assessment of the importance of experience led us to a brief discussion of emotional stability and the ability to deal with other individuals in the workplace. Quite simply, successful leadership will not be achieved without careful attention to human relations, i.e. an ability to be aware of the individuals whom one is attempting to control and to develop social understanding and operate social skills when in contact with the workforce. If a leader is able to achieve this it will illustrate that he possesses not only an understanding but a respect for the people who are working with him. In turn it is then likely that this respect and understanding amongst the workforce will be reciprocated, thus creating a harmonious and efficient set of working relationships.

Achievement and motivation

In Chapter Six we discussed the importance of motivation as a factor contributing to the drive and sustained application of individuals in the workplace. As long as an individual has needs he will be motivated to fulfill them. Maslow's analysis centred upon a hierarchy of needs, arguing that once our lower-order needs are fulfilled we tend to seek out and attempt to fulfill other higher-order needs.

Clearly the motivation to fulfill these needs will vary from individual to individual, but it is likely that an individual who is attempting to become a successful manager will be in possession of higher-order needs. Indeed, we may argue that for any leader to be successful he *must* possess these higher-order needs. Without constantly seeking to achieve goals, fulfilling needs and reaching objectives, the leader is likely to stagnate, weaken and eventually lose the understanding, respect and control that he previously may have cultivated.

We may further argue that a successful leader will, in Maslow's terms, be continually striving for the goal of "self-actualisation" or "self-realisation", i.e. the very pinnacle of the needs hierarchy. His success will hinge upon his desire to explore new areas, accept challenges and to take on responsibility. At the same time, however, he will have to be seen to be achieving these motivational goals, otherwise his workforce is likely to lose confidence in and respect for his leadership.

Before moving on to a discussion of the various types of leadership we should finally point out that the factors dealt with above which contribute to successful leadership must be seen in a given context or situation. These factors provide us with an outline so that we may be aware in *general* what contributes to successful leadership. We must be aware that in any situation different leadership qualities will be called upon; the success of any leader will be measured in his ability to cope efficiently with every individual, every group, every event or unforeseen circumstance that may arise in any working day.

LEADERSHIP TYPES

The concluding remarks of the preceding section may lead us to believe that if successful leadership is measured in terms of effectiveness in given situations, then a discussion of types of leadership will be fraught with difficulties. How may we talk in general terms about leadership types when we need to analyse each individual leader in terms of each situation he has to deal with?

We are clearly talking here about two extremes and it is necessary to achieve a balance between viewing each specific case relevant to leadership quality and talking in general terms about leadership types. This will be achieved by first of all attempting to distinguish between various types of leadership, determining in what ways they overlap or may be linked, and finally assessing the way in which they may be applied to or be successful in a number of given practical situations.

We may distinguish between the various types of leadership by examining the way in which they exercise the *power* that they have and also the way in which they organise *decision-making* within the organisation. We will examine the three most commonly accepted styles of leardership—authoritarian, democratic and laissez-faire—and discuss each in turn.

Authoritarian

The authoritarian or autocratic style of leadership is the most common form of leadership, traditionally found not only in the catering industry but in industry and commerce in general. In simple terms it is a style of leadership which possesses the greatest degree of individual power and decision-making. The authoritarian type of leadership entails the view that any form of consultation is a weakness and that the individual who is in a position of responsibility should have sole authority over the decisions that are to be made within the organisation.

Advantages
Clearly the authoritarian leader will exert a considerable amount of power within the organisation and will therefore determine the manner in which it develops and, ultimately, its degree of success. By taking

control of the decision-making process the authoritarian leader takes full responsibility for the decisions that are made and therefore his success or failure will be easily measurable.

The advantage of this position is that decisions can be made quickly, without having to deal with the consultative process, and acted upon accordingly. Within the catering industry there are numerous situations where speed of decision-making is absolutely necessary. For example, during food service, where timing and co-ordination has to be exact, inefficiency would probably arise if too much time was devoted to discussing and then deciding upon courses of action to take.

In addition the authoritarian leader is positive in his approach; he should be able to motivate the workforce to achieve goals *for him*. Individuals in society are, in varying degrees, brought up to expect authoritarian leadership; parents, school teachers, policemen all represent examples of authoritarian figures. Indeed many individuals expect to be led because, as they have grown up, they have been used to different forms of authoritarian control in the home, at school and in the wider society.

Disadvantages

However the negative effect of this type of leadership is that the workforce may reject the authoritarian approach; they may not respect this form of leadership, feeling that they are uninformed and looked down upon. The effect of this may be quite damaging for a given operation in that motivation and morale amongst the workers may decrease. This may in turn have the effect of decreasing the productivity and the efficiency of the organisation as a whole.

Democratic leadership

Unlike the authoritarian style of leadership, this allows the workforce to participate in the decision-making process. This has the effect of decentralising power and delegating responsibility amongst the workforce rather than vesting it in the hands of one manager. Consultation here would be regarded as a positive contribution to the process of decision-making, encouraging the workforce to make suggestions and put forward ideas about aspects of their work. However the manager using this style of leadership should in no way be seen to be abdicating any responsibility, but rather as engendering co-operation and involvement amongst the workforce.

Advantages

The intended effect of this approach is to raise the general interest in the job, making the individual worker feel that his contribution is of value and that he is an integral part of a team involved in the goals of the organisation. It may be particularly useful when decisions have to be made regarding such things as working out duty rosters, overtime schemes, work-study programmes, etc., where speed is not necessarily essential and a range of contributions from members of staff is valuable.

Disadvantages
In contrast to the authoritarian style, democratic leadership tends to be slower in that decision-making cannot function so quickly and therefore may not be so effective in emergencies or situations of extreme pressure, e.g. food service.

Laissez-faire leadership
Laissez-faire is a French phrase which literally means "leave well alone" or to give a "free rein". Successful operation of this style of management might occur in a situation where the manager can afford to leave the responsibility for decision-making and the running of an operation or section to a group of trusted, well-motivated workers.

Advantages
The use of laissez-faire leadership may have the positive effect of making the workers who are involved feel responsible, important and trustworthy, thus motivating them to achieve good results within the sphere of work.

Disadvantages
On many occasions, however, the use of laissez-faire leadership does not have these positive effects; it may often provide excuses for inefficient or weak management, allowing the motivation of the workforce to decrease so that production and efficiency eventually suffer.

The negative effect of the laissez-faire approach is that it does not allow for the inspiration of an individual leader, and in the catering industry, where "pressure points" exist, in many operations this lack of positive leadership might be damaging to the overall efficiency of the organisation. For example, if the front office team is using the laissez-faire approach it is possible that junior or inexperienced receptionists may not be able to cope with the complexity of requirements they are confronted with during busy checking in and out periods. This may lead to queries, hold ups and, more importantly, frustrated guests anxious to check in to their rooms or leave the hotel. In this situation the organisational skills and experience of a manager with a more authoritarian approach may be able to take control of the situation and overcome the problems involved.

The laissez-faire type can be effective providing it is not an excuse for weak leadership and it does not have to operate under excessive pressure.

LEADERSHIP AND THE CATERING INDUSTRY

Management styles

For a variety of differing reasons, management styles may be applied more flexibly in the hotel and catering industry than in other industries. The need for this greater flexibility of management style and approach is often dictated by location, the labour force available, the market catered for, the individual geography of an operation and the attitude or policy of the owners, whether they be a single-unit operation or part of a national group.

Large-scale operations

A large hotel may well employ a manager to run each department according to the standards and policy set down by the owners. In this case the manager may well have a democratic style of leadership with his departmental heads, or even a laissez-faire style (provided standards are adhered to) if he does not possess the specific skill necessary to run a department, e.g. the kitchen. Although he might have a knowledge of the product and the standard or quality expected, he may well have to leave menus or dishes to his chef's interpretation or individual skills.

However, away from his heads of department, personnel working in his establishment may well find his leadership style authoritarian. This may present an "ivory tower" image of management to staff in large-scale operations, although this need not be damaging. The approach enables management to communicate socially with the public and hotel guests, which itself is an important management function. The successful delegation of authority in key areas frees management to engage in this kind of necessary social contact.

Medium- and small-scale operations

Heads of departments and management in medium-sized operations have more direct contact with staff in a working situation than in large operations; from time to time they may well be working alongside staff when there are pressure periods, e.g. during banquets and at peak periods during food service or when guests are checking in and out of the hotel in groups. This calls for knowledge of day-to-day systems, being able to assess pressures in advance by reasoning from past experience and being aware of limitations of staff or equipment.

Coping with crises

Supervisors may well be involved in implementing working systems and training staff in the operation of these systems. However these systems are only meant to cope with the normal day-to-day operations, and when the unexpected happens, such as a machinery breakdown, the ability to reorganise and redeploy staff is essential.

An example of this might well be when a dishwashing machine breaks down during breakfast, necessitating dish-washing by hand. Time is obviously important in such a situation, as plates, cutlery, etc., will be needed for a second sitting of breakfast or for lunch. Consequently pressure is on the supervisor to ensure that the customers are not affected.

Fortunately the customers may never be aware of such crises, but in the event of this happening the supervisor's skills can well be stretched if, as well as implementing a system to cope with a crisis, he or she also has to pacify guests or apologise or explain new procedures to them as well. A mature, stable approach is needed to cope with such a situation.

Employee motivation

In situations where essential work in the operation of the hotel can be monotonous, such as room cleaning or control procedures, the supervisor or management must consider the motivation of employees. For example, some hotel companies pay by the number of rooms cleaned, in which case it is up to the supervisor to maintain standards as the employee's main motivation is money. Here we can find authoritarian styles of leadership an advantage; if the employee was left unchecked standards would soon drop and, consequently, in the long-term, revenue also.

In the employment of career-motivated staff one may well find it more advantageous to adopt a laissez-faire style, in the hope of stimulating potential senior employees in the creation of new ideas. Obviously before adopting such a style, the staff background must be carefully considered to ensure they have the experience to be put in such a position.

Layout of establishment

The physical layout of the building may have some influence on styles of leadership. Hotels are often large rambling buildings, which means that management is not able to constantly watch over staff, which in turn can often influence the type of leadership adopted, necessitating a more democratic style.

This may also influence selection procedures, as considered later in the text (see page 113).

CONCLUSION

We have made an analysis of the factors which contribute to successful leadership and we have also examined some of the types of leadership that may be found in a variety of situations within the catering industry. In summarising this chapter, one important point requires emphasis. Any appraisal of successful leadership must hinge upon the context in which it is viewed; in other words it must be viewed in relation to the particular situation in which it operates. We cannot generalise and say, for example, that the democratic style is most suited in all industrial situations or that the human relations attitude is of primary importance in successful leadership. We must assess each situation and attempt to understand its requirements; then we may be able to understand the most suitable leadership approach.

Ultimately, the leader in any given organisation is required to motivate the workforce to achieve the goals and objectives prescribed by the organisation. Thus if the organisational goal is profit through production then the successful leader will work to bring about this goal, adapting the various types of leadership to different situations and being constantly aware of his own position and performance within this working framework.

SELF-ASSESSMENT QUESTIONS

1. What are the four basic factors mentioned in the text which contribute to effective leadership?

2. List the three main leadership types.

3. Give three examples of an authoritarian figure.

4. Describe a possible negative effect of laissez-faire leadership in the catering industry.

5. What influence might the geographical layout of a hotel have on the style of leadership used?

CHAPTER NINE

Personnel Functions

CHAPTER OBJECTIVES

After studying this chapter you should be able to:
* understand the personnel function in a hotel and catering operation;
* know the considerations made in personnel organisation structures;
* understand the factors which determine staffing levels.

INTRODUCTION

Wherever people are employed there is a personnel function, the size and organisation of which will vary according to the number of employees and the individual needs of the organisation. This therefore leads us to assume the greater the number of employees, the more complex the administration of the personnel department will be. The wide range of skills involved in hotel and catering operations also increases the complexity of the personnel department, in that they have to place the right person in the right job for the right period of time.

The personnel department should recognise the needs of the organisation, both economic and functional, as well as the needs of the employee during his employment with that organisation. These factors should be uppermost in the mind when the personnel policy is formulated and its procedures administered. Some sections in this chapter have been dealt with more fully than others as the areas of recruitment, training and legislation are detailed in later chapters.

THE ROLE OF THE PERSONNEL FUNCTION

Personnel and industrial relations policy

When the overall policy of a business organisation is formulated as to its aims and objectives, policies relating to all aspects of management, whether they are financial, marketing or personnel, will be formed to meet those aims and objectives, all of which will be interrelated.

The personnel policy will be to recruit, select and train staff, as well as to design methods of remuneration and reward for those in employment within that particular organisation. The objective is ultimately to supply a workforce that fulfills the need of the organisation's management in the satisfactory provision of the product or service offered. There is also a need to satisfy legislation for the protection of the public and employees in the fulfilment of these objectives, both in the workplace and as regards the product or service supplied.

Personnel policy should therefore embrace all these considerations as an integrated part of the overall company policy.

Recruitment

The recruitment methods used in the hotel and catering industry will be discussed more fully in the next chapter; it does, however, form one of the major roles of the personnel function due to the transient nature of the industry's workforce. Methods of recruitment will vary according to the type of position available, whether it be management, skilled, semi-skilled or unskilled. Other factors may also influence methods used, such as the urgency of the need to fill a post, the location of the work-place with regard to its accessibility, and specialist requirements of the job and establishment.

A recruitment policy itself needs to be formed within the framework of the personnel policy. Recruitment can prove expensive; hence the need to be able to use the best method for any vacancy that may occur in order to make suitable applicants aware of vacant posts. It may be argued that during periods of high unemployment recruitment is easier than during periods of full employment. However when specialist skills are required it is still in the best interests of any business organisation to recruit the most suitable person for a particular position.

Selection and appointment

Selection involves the assessment of candidates who have applied for a particular vacancy, with the objective of engaging the most suitable person who will fulfill the general needs of the organisation and the specific needs of the post available. There are various methods of selection which can be used, depending on the particular requirements of the vacancy. However, different business organisations will have laid down procedures on staff selection. For example procedures set down by government organisations such as the National Health Service or local education authorities have been negotiated with trade unions as regards recruitment, applications, interviewing and appointment of all employees, whether externally or internally appointed. Selection procedures in the commercial sector of industry may not be so rigid, but the method of assessing candidates must be formulated from the application through to the appointment of the successful candidate and notification of the unsuccessful applicants.

Methods of selection and appointment will be considered in greater detail in the following chapter, but it must be emphasised here that the objective of selection and appointment is to place the right person in the right vacancy, choosing from the candidates that are available.

Remuneration benefits

It may be said that the financial incentive is not the only incentive. However the amount of take-home pay must, by necessity, be of vital importance to most employees and their families. Wages paid in the hotel and catering industry are a sensitive topic and are often regarded as a bone of contention between employers and employees. This is due to anomalies such as tipping, service charges, accommodation and meals on duty that are provided for staff as extra benefits in addition to wages.

Irregular hours are worked by most employees in the hotel and catering industry, and a large proportion of the services provided are labour intensive, thus creating high labour costs. Being an industry where minimum rates of pay are set by wages council, employers tend to pay what they can afford or, in some cases, the basic minimum as set down by the wages council. This puts an even greater emphasis on the extra benefits staff have through living in. Whilst these extra benefits can well be costed out in monetary terms, there is often resentment from staff because of the discrepancy in the standard of accommodation and food they receive in comparison with the product being sold to the customer.

There is an increasing trend in the industry to make extra payments to staff through incentive schemes or bonuses, as a reward for achieving targets set down by management. Examples of these may be sales bonuses to receptionists, profitability bonuses to chefs or customer-recommended good-service bonuses to porters or floor staff. Seasonal establishments often make end-of-season payments to staff as an incentive to them to complete the agreed period of work. The payment of bonuses is arguable on both sides, as is that of service charges and tipping; they can all often lead to discontentment amongst staff and require delicate handling by the personnel department and management alike.

The policy of remuneration within a hotel and catering organisation therefore has to be finely balanced, taking into consideration all the points mentioned above. It must then be presented to the staff as a complete package.

Induction procedure

The induction procedure is to acquaint the new employee with the organisation and with his work colleagues. This procedure should start at the initial stage of the prospective employee's recruitment and job application, when he or she should be informed of the company and the actual job applied for.

When the employee actually starts work for the organisation, the first period should be spent introducing the employee to his new work environment, its systems, procedures, rules and regulations. Whilst induction programmes will be dealt with more fully in Chapter Eleven it must be emphasised here that the introduction of employees to any new work is essential, whether the new employee be a general manager of an organisation or a kitchen porter. The procedure involved will be similar in content for all employees at the outset, although more relevant details regarding specific departments or jobs may be adopted at a later stage of induction, according to the scope of the job and the needs of the individual.

Many large organisations have realised the need for formal induction to the workplace and have planned induction programmes which take place every week for new employees. One role of the personnel department might therefore be to organise such programmes and ensure that all employees start work on say a Monday, when such a programme would function, and that all departments of an operation are organised to contribute to it as and when necessary.

Various management surveys have shown that the highest level of staff turnover occurs during the first two months of employment, which indicates that either the candidate recruited for a position was wrong or that he or she was not introduced to the workplace adequately. This in turn indicates a need for induction procedures whatever the size of the organisation or the vacancy within it. Proper induction procedures are therefore beneficial to the organisation and the employee alike.

Records and performance appraisal

The need for detailed information on staff in every type of establishment is necessary to carry out the personnel function. This information will have a variety of purposes, both administrative and welfare related. How a business goes about organising and obtaining this information will depend on a variety of factors ranging from size, i.e. number of persons employed, training procedures, promotion and staff development policies, statistical purposes, wages compilation, after-employment testimonials, disciplinary actions, timekeeping and absences.

In a small organisation, apart from basic personal details and wages records, the employer will probably rely on memory and personal contacts for his information regarding his employees. However the larger the organisation the more impersonal the relationship between employer and employee becomes, and this necessitates keeping detailed records of employees and their history with the company.

The process could start with the employee's application form, giving personal details and background preceding employment with the organisation. This may be substantiated by past testimonials or references, copies of certificates, etc. Once an employee has joined the organisation a personnel record card should be completed (as illustrated in Chapter Eleven, see Fig. 31); this will record the employment of the individual with the company with regard to jobs performed, wage details and changes, training and other relevant details. Any supporting documents should be attached to this as and when necessary. The wages and salaries department will keep records regarding hours of duty and timekeeping, e.g. clock-cards, timesheets and duty rosters, in order to prepare the employees' wages. They will also keep ongoing records to cover PAYE details and national insurance contributions; this they are required to do by law.

Records of employees are an essential part of the personnel function as they serve many useful purposes and can be referred to by management or supervisors with regard to training needs, promotions and transfers, wage increases, disciplinary action and other aspects of performance appraisal. The statistical function in large organisations might also be linked to such records, e.g. for the preparation of staff turnover, training, absence, overtime, timekeeping, accidents and welfare statistics.

Employment records may be kept in a variety of ways. In the past they have been kept in folders containing all relevant details applying to individual employees, or by card index. With the increasing use of computers in the industry, and a corresponding increase in the software systems available, records are now kept on computer tape or disk by many medium-sized and large organisations. The use of computers has obviously increased the flexibility and use of employee records, allowing the employer to keep a much closer watch on personnel developments.

It must also be emphasised that security regarding employees' records must be very strictly adhered to. Because of their very confidential nature, access to such records must be limited to senior personnel or personnel department staff within an organisation. Where physical records are kept either in files or folders, they should be locked away in steel filing cabinets in the personnel or wages office; in the case of computers, access to codes, tapes and disks should be strictly limited. As a protection against loss through fire or other disasters, fireproof cabinets may be used or it might be necessary to keep duplicate tapes or disks in a separate place.

The maintenance of an adequate system of employee records will therefore enable an organisation to follow the personnel policy efficiently and give accurate appraisal of its employees regarding all decisions concerning their employment.

Training and development

The training and development of employees within an organisation will form a major part of the company's overall personnel policy. Whilst the company may have a general policy, one of the major considerations contained therein will be the individual needs of the employee. Therefore a training policy can only be general until the needs of the individual have been considered by his manager, supervisor or training officer. The training policy should also consider the changing factors within the industry and organisation with regard to the need to retrain or update staff as and when necessary because of new technology, systems and legislation.

Training, it can be said, starts at the selection stage of an employee's stay with a company and finishes when the employment is terminated for whatever reason. During this period the employee is at first introduced to the working situation by induction training; this is followed by training in the job he has been engaged to do, which is in turn followed by retraining as and when necessary. Training may also be seen as a part of a staff development programme; e.g. when an employee shows the qualities necessary for supervisory, management or senior management positions. It may be necessary to train them in supervisory skills or more advanced management techniques, e.g. budgeting, interviewing and selection techniques or industrial relations procedures. Legislation demands that staff have adequate training in all aspects of safety and fire precautions, which increases pressure on all organisations to have a well-planned and closely monitored training plan.

In Chapter Eleven a closer consideration is given to the various types of training programmes and how they should be planned, organised and monitored.

Termination of employment

An employee can terminate his employment with an organisation in most instances by resignation, through retirement or redundancy or through dismissal by his employer. It must be said that one of the primary functions of personnel practices is to minimise staff turnover, as it can prove to be very expensive in monetary terms through lost productivity, recruitment and training costs as well as harm to the goodwill of the organisation as an employer. Whilst procedures regarding termination are often vague in most business organisations, it can prove most worthwhile to establish a practice to be followed which may be varied according to the circumstances involved.

Dismissal from employment by the employer is covered by various statutes, which are explained further in Chapter Thirteen, and disciplinary procedures are further discussed in Chapter Fifteen. However the establishment of procedures may be set up in joint consultation with trade unions. The personnel department must make all departments aware of such procedures to avoid any allegations of "unfair dismissal", which can prove expensive to the employer.

It must be made clear to management and supervisors exactly who has the power to dismiss staff; some organisations leave this responsibility to departmental managers whilst others see it solely as a function of the personnel manager. This will obviously vary according to the organisation, structure and size of the company; however it ought to be recognised that dismissal should not be left to one person alone and that some consultation with superiors or personnel should take place to avoid recriminations, either legal or otherwise.

The personnel department may also have to act as a mediator in such situations and make certain recommendations to management or the employee. A final function in the dismissal procedure may be to hold an inquiry to establish certain reasons for a dismissal and make recommendations so as to prevent a recurrence of the situation.

Staff resignations have, in most cases, some substantial reason on the part of the employee, though it can be said that in the hotel and catering industry the transient nature of the workforce is responsible for a fair proportion of staff turnover. A periodic analysis of reasons for staff resignations can often establish flaws in company policy, either overall or in personnel policies. Examples of reasons for resignation, established by such an analysis, may be that competitors are offering better conditions of employment and wages, that there is dissatisfaction with supervisors or management, that poor recruitment practices are placing the wrong people in the wrong jobs, that there is a lack of training both in induction and job training or that there is a lack of career development opportunities.

On reviewing any analysis, personnel are then able to make recommendations to the company's senior management with a view to changing company policy in order to eliminate or minimise labour turnover. Some organisations have their own policy with regard to resignations. In certain circumstances when an employee gives his notice of termination to the organisation he is paid off immediately and asked to leave, the argument being that he can do damage to the establishment if he stays on or that he will be non-productive and cause disruption. This sort of practice is frowned upon in the catering industry as it does not encourage goodwill between the company and its employees. It also causes disruption to the work situation and can often lead to hasty recruitment of a replacement, as well as the extra costs involved either through the payment of temporary staff or loss in business. Procedures regarding termination of employment by either party should be made clear to employees at induction, so that the employee is fully aware of his obligations.

Redundancy occurs when a job ceases to exist through business reorganisation, mergers between two organisations or bankruptcy. The employer has certain obligations to fulfil as laid down by law, e.g. redundancy payments; these are dealt with further in Chapter Thirteen. In the negotiation of redundancy the employer is obliged to negotiate with the employee or his trade union in order to minimise the effects of redundancy, whether through early retirement or the phasing out of certain positions, and to provide adequate compensation.

A form of redundancy also occurs in seasonal operations where staff are engaged for a limited period of time, e.g. at holiday resorts or when business falls off sufficiently to make it financially unviable. In these types of operation the employer must make it clear to the employee the exact terms of the agreement or contract of employment as to how long the employment will last and any practices that take place regarding the payment of bonuses, etc.

Retirement must be recognised as a great change in a person's life, and employers should attempt to recognise this in their personnel policies. Not only should an employer consider pensions and other gifts or presentations but consideration should also be given to some form of preparation for his new status in life, involving as it does loss of contact with work and working colleagues, decrease in income and increase in spare time. This aspect is dealt with more fully in Chapter Twelve.

It is therefore necessary for a business organisation via its personnel policy, to consider the various aspects of termination of employment, both voluntary and involuntary. The objective should be to reduce labour turnover, which can be costly, contributes very greatly to in-efficiency and affects the overall policy of the organisation with regard to profitability and goodwill.

ORGANISATION AND OPERATION OF THE PERSONNEL FUNCTION

The organisation of the personnel function in hotel and catering organisations will be dictated by the size either of the individual opera-tion or of the company and its relative complexity.

In a small hotel the manager will have responsibility for all aspects of personnel, but as the size of an operation increases so the responsibility will be delegated to assistant managers. It is not until the hotel has more than 200 rooms that it will warrant a personnel officer who will have responsibility for all personnel functions. As the size of the operation in-creases further, so the organisation of the personnel department will become more complex, until the structure illustrated in Fig. 12 is reached.

The operation of personnel practices in individual establishments which do not have company policies and services to rely on may on occasions be disjointed. Departmental managers will have responsibility for staffing in their departments, subject to budgetary restrictions, and will rely on the personnel department for administrative procedures only. In operations such as this it is essential that there is adequate communication between them and that powers of authority are clearly defined.

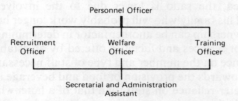

Fig. 12.   *Personnel department's organisation chart for a 650-bed hotel.*

The large hotel and catering groups will have a two-tier system of organisation as illustrated in Fig. 13 for a company employing 4,000 employees in 20 outlets. Head office will be responsible for setting and interpreting company policy from boardroom level down and communicating it to the unit personnel officer. Its second responsibility will be for personnel management of head office staff, managers and assistant managers in the units of its operation. The personnel officer at unit level will be directly responsible to the unit manager, as well as acting as the representative of the group's personnel manager in carrying out company policy. This two-tier system is clearly defined in its responsibilities. By the nature of its size it should provide an efficient personnel function at head office level, using the services and skills of specialist staff. At unit level there will be the flexibility necessary to implement the personnel policies of head office whilst considering the specific needs of the unit and its workforce.

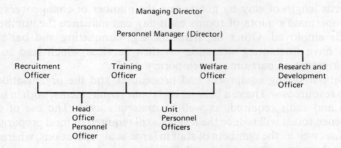

Fig. 13.   *Personnel department's organisation chart for a hotel and catering group.*

DETERMINING HOTEL AND CATERING STAFFING LEVELS

There are many factors which determine the level of staffing in a hotel and catering operation. The number of bedrooms or guests and number of covers served by the food and beverage department is obviously important. Large operations tend to have a higher ratio of customers or guests to staff, whereas in smaller establishments, which tend to be privately-owned, the ratio is lower due to the involvement of the proprietor and his family who will probably work longer hours. This indicates that ownership can be another factor in determining staff levels.

The range of services and facilities offered by an establishment will have an influence on the number and type of staff necessary to provide them. A bias towards the provision of food and beverage in a hotel will indicate a greater reliance on staff than that of a hotel which is biased merely towards the provision of accommodation. An analysis of hotel labour costs shows on average that 40–50 per cent of the total wage bill is attributed to the provision of food and beverages, against 25–30 per cent for the provision of accommodation services.

The method by which a service is provided is another influencing factor, both in the number of staff and the skills necessary from them. This may be best illustrated by the various methods of service used in the provision of food, ranging from gueridon or full silver service to self-service or the use of vending machines.

The layout of premises and equipment provided for the provision of food and services again influences the number of staff and their respective skills. Modern hotels are purpose built, with labour-saving designs of layout and furnishings, whereas older buildings tend to be more sprawling in their layout, with more traditional furniture and furnishings. An example of this is in the number of rooms a chambermaid may be expected to service; it can range from 18 in a modern hotel to 8–10 in an older building.

In accommodation-biased operations, frequency of demand as regards length of stay by guests and the number of changeovers in a chambermaid's quota of rooms each day can influence the number of maids employed. Other departments, e.g. banqueting and bar-staff, may have fluctuating demands on their services which lead to the employment of part-time or temporary staff.

Labour-saving equipment and procedures and the organisation of such resources will have a bearing on labour requirements, both in numbers and skills required, as well as materials used. The use of convenience foods will reduce the level of skill required of food preparation staff, as well as the numbers of staff in large-scale operations, whereas if all fresh unprepared food is used the labour involved increases rapidly.

Conclusion

Increases in modern technology, e.g. the introduction of computers and other electronic methods, have created a demand for new skills. This is best illustrated by the introduction of computers in front office operations. This has taken a considerable administrative workload off this area and has therefore made more time available to the receptionist so that she can use different skills in her job, e.g. through increased guest contact she is better able to sell them the hotel's services.

It may therefore be said that hotels and their staffing pose particular problems for management and the personnel function, due to the complexity of their structure and organisation, the range of services offered and the fact that industry relies heavily on the workforce and their skills to achieve its business objectives.

SELF-ASSESSMENT QUESTIONS

1. List the separate functions of the personnel department.
2. Explain the remuneration package.
3. Explain the purpose of personnel records.
4. Briefly explain the reasons for terminating employment.
5. Explain the role the personnel department plays in a large luxury hotel.
6. Explain the factors which determine hotel staffing levels.

CHAPTER TEN

Staffing, Recruitment and Selection

INTRODUCTION

By the nature of the variety of services offered by a hotel and catering operation it is obvious that there is a high degree of labour involvement. This is further supported by labour costs in the industry, representing 20–25 per cent of turnover or a third of expenditure of any hotel operation. Obviously these figures will vary according to the specific operation and the service it offers, but it is apparent that the industry relies heavily on its manpower merely to exist.

At the upper end of the market, representing 15 per cent of the hotel industry, there is a very high involvement of labour; statistics show that on average there are 0.85 employees per room. There is not such a high degree of labour involvement in the middle and lower sectors; for example a small private hotel or guest-house would have one employee to every four rooms.

These facts show the great importance within the industry of determining staff levels, and recruitment and selection of suitable employees for the many varied positions necessary to run a successful hotel and catering organisation. The major emphasis and effort of the personnel function is therefore in this area and this chapter looks in detail at staffing, recruitment and selection techniques and the importance of job descriptions in all aspects of the personnel function.

JOB DESCRIPTIONS

A job description may be defined as a statement of the purpose, scope, organisational relationships, responsibilities and tasks which make up a particular job. It is an integral part of any personnel function, and is said by some writers to be the "hub" of personnel management. The job description is an aid to writing job specifications, to interviewing, to planning induction and job training, as well as being a yardstick for job evaluation and for fixing remuneration.

Inaccurate job descriptions can be blamed when employees are either not informed of the scope of a job or not told of some of the duties involved. Invariably those duties omitted are the more unpleasant ones, and this can be a contributory factor to high labour turnover in the early stages of employment. This is therefore a justification for accurate and precise job descriptions; they will lead to less misinterpretation of the duties involved in a job and a more efficient use of labour.

A job description must not be confused with a job specification; the latter is dealth with later in this chapter. It is necessary for a job description to be prepared before a job specification or job analysis is drawn up, in order that any specification or analysis is a true and worthwhile representation of the job to it applies.

Purposes of job descriptions

The purpose of a job description is that an employee understands his or her duties, responsibilities and status in the organisational structure within which he or she works. The employer will thus be able to assess an employee's performance, evaluate a job with regard to grading and remuneration, and plan recruitment, selection and placing of employees and their induction and training.

A job description should be split into two parts. The first part deals with the details of a job that are relevant to the contract of employment and all conditions that may be contained therein. In the hotel and catering industry, because of its long and varied hours of operation and particular demands placed on employees, it is not always practically possible to be precise as to working hours. If this is the case then it should be mentioned in the job description. The same may be said for payment, i.e. basic pay and what it means, overtime (either compulsory or voluntary) and any bonuses. Uniforms and protective clothing and the necessity for them in particular jobs must be properly explained.

The second part of the description provides information as to the job itself and is best split into definitive sections.

Job title

This should be as precise as possible and is essential as a means of indentification, e.g. the breakfast and vegetable chef describes a chef in a hotel who is engaged in that specific area of food preparation.

Department

This describes the department in which the employee works in that particular establishment. This is necessary due to varying organisation structures; in some cases, especially in smaller establishments, employees may work between two or more departments, e.g. general assistants.

Duties

The description of these can be as detailed as the situation requires. In some cases they may be expressed in more general terms; for example the duties of a chambermaid could be described as "to clean guests' bedrooms, bathrooms and toilets to the satisfaction of the housekeeper". Other descriptions of duties may be more definitive, giving a complete breakdown of duties, even to the extent of timing involved. Duties may also be split into regular, irregular and emergency as a particular job may demand.

Responsibilities

In certain cases this part of a job description is an extension of the duties. However most jobs do have certain responsibilities regarding either equipment, customers, stock, money or all of the aforementioned. An employee should be aware of his or her responsibilities and the effect they have on the organisation. Employees should also be made aware of who they are responsible to in the organisation structure of their particular operation and, similarly, who they are responsible for in the case of middle management and supervisors. Middle management and supervisors should also be made aware of where they stand in the overall organisation of an operation with regard to lateral communication.

There is often confusion in medium- and large-scale operations as to the status of heads of department with regard to each other. This can lead to friction between them, with the result that their departments may not be working towards a unified approach in achieving the operation's objectives.

How a job description is set out will vary from one establishment to another, according to the individual needs of the particular operation. When a job description is initially prepared it should be done so in direct consultation with the current employee in the job concerned and be reviewed and updated in a similar manner when there is thought to be the need. If there are areas of concern in the preparation of a job description it may be thought worthwhile for an independent view to be sought regarding the scope, duties and responsibilities of a job.

Figures 14 and 15 show two examples of job descriptions and how the approach and content may vary. Whilst both job descriptions have a similar format, the content varies according to the scope of the job. The post of housekeeper in a 100-bedroom hotel is a senior management position. In an operation of this type the duties and responsibilities are drafted in more general terms because of their nature; a housekeeper with the right background would understand what is entailed from the general description. This is not the case with the job description for a waitress. Here the duties are more specific and, whilst it may be necessary to employ a person with waiting skills, such jobs will vary according to the establishment and it is necessary to be precise in their description to avoid any misunderstandings.

JOB SPECIFICATIONS

In writing job descriptions one must realise that it may be necessary for a candidate to possess certain skills in order to carry out the job. In both examples of job descriptions shown in Figs. 14 and 15, certain qualifications, experience and skills will be required; these would be contained in the job specifications. A job specification or operation manual may also be necessary to expand on details regarding duties.

A job specification therefore contains more detail than a description, although its content will depend on its purpose. If the purpose is to specify the qualities required of an employee with regard to a certain post or to expand on the duties performed by an employee for training purposes, then this must be considered when preparing the specification. Whilst joint consultation with existing operatives and their superiors should take place, the specification should be prepared by the personnel department if it is for recruitment purposes or by a training officer if it is for a training purpose.

The examples of job specifications shown in Figs. 16 and 17 are based on the two examples of job descriptions given in Figs. 14 and 15, and show how the specification may vary according to the job and the needs of the establishment.

Once prepared, specifications may be used in recruitment, selection, training and job evaluation as needed by the personnel function and as set by the standards required by an establishment.

METHODS OF RECRUITMENT

One of the main functions of the personnel department is to place the right person in the right job. In order to do this the right person must be

TITLE:	Housekeeper
DEPARTMENT:	Accommodation, Fistral Beach Hotel
SCOPE OF JOB:	The provision of accommodation services and cleaning of all areas except those directly relating to the preparation or service of food and beverage
RESPONSIBLE TO:	General Manager
RESPONSIBLE FOR:	Staff: Assistant Housekeeper, all chambermaids and cleaning staff. Equipment: All furniture, furnishings and fittings contained in guests' rooms, public areas and offices in the hotel, except food and preparation areas.
DUTIES:	The organisation and supervision of the servicing and cleaning of guests rooms, corridors, ladies cloakrooms, public lounges and areas, reception and managers' offices. The day-to-day maintenance of all furnishings, linen and cleaning equipment in the hotel. Maintaining stocks of cleaning materials and linen for the hotel, including uniforms and protective clothing. Security of all keys and stock related to the department. Selection and training of chambermaids and cleaners. Preparation of duty rotas. Provision of floral decorations in public areas within the hotel. Preparation of departmental budgets in joint consultation with Assistant Housekeeper and General Manager.
LATERAL COMMUNICATION LINKS:	Head Chef, Head Waiter, Head Receptionist, Head Porter.
AUTHORITY LIMITS:	Staff: Appointment and dismissal of chambermaids and cleaners, with regard to Assistant Housekeeper. Appointment and dismissal in joint consultation with General Manager. Financial: Authority of expenditure within agreed limits of departmental operating budget. Maintenance and capital expenditure in joint consultation with General Manager.

Fig. 14.   Job description for a hotel housekeeper in an independently-owned hotel of 100 bedrooms.

TITLE:	Waitress.
DEPARTMENT:	Directors' dining room.
SCOPE OF JOB:	Preparation and cleaning of dining room. Service of all foods and beverages to directors, senior management and their guests.
RESPONSIBLE TO:	Unit Catering Manager.
RESPONSIBLE FOR:	No surbordinate staff.
DUTIES: Regular:	Laying up of tables and sideboard. Preparation of cruets, condiments and accompaniments. Taking of orders. Service of all foods and beverages. Stripping of tables, clearing of restaurant.
Irregular:	Cleaning of floors, furniture and equipment in restaurant. Maintaining stocks of linen in restaurant linen cupboard. Day-to-day orders of condiments. Reporting complaints to Catering Manager. Handing in lost property to security. Reporting accidents to Safety Officer.
LATERAL COMMUNICATION:	Cooks.
LIMITS OF AUTHORITY:	Staff: None Financial: None

Fig. 15.   *Job description for a waitress in a company directors' dining room.*

TITLE:	Housekeeper
DEPARTMENT:	Accommodation. Fistral Beach Hotel.
AGE:	25 - 40
QUALIFICATION:	OND or BTEC Diploma or similar level in Hotel, Catering and Institutional Operations, or City and Guilds 708.
EXPERIENCE:	2 - 3 years as a supervisor in a larger operation or as an assistant in a similar operation or as a housekeeper in a smaller operation. Experience of handling staff. Experience in controlling linen and cleaning materials. Experience in staff selection and training (registered HCITB trainer desired). Experience in flower arrangements. Knowledge of hotel budgeting.
QUALITIES:	Pleasant appearance and manner. Above average intelligence. Ability to communicate.
OTHER REQUIREMENTS:	Able to work 8.00 a.m. to 4.30 p.m. plus occasional evenings. Live out position.

Fig. 16.   *Personnel specification for hotel housekeeper.*

DUTY:	LAYING UP OF TABLES AND SIDEBOARD
	Ability to lay a tablecloth. Ability to polish cutlery, crockery and glassware. Knowledge of cutlery required for different dishes. Ability to lay up a cover in the correct order for different menus. Ability to fold serviettes. Knowledge of serving equipment required on sideboard for different dishes. Preparation of water jugs. Ability to lay up a sideboard for meal service.
DUTY:	CLEANING OF FLOORS, FURNITURE AND EQUIPMENT IN RESTAURANT
	Ability to clean and dust restaurant systematically and effectively. Ability to use a vacuum cleaner correctly and detect faults. Knowledge of treatment required for stains to carpet and furniture. Knowledge of cleaning materials and polishes used for furniture and equipment and their effective use. Ability to check equipment. Ability to detect damage or wear in furniture and linen. Ability to make a report either verbally or written.

Fig. 17.   *Sections from a job specification for a waitress in a directors' dining room.*

attracted to apply for a vacant position. There are a variety of methods which may be used to attract applicants for different vancancies. However, in order to be effective, certain considerations must be made before a method or a variety of methods of recruitment are used.

Large companies have set methods of recruitment according to the status, skill and type of employee required. These methods take into consideration company policy and finance available for recruitment, which may be on a sliding scale according to the stature of the position. Economy must be emphasised, as some methods of recruitment such as newspaper advertising or use of employment agencies can prove very expensive. Another factor which can influence the method of recruitment is the urgency of the need to fill the vacant post. It may be preferable to fill the post temporarily rather than recruit hastily and engage the wrong person, thus involving additional expense and inefficiency.

We will therefore look at methods that are effective, economic and that fill the vacancy within a reasonable time. Once a personnel specification is prepared or is readily available (see Figs. 16 and 17) the personnel department can decide which is the best method of recruiting for a particular post.

Internal methods
The first method to consider should be internal recruitment,

especially in the case of supervisory positions, i.e. looking at existing operatives and their suitability for promotion. This should be done in liaison with heads of departments and should be conducted democratically, making staff aware of the vacancy by internal advertising so as to avoid accusations of favouritism and resentment. Promotion of existing employees can act as a motivator to staff, enabling them to see the possibility of advancement in their careers. It can, however, lead to resentment on the part of unsuccessful applicants.

Other positions of a more junior nature should also be advertised internally, as friends of existing staff can be excellent sources of recruitment. This method of recruitment encourages teamwork and can help the general work atmosphere. The disadvantage of employing friends of staff is that it can lead to a "closed shop" or "jobs for the boys" situation which may affect productivity and efficiency. If this method is considered, the departmental head should decide if it would be suitable for the department and his staff. Applicants through this method should be closely vetted to ensure that they match the personnel specification and will not be a "passenger" or disrupt the working atmosphere of the section or department.

External methods
External methods of recruitment are used to encourage applications from employees outside the working environment.

All vacancies should be notified to the Department of Employment. The services of this government department are free and it has specialist departments nationwide for the hotel and catering industry and management. It is worthwhile noting that most unemployed persons use the Department's service, as well as persons already in employment. This method of recruitment is probably more suitable for junior members of staff and for unskilled and semi-skilled jobs, e.g. chambermaids, catering assistants, porters, etc.

When employees with basic or semi-skilled training are required, college catering departments should be informed, although students tend to be available only at the end of the college year.

Advertising
Notices in shop windows can be used for attracting local people for semi-skilled positions or for part-time staff, as can local newspaper advertisements.

Advertising through local newspapers is not costly and, depending on the size of the locality and the newspapers' circulation, can reach a great number of people. In fact, depending on the type of locality and the current unemployment situation, this method can be most effective for all but the most senior of appointments.

An important consideration to be made in deciding whether or not to recruit locally for any position is the accommodation available for the person appointed, i.e. whether or not the hotel has living-in facilities or other local alternatives.

If it is necessary to recruit from another area, which may well be the case with skilled or senior management positions, then other methods must be considered. National newspapers or specialised trade publications are read by vast numbers or specific groups of people respectively, although advertisements in these publications are expensive and money can be wasted if they are not effectively used.

The first consideration of advertising is to decide which types or groups of people you want to get your message across to. If the post requires a high degree of specialised knowledge or skill, then it is best to use trade publications. However if your requirements are more general or there are a number of posts available, national newspapers may suit your needs. The most effective use of the advertising space must also be considered; whether it is a small ad in a local newspaper or a quarter page in the *Caterer and Hotelkeeper*, the same information must be conveyed to prospective applicants.

Illustrated in Figs. 18–21 are examples of newspaper advertisments of different types, all of which convey similar basic information according to the needs of the advertiser and what the reader will want to know. This information usually consists of job title, description, details of the employer, person required, conditions of employment and how to apply. How much detail should be contained in an advertisement will depend on the space available and how much information needs to be conveyed.

In Fig. 18 a reasonable amount of information about the establishment, a short job description, brief details of the person required and a summary of the main conditions of employment are included; it is to be expected that a person of the stature required for the post would want to know at least that amount of information before considering an application. The advertisement also informs people of the exact type of person you require with regard to experience and qualifications, and thus eliminates unsuitable and time-wasting applications.

The advertisement in Fig. 19 is for the housekeeper as detailed in our job description and personnel specification in Figs. 14 and 16. The information conveyed is similar to Fig. 18 in its content, but it may be reasonable to assume that, as it is being advertised locally, the readers will have some knowledge of the hotel. Before placing such an advertisement the employer will have assessed, from local knowledge of the labour market, whether or not it would be worthwhile to attract local applications.

Classified advertising is used for more junior or part-time vacancies

WINDSOR HOTEL
SOUTHAMPTON ROW
LONDON WC2

Invites Applications For The Position Of

HOTEL ACCOUNTANT

With this prestigious 500-bedroom hotel situated in London with conference facilities for 600 persons, a large food and beverage operation and a staff of 550.

The successful applicant will be one of the management team reporting directly to the managing director for the entire accounting function of the hotel. He/she will also be responsible for the preparation of budgets with management and departmental heads and have control of a staff of 20.

Applicants aged 25-35 with professional qualifications in accounting or HCIMA membership with at least 2 years experience in a senior accounting position in a similar type of hotel operation. Experience in hotel computer systems desirable, as well as being used to dealing with people.

The renumeration package is excellent with a salary of £12,000 pa, free medical and life insurance, company pension scheme and 5 weeks annual holiday.

APPLY IN WRITING TO:
D. PERRY FHCIMA,
MANAGING DIRECTOR,
WINDSOR HOTEL,
SOUTHAMPTON ROW, LONDON WC2.

Fig. 18.   *Quarter-page feature advertisement in a catering journal for a senior executive.*

and generally appears in two formats, as illustrated in Figs. 20 and 21. The first example may be used for a skilled operative such as a waitress for the director's dining room previously illustrated in Figs. 15 and 17, where basic details are required to attract the right applicant. In Fig. 21 very brief details are given as the range of applicants will be broad due to the fact that no experience is necessary; telephone applications are requested and more details regarding the post can be given at that time.

When compiling advertisements, make sure that they are precise and give the information that any prospective applicants will want to know when considering whether or not to apply; make sure they know how to apply and who to apply to. The legal aspects of advertising for staff recruitment are dealt with in Chapter Eleven.

FISTRAL BEACH HOTEL

NEWQUAY

☆ ☆ ☆

This 100-bedroom, 3 star hotel requires a

HOUSE KEEPER

The ideal applicant for this demanding position
will be at least 25 years old, college trained
with a minimum of 2 years experience in managing
accommodation services.

The position involves the organisation and
control of all accommodation services in the
hotel and responsibility for a staff of 10.
Knowledge of staff training and budgeting would
be an advantage.

In return for a 5-day 8-4.30 week and occasional
evenings we offer a salary of £6,500, free meals
on duty, annual bonus and 4 weeks holiday.

If you think you are suitable and wish to advance
your career, apply in writing to:
Peter Catchpole, Manager, Fistral Beach Hotel,
Newquay, Cornwall.

Fig. 19.   *Display advertisement in a local newspaper for a head of department.*

Employment agencies

Another method of recruiting staff is the use of employment agencies,
some of which specialise in hotel and catering staff. One of the main
advantages of this source is that they have already conducted screening
interviews and should only send you suitable staff, providing you have
conveyed your requirements correctly. They are also usually able to
meet your requirements quickly, which on occasion may be necessary.

A lot of businesses use such agencies for temporary staff or in
emergencies. Their main disadvantages are that some are not as
thorough as others and do not screen their applicants properly, and when
under pressure do not always send the most suitably experienced
people. They can also prove costly. Their charges range from one to two
weeks' wages, payable when the employee has stayed with the new
employer for a month. An added disadvantage is that people on their
registers tend to move from one job to another and consequently may
not stay in your employment very long, thus leading to the position
becoming vacant again.

Offering the job to persons working elsewhere

One method of recruitment which is often practised in the hotel and

PENWITH OIL plc

Experienced silver service

Waitress

For their directors' dining room
at Victoria, London SW1.
To serve lunches only and be
responsible for dining room.

Monday - Friday 9.30 - 4.30.
£2.50 per hour plus meals on
duty.
3 weeks holiday. Uniform provided.

Telephone applications to:

Catering Manager
01-828 2211, ext 249

Fig. 20. *Block classified advertisement in a local newspaper for a skilled
operative.*

catering industry, more so than in others, is to offer the job to someone
working elsewhere. This is often practised with chefs if they have a local
reputation or are renowned for their skills. Whilst ethically frowned
upon by some, it can firstly solve a problem and secondly enhance the
goodwill or reputation of a business because of the person's prowess.

This method can be used for all types of position which involve
special qualities or skills. However if you do use this method it may be
best to tie the candidate down to some sort of contractual agreement, as
a person of this quality may well be in demand and could easily be
tempted away from you.

BAR PERSON.   Training given.
Thursday - Saturdays inclusive.
Evenings only. £2.20 per hour.
Telephone Doris Green
Dolphin Inn, Plymouth 50501.

Fig. 21.   *Classified advertisement in a local newspaper for a non-skilled part-
time vacancy.*

Whilst we have dealt with methods of recruitment in detail, it has to be remembered that they are only part of the overall recruitment procedure. Once the method has been established as suitable for a particular vacancy and has been carried out, all persons concerned with that vacancy must be made aware that this has taken place. Whatever method of application is being used, the person dealing with it should be available to deal with enquiries and send out acknowledgments or application forms as the procedure requires.

In Table 1 the different methods of recruitment are shown for a variety of vacancies in the industry, bearing in mind the considerations previously discussed. There may be some variations in the methods used due to the location of the establishment and the local employment situation, as well as the personnel policies of the organisation itself.

It is also worthwhile assessing the success of the methods of recruitment used for different posts. This may be done by comparing the number of responses or applicants against the cost that has been incurred in recruiting. This can be an aid to the personnel department in future planning.

SELECTION PROCEDURES

The procedure involved in the selection of applicants will vary from business to business according to their policy, the urgency of the need to

TABLE 1 METHODS OF RECRUITMENT FOR VACANCIES IN A VARIETY OF CATERING OPERATIONS

Vacancy	Type of establishment	Methods of recruitment
Commis waiter	Restaurant	Local college Jobcentre Local newspaper advertisement
Still-room assistant	50-room hotel	Friends of existing staff Jobcentre Card in local shop Local newspaper
Assistant cook	300-bed hospital	Local newspaper Jobcentre
Trainee manager	150-room hotel	Local college Jobcentre Caterer and Hotelkeeper
General assistant	30-room hotel	Local college Jobcentre The Lady magazine
Receptionist	100-room hotel	Local newspaper Brook St Bureau
Domestic bursar	University hall of residence	HCIMA Journal Local newspaper Caterer and Hotelkeeper
Head chef	400-room hotel	Catering Times Offers to known persons Alfred Marks agency Caterer and Hotelkeeper
General manager	200-room hotel	Caterer and Hotelkeeper
Personnel manager	500-room hotel	IPM Journal Daily Telegraph Caterer and Hotelkeeper
Wine waiter	Restaurant	Local advertisement Alfred Marks agency
Counter assistant	Store cafeteria	Local newspaper Friends of existing staff Jobcentre
Part-time banqueting staff	Hotel	Friends of existing staff Card in local shop Local college

fill the vacancy and the stature of the position. Whichever method of application is used the procedure involved will be to assess all applications, draw up a short list of those most suitable for interview and appoint the best candidate from these.

Telephone applications
Telephone applications are usually used for more junior positions and may be regarded as the first stage in the selection process. The employer or his representative should at this stage eliminate all unsuitable persons by posing questions over the telephone regarding skill, experience and availability. The basic details and working conditions could also be given as they would probably not have been contained in the advertisement.

This then enables both parties to establish whether or not the application should be taken any further. If the employer feels it should then an interview should be arranged. The applicant should be informed of the date, time and place of interview, any directions, whom he or she should ask for and whether or not he or she should bring any documents or testimonials.

Letters of application
Letters of application should be read thoroughly and the contents assessed as to the suitability of the candidate, taking into consideration the personnel specification. Other details that can be assessed from a letter are the ability of the applicant to communicate and the layout and neatness of the application, especially if such skills are involved in the carrying out of the position applied for.

When the most suitable applicants have been sorted out they should be informed of the details of interview. They should also be asked to confirm either by telephone or in writing whether or not they will be attending the interview.

It is important to inform other applicants that their application has been unsuccessful and thank them for applying, as it is bad manners not to acknowledge them and can harm the employer's reputation.

Application forms
The use of application forms for vacancies has the advantage that information is systematically laid out as the employer requires it. Applicants should be informed in the advertisement that application forms are to be used, for example using a phrase such as "Prospective applicants are asked to write or telephone for an application form and further details." This hopefully prevents an applicant from wasting time by writing a formal letter and then repeating the details in a subsequent application

form, although some employers do use such a two-stage system of assessing applicants for a post.

An application form is most useful as an aid to the interviewer as all the information is in front of him in a concise manner. Application forms are also used as a basis for personnel records, as explained in the previous chapter. The layout and content of application forms are illustrated in Figs. 21 and 22 and will vary according to the needs of the employer. It is worthwhile all employers using them as it then gives them necessary information about their employees.

In Fig. 22 the operation would probably also use the application form as the only personnel record, with the exception of a wages record. The form could be filled out by the applicant whilst waiting for an interview, excepting in the case of senior positions where applicants would have to be asked to complete the form at an earlier stage of their application. Their use in the interview is explained in the next part of the chapter.

With a national catering company (see Fig. 23) the application form is completed by all employees and thus would be an integral part of their employees' records as well as an aid to selection.

The information requested in both examples illustrated is similar, although with the small organisation it is possible to be more specific with regard to location and experience. Application forms for large organisations tend to be more general and the information requested more varied, due to the wide range of positions available within them. It should also be noted that information requested does not often apply to all vacancies, especially those for more junior, semi- and unskilled operatives.

INTERVIEWING

The purpose of an interview is threefold:

(a) to select the most suitable candidate for a specific or, in the case of trainee posts, general vacancy;

(b) to present an employer or job in greater detail;

(c) for the employer and employee respectively to offer and accept the post.

With these purposes in mind, this is how an interview should be conducted.

There are certain golden rules to be followed in interviewing.

(a) The interview should, whenever practicable, be conducted at the place of employment.

(b) It should be at the time stated.

(c) Interviewees should have the opportunity to present themselves

```
┌─────────────────────────────────────────────────────────────────┐
│                 PHEASANT HOTEL, BUDE, CORNWALL                    │
│                 APPLICATION FORM FOR EMPLOYMENT.                  │
├─────────────────────────────────────────────────────────────────┤
│  POSITION APPLIED FOR: _____ DATE: _____        │
│                                                                   │
│  NAME: _____   ADDRESS: _____        │
│                                                                   │
│  DATE OF BIRTH: _____        _____        │
│                                                                   │
│  NATIONALITY: _____          _____        │
│                                                                   │
│  MARITAL STATUS: _____   TEL. NO: _____        │
├─────────────────────────────────────────────────────────────────┤
│  EDUCATIONAL QUALIFICATIONS:                                      │
│                                                                   │
│                                                                   │
├─────────────────────────────────────────────────────────────────┤
│  EXPERIENCE TO DATE (WITH DATES OF EMPLOYMENT):                   │
│                                                                   │
│                                                                   │
│                                                                   │
├─────────────────────────────────────────────────────────────────┤
│  MEDICAL HISTORY (list any disabilities and time off work in      │
│  the past 3 years):                                               │
│                                                                   │
│                                                                   │
├─────────────────────────────────────────────────────────────────┤
│  REFERENCES (list two names, one of whom must have been a         │
│  recent employer):                                                │
│  1.                                                               │
│  2.                                                               │
├─────────────────────────────────────────────────────────────────┤
│  Period of notice required in present position:                   │
│  Present salary:                                                  │
│  Live in/out:                                                     │
├─────────────────────────────────────────────────────────────────┤
│  I certify that the above information is true in every respect    │
│  and if I am selected for employment the references listed above  │
│  may be taken up.                                                 │
│                                                                   │
│  SIGNED:                        DATE:                             │
└─────────────────────────────────────────────────────────────────┘
```

Fig. 22.   *Application form for a medium-sized hotel with 60 bedrooms.*

and feel that they have had a fair interview.

(*d*) The interviewees should be able to ask questions relevant to the job applied for.

It must always be appreciated that the interviewees are also deciding whether or not they want the vacancy. If the interview takes place at the establishment where they are going to work it should be possible for

APPLICATION FOR EMPLOYMENT

SURNAME	CHRISTIAN NAMES		MR MRS MISS
ADDRESS		HOME TELEPHONE	

DATE OF BIRTH	NATIONALITY	MARRIED/ SINGLE	NO. OF CHILDREN

NEXT OF KIN	POSITION APPLIED FOR	CURRENT SALARY	DATE AVAILABLE FOR EMPLOYMENT IF OFFERED

HEALTH
(All senior employees are required to pass a medical examination. Please state if you have any physical handicaps or have had any serious illnesses.)

EDUCATION   PERIOD (from - to):
Names of schools attended:

Scholarships gained, degrees, diplomas or professional qualifications (please give details and dates)

Please show here any additional information about yourself you would like us to know, e.g. hobbies, interests, ambitions, membersip of clubs, societies and other bodies.

(a)

PREVIOUS EMPLOYMENT: All previous employment must be shown, giving employer's name and address and dates employed.
NB Your present employer will not be contacted unless you give permission.

Name and address of employer and nature of his business	Position held including duties and responsibilities and the number of staff controlled by you	PERIOD		Finishing salary	Reason for leaving
		From	To		

I certify that the information given on this form is true in every respect, and that if offered a position the Company will take up my references. I realise that my engagement may be subject to my passing a medical examination and to my references proving satisfactory.

SIGNED	DATE

(b)

Fig. 23. *Application form for a national industrial and institutional catering organisation. (a) Front. (b) Reverse.*

them to see the workplace and environment, to see the living accommodation if applicable, or be made aware of transport problems. They should also be able to meet prospective colleagues, examine equipment and have specialised systems explained to them. The interview should be at the time arranged. Lateness gives the impression of inefficiency on the part of the employer and can be unnerving to the interviewees who may not give the best of themselves as a result. Because of the confidential nature of the questions, the interview should be held in private. The interviewer should make sure he is not interrupted during the interview as this is distracting to both parties.

During the interview the interviewees should have the opportunity to put their case and answer the questions they have been asked, as well as to ask questions regarding the organisation, the job applied for, their conditions of employment, career prospects and any other questions they feel are important.

Not only do different interviewers have different styles, but specific vacancies will also warrant different styles or types of interview. Despite this, there is usually a fairly set pattern to follow in most interviews, and the interviewer must be aware of this and of the time that is being spent; his time should not be wasted. Therefore an interview should be conducted in stages, with the interviewer deciding whether and when to take the interview into the next stage.

The first stage of an interview is to assess the interviewee. The candidate should be made to feel relaxed and comfortable, perhaps by asking if he or she had any problems in getting to or finding the establishment. From this type of question the interviewer can assess whether the person would have similar problems in travelling to work, especially if unusual hours may be involved in the job. The interviewer can then assess the candidate, maybe by going through the application form, asking relevant questions in order to elaborate on the facts contained therein. The interviewer should be careful not to repeat direct questions already asked on the form or to dwell unnecessarily on irrelevant details.

Candidates should be asked specific questions on their experience, duties involved in particular jobs, equipment used, reasons for leaving their previous job, wages, etc. It is also worthwhile at this stage establishing the candidate's availability to take up a post. Married women might be asked if they have any children and, if so, what provisions would be made for them during periods of sickness and holidays. Work permits, if applicable, should be discussed with foreign nationals. Questions on social activities and interests can be used to assess whether or not the applicant would fit into the workforce already employed.

Whilst questioning applicants the interviewer should always be assessing their suitability for the post applied for; if several candidates are being interviewed the interviewer should make notes on each candidate.

At the end of this stage of the interview the applicant should be told of the finer details of the job and the conditions of employment, and should be given an opportunity to ask questions. The interviewer should then be able to assess, by the reactions of the applicant, how motivated he or she is towards the post applied for. It is worthwhile at this point for the interviewer to ask the applicant whether, if the post was offered, he or she would be prepared to accept it.

The interviewer should now know whether or not the applicant is suitable for the post. If this is the case the suitable candidate might then be presented with the offer of the job.

At this stage of the interview, and if both parties are in agreement as to the suitability of the applicant for the post, any special skills should be tested. In some vacancies, such as for chefs, these can be tested by questions and answers on the skills or knowledge necessary to carry out the job. Cashiers or receptionists may be tested on the use of accounting machines or computers, wine waiters on their knowledge of wines, barstaff on the preparation of certain drinks or on their numeracy with regard to charging customers. When testing skills the interviewer should be patient and helpful, and always remember the falseness of the situation and the nervousness of the applicant. Diplomas and testimonials should be checked against the application form if necessary.

Before the interview is completed the candidate should be informed of any decision that has been made or when and how he will be informed of the decision. It is important that candidates are given this information as it is not fair to keep them in any unnecessary suspense; failure to do so would not give a favourable impression of the employer.

If at this stage references are being taken up, then the candidate should be informed and, if necessary, his or her permission requested. References from past employers can be misleading, and where practical, are best taken by telephone due to the fact that some people do not wish to commit themselves in writing as to another person's faults. If on receiving a written reference it is not satisfactory, or you feel "you can read between the lines", then it should definitely be checked by telephone. It should always be remembered that references are confidential documents and should be treated in such a manner. Some organisations send out questionnaires on prospective employees to their past employers; whilst these have distinct advantages, being able to ask specific questions as to a person's suitability, they can also be inflexible or restrictive as to the answers given.

Some applicants may not wish their present employer to know that they are applying for other jobs. If this is the case it would be loyal to the applicant for references not to be asked for unless he or she is appointed.

APPOINTMENT OF APPLICANTS

When the final decision has been made as to a candidate's suitability, he or she should be informed as quickly as possible. If the candidate is appointed at interview or verbally informed by telephone that he is successful, he should also be told that he will be sent a letter confirming his appointment.

This letter of appointment may, in some organisations, be used as a contract of employment. If this is the case then it must comply with the legal requirements of the Contracts of Employment Act. The contents of the letter should therefore include the following:

(a) the offer of the job and the commencing date;
(b) the job description, or a copy, attached to the letter;
(c) rate of pay, other benefits and how they are paid;
(d) hours of employment and overtime conditions;
(e) holiday entitlements;
(f) details of sick pay and pension schemes;
(g) periods of notice applicable to both parties;
(h) grievance procedures;
(i) other conditions applicable to the post;
(j) request for a written reply confirming the offer of the post and the acceptance of the working conditions;
(k) starting time and who and where to report to on the first day.

When such a letter is used as a contract of employment a copy should be sent to the person appointed. He should then sign and return it to the employer as his form of acceptance.

Other procedures to be followed will vary according to the organisation and its systems. However departments and persons affected by the appointment should be informed of details relevant to them, in order that the arrival of the employee is anticipated.

SELF-ASSESSMENT QUESTIONS

1. Explain the purpose of a job description.
2. Draw up a job description for a canteen assistant in your college refectory.
3. Explain the purpose of an employee specification.
4. Draw up a job specification for a still-room hand in your department's restaurant.

5. List the methods of recruitment that are used in the hotel and catering industry.

6. Explain the types of newspaper advertisement you would use for different employees in a small hotel (40 rooms).

7. Explain a suitable selection procedure for a hotel manager.

8. Explain the purpose of an interview.

9. Draw up a plan of the order of how an interview should be conducted.

10. Explain the procedure to be followed on appointing an applicant for a vacancy.

CHAPTER ELEVEN
Training

CHAPTER OBJECTIVES

After studying this chapter you should be able to:
* identify training needs;
* understand the methods of training used;
* understand the considerations made when formulating a training plan and programme;
* prepare an induction programme;
* prepare a job training programme;
* understand the need for task analysis;
* prepare a succession plan for a business organisation;
* draw up an appraisal system;
* understand the types of management development programmes.

INTRODUCTION

Training may be defined as the systematic development of an employee's ability to carry out a task or job and of his standard of work, thus supplementing his education.

Bearing this in mind we must first look at who is involved with training. Here there are two groups of people, those who are responsible for giving training and those who are actually receiving the training. Those responsible for giving training again fall into two categories, the government and the employer.

By legislation the government has to provide formal education for all persons up to the age of 16, and then further education to those who need it. Where education ends and training starts is an almost impossible argument to resolve and has been the subject of much debate by theorists on either side. However when there is a need for training on a large scale, for example for people completing their formal education, or for people in declining industries who need retraining, it is generally accepted that it is the government's responsibility. Such training is provided by the government in a variety of ways. Primarily it is provided via finance for colleges of further and higher education and for training centres as well as via the awarding of grants or training allowances to those persons attending such establishments. In addition, government has also passed legislation setting up training boards to organise training in certain industries, giving them powers to raise levies from employers in order to finance the training given.

The employer also obviously has a duty to provide training; indeed it would be logical to say that it is in his own best interests to do so. Such training given by employers will be designed to meet their own specific needs. This may be done on an individual basis or by participating in the group schemes of the Hotel and Catering Industrial Training Board. The role of the Training Board is explained in greater detail in the next chapter.

Final responsibility for training falls on the person or group of persons being trained. No matter what provisions are made by an employer, if the right attitude towards training is not there on the part of the trainee then it is destined to fail. Again, it is in the best interests of employees to be trained to do a job efficiently and properly.

We must be aware that training, from job training through to management training, takes place from the day of engagement to the termination of employment and at all levels of employment. In this chapter we will look at the need for training, how training is carried out and the structure and content of different types of training courses.

IDENTIFICATION OF TRAINING NEEDS

The need for training generally arises either due to the failure to achieve the objectives set out in the policy of the organisation or due to changes in the working environment caused by the introduction of new systems of operation or of equipment. In this section we take a closer look at these reasons and establish the type of training that can be given to overcome them.

Whilst the failure to achieve certain business objectives may not necessarily be due to a lack of or inadequate training, it can generally be accepted as a contributory factor at some level, e.g. if a kitchen has been badly designed, causing inefficient operation, it could be that the kitchen designer needs training in kitchen workflow or designing. We therefore have to look for signs in the business operation that indicate a need for training.

High levels of staff turnover indicate job dissatisfaction; further analysis of the statistics may give clues to reasons for this. For example, if the analysis reveals that staff tend to leave during the early period of employment, it may be that the induction procedure needs revising or does not exist at all. Analysis may reveal other reasons for departure, e.g. inadequate supervision or job training, or lack of career development, giving rise to a need to examine procedures in those areas.

A high level of resignations in certain departments may indicate isolated training needs in specific areas. For example, a failure to achieve sales targets may indicate the need for sales training in all or certain departments in a hotel or similar organisation. A failure to reach profit targets or expense budgets may indicate other inefficiencies due to inadequate training. Complaints from customers about inadequate or slow service may indicate poor supervision or an inability on the part of the staff to do their job properly, while a high level of accidents or breakages would indicate a need for safety training. Low morale of staff, arguments and friction between staff or departments can also reveal training needs.

Changes in the working environment, perhaps caused by organisational adjustments or the introduction of new technology or systems, would also indicate a need for training. Listed below are examples that would involve job training:

    (a) the introduction of new menus and other methods of food preparation or service;
    (b) the introduction of a computer into the operation;
    (c) purchasing of new kitchen equipment;
    (d) a takeover by a new company or new management;
    (e) changes in the market attracted to the operation;
    (f) introduction of new products or services, e.g. draught beer.

In contrast, the following examples indicate a need for supervisory or managerial training:

    (a) the introduction of new budgeting or accounting systems;
    (b) a new promotion policy caused by expansion;
    (c) departmental reorganisation;
    (d) retirement or promotion of staff;
    (e) new ownership or management;
    (f) failure to achieve sales targets or expense and profit budgets.

When training needs have been identified the training plan should be structured and organised to meet those needs. The priority in the overall training plan should be given to areas which need the most urgent attention, although consideration must also be made regarding the day-to-day running of a department and any disruption that training may create; for example, at peak periods of operation it would be impractical to organise training. Consideration must therefore be given when planning training, firstly, to meet the demands that such peak periods create and secondly not to disrupt such periods. Training courses at peak times will only lead to antagonism towards the course by trainees, colleagues and superiors alike. Seasonal hotel operations, for example, recruit their staff at the beginning of the season in order to train them whilst business is slack, ready for the subsequent demands of the high season. Similarly, in city hotels training courses often take place at weekends when the demands of the business are low. Job training in kitchens, restaurants and bars is best planned to take place in the afternoon when these departments are closed.

FORMULATING A TRAINING PLAN

Whilst a business organisation will have prepared a training policy as an integral part of its personnel objectives, as discussed in Chapter Nine, it is still necessary to plan the actual training in order to achieve those objectives. In order to do this, the training officer of an organisation, or the person responsible for this function, must take a long-range view of the training necessary and what such training is intended to achieve. For example, it may be necessary to hold certain courses regularly, e.g. induction courses, some when a specific need arises, e.g. introduction of new technology, and others at intervals in order to cope with the ongoing demands created by the business operation, e.g. supervisors' courses and job training.

To explain this more fully we must look closely at the demands put on the training function and analyse the various needs which give rise to this training. On the other hand if training is looked upon as prevention rather than cure with regard to inefficiencies in a business, such training is likely to be more effective and to be held in high regard. However if someone is sent on a training course because of a failure to achieve targets or as a result of customer complaints, it will be regarded as a punishment or a slight against their ability. In formulating a training plan the short-, medium- and long-term needs must therefore be assessed.

Induction courses will be held weekly in most organisations employing large numbers of people because of the constant staff turnover in such establishments. An induction course should therefore be planned for every Monday and all new employees should start work on that day in order to be inducted properly. Job training, however, should take place on a regular basis and plans should be made to link it with day release courses at local colleges. The timing of such training, and the work loads, should be carefully considered both for trainers and trainees alike; if the trainee is overloaded the training becomes ineffective. If departmental staff are changed, health and safety training must be checked to make sure that all staff are up to date with their training. The introduction of a computer will mean that training for all staff concerned will have to be planned; to ensure the smooth transfer from one system to another such training may have to be carried out in isolation from other training. Once such a computer is installed and running, the subsequent training will then have to be planned systematically, in line with training for updating other staff and for new personnel.

Training for prospective supervisors and for other forms of staff development must be planned in line with the organisation's development and promotion policies to ensure that there is an adequate supply of trained personnel for all functions. It may be all very well to have a supervisors' course every six months, but does the organisation have the demand for that number of supervisors, or conversely, is there a shortfall from time to time? The number of trainees on such courses has to be regulated in order to provide the correct numbers of trained staff; it can be most frustrating for someone to attend a course and then not be promoted or not be able to implement what he has learned.

Final considerations when formulating a training plan will be the facilities and equipment available for certain types of training and the adequacy of the training budget and finance.

METHODS OF TRAINING

There are two methods of training, on-the-job training and off-the-job training. The method used will vary according to the needs of a particular training course, its content and the trainee.

On-the-job training

On-the-job training is generally used to train operatives in new skills, both manual and social. By the very nature of the hotel and catering industry, almost all training tends to be on the job as the majority of jobs involve the ability to perform certain functions in front of the customer. There is therefore a need to practice both the manual and social skills simultaneously. For example, a waiter serving food by silver service to a customer needs the technical skill in using a spoon and fork and the social skill of being able to communicate with the customer. Whilst the technical skill can be taught away from the job, the use of both types of skill, one of which has to be practised in front of the customer, indicates the need for training to take place on the job.

When considering on-the-job training, we must first decide how it is going to be done and who is going to do it. Later in this chapter we shall look in greater detail at job training programmes and how they should be planned. However we must remember at this point that the trainers are an important part of the training, and that they in turn require training in instruction and communication techniques.

"Sitting by Nellie" is a phrase which has been used for many years. It means that the trainee is shown how to do a job by an existing operative by watching her and then practising the task. This method is all very well but does "Nellie" in fact know how to do the job properly? She may take short cuts or she may pass on bad working habits to the trainee; she may not be trained in communicating with the trainee or in breaking the job down into component parts.

Trainers should therefore be trained in instruction techniques, and to this end the Hotel and Catering Industrial Training Board (HCITB) runs short courses in on-the-job training for skilled operators or supervisors so that they can be trained in these methods. The courses show prospective trainers how to plan a training programme, the techniques of job analysis, how to communicate their training and how to measure its success.

The trainer must always be aware that skills are learnt when the trainee participates in the training, using all his functions to carry out and measure the success of a task. It must also be remembered that a training group consists of individuals who learn at different speeds—some, for example, might be affected by nervousness or lack of confidence. All this supports the view that group training is not as effective as individual training in which individual needs can be catered for.

When on-the-job training takes place, customers should be made aware of the situation, and if necessary, considerations should be made in pricing. This avoids complaints which may prove embarrassing to the trainee and the customer and could have a detrimental affect on the training being given.

Off-the-job training

Off-the-job training means that training takes place away from the workplace, or at least takes place whilst the workplace is not functioning in its usual capacity. This type of course is usually used for the teaching of knowledge, although in some cases skills are also taught in this way, e.g. when training chefs in certain practical tasks.

Knowledge is imparted in a different way to skills and consequently a different approach must be adopted, depending on the course content, the level of personnel attending the course and the measurement of success that is used or is necessary. Off-the-job training usually takes place in groups and consideration must be given to the balance within a group and the individual needs of its members.

Knowledge is best communicated by lectures or talks, perhaps supported by visual aids such as films, slide presentations, diagrams, etc. Seminars and discussion groups can be used as more informal methods of teaching when necessary, to expand on certain topics or to discuss the practical application of theoretical topics. When skills are being taught, the use of demonstrations or role-playing may be used to support theoretical knowledge. Practical examples can involve the use of case studies and can, again, include role-playing.

As with on-the-job training, the trainer plays a very important role. Again he should be trained in what he is doing in order to communicate effectively. Hotel groups and other bodies often use senior executives who, whilst being competent in their jobs, make ineffective speakers either because they do not plan their talk and its delivery or because of their attitude. For this reason HCITB runs more expanded trainer courses, as do other organisations.

Measurement of success is more difficult in group-based courses unless tests or examinations are used. Where delegates on a course are split up into smaller groups to analyse or discuss problems, some members may not be able to or have the opportunity to contribute, and in some organisations this will be held against them, through no fault of their own. When considering off-the-job training it must therefore be remembered that the course should be designed to achieve its objectives and fulfill the needs of its delegates both collectively and individually.

PREPARING A TRAINING PROGRAMME

A training programme must be systematically approached, remembering that it is an integral part of the training plan as a whole.

The first thing to decide is what are the objectives of the programme that is being planned, what subject areas are to be covered and to what level or depth should they be taught? Other factors that influence such preparation are the number of trainees and any financial restrictions that are involved. The method of training most suitable for a particular type of course and for the different types of trainees must also be considered, bearing in mind where and when the course is to take place and the availability of all concerned. When planning the programme for the course and the topic areas that have to be covered it is important that there is a logical progression from one topic to another; in educational and training terms this is called "leading from the known to the unknown".

Later in the chapter there are two examples of course programmes (see Figs. 24 and 33) and it should be noted that a fragmented breakdown is given in both cases. The reason for this is that it is of far greater value to break a course down into short periods of 45 minutes' learning on a regular basis than have a continuous six-hour programme during which the trainee ceases to learn anything after the first two hours. This breakdown is not possible with induction programmes and other courses which last a whole day or longer. However in such cases it may still be possible to break down the course content into topic areas lasting no longer than an hour, each topic area being separated by a break either for refreshment or for some activity such as a tour of the establishment. Where possible either the speaker or the method of presentation should be varied in order to alleviate boredom, and time should be made available for questions (this should be indicated to trainees either in the programme or by the trainer).

All members of staff within an organisation should be informed of the fact that a training programme is taking place; this is perhaps as important as the courses themselves. On occasions when volunteers are required to attend courses, e.g. first aid courses, the programme should be advertised to all levels of employee. By so informing all members of staff of courses, as well as making course members aware, it allows departmental heads to plan work rotas and generally to minimise disruption.

INDUCTION TRAINING

The purposes of induction courses are to introduce new employees to the organisation and to help them fit into it. This is done by providing them with all the necessary information they need to know at the start of their employment.

New staff invariably feel anxious in strange surroundings and may have to guess at what they are expected to do; consequently they are likely to make mistakes and irritate customers and lose sales. Because they have to be more closely supervised the supervisor's time is wasted and the new employee may feel less secure.

Nowadays an organisation has to earn the loyalty of new staff; it cannot be taken for granted. Good induction procedures convey to an employee the notion that the company cares about its staff; as such first impressions count for a great deal, the employees thus form a better impression of the organisation.

Whilst induction procedures may vary from employee to employee in how the content of a course is related to their specific employment, the topics covered are similar. Listed below is a checklist and specific details of relevant topics that should be covered in an induction course, although these will vary according to the establishment's individual procedures.

Conditions of employment
   (a) Hours of work—shift systems, rotas, overtime and lateness.
   (b) Holidays—annual entitlement, when taken, payment.
   (c) Sickness—who to inform, certificates, payment.
   (d) Noticeboards—location, purpose and uses.
   (e) Contract of employment—what it means and contains, signing.
   (f) Pay arrangements—pay periods, pay day, where and when.
   (g) Bonuses—how calculated, when paid.
   (h) Company rules and regulations—use of hotel facilities/bars.

Welfare and social facilities
   (a) Staff eating arrangements—procedure, where and when.
   (b) Cloakroom and toilets—location, security, hygiene.
   (c) Sports and social facilities—membership, privileges.

(*d*) Protective clothing and uniforms—issuing, returning, responsibilities.

(*e*) Staff accommodation—cleaning, security, responsibility.

(*f*) Staff complaints—procedures involved.

Fire precautions

(*a*) Fire routine—drills, checking and reporting, training.

(*b*) Fire-fighting equipment and alarms—location and uses.

(*c*) Means of escape—staff and customers, location.

(*d*) Fire prevention—procedures, safety, hazards, reporting.

The company/establishment

(*a*) Development and history of the company—aims and objectives.

(*b*) Who's who—organisation structure, their place.

(*c*) Customer relationship—formal and informal, social skills.

Training schemes

(*a*) Aims of training schemes—hotel and individual.

(*b*) Training courses—types, opportunities and availability.

Introduction to department

(*a*) Supervisors—names, responsibilities, communication.

(*b*) Introduction to colleagues—names, status.

(*c*) The job—description, workplace, location of equipment.

(*d*) Human relations—colleagues, supervisor, customers.

(*e*) Waste disposal—procedures, safety.

(*f*) Accident prevention—obstructions, electricity, safety.

(*g*) Accident procedures—reporting, procedures, records.

(*h*) First aid—procedures, location, persons, training.

(*i*) Personal hygiene—uniforms, equipment, rules and procedures.

Whilst the above may be regarded as checklists for topics to be included in an induction programme or course, it must be remembered that some subjects may well have been explained at the interview or on appointment.

The programme itself must package all the appropriate topics together in some logical order which will be of interest and use to the employee. The use of induction manuals for staff is practised by many large organisations and can prove extremely useful, providing they are fully explained and any questions or queries answered. If a manual is not used it is useful if handouts, containing the relevant information, are given to employees; if an induction course lasts a whole day it would be unfair and confusing to expect them to remember all the information that they are given.

Illustrated in Fig. 24 is a typical induction programme for a 300-bed hotel, showing how the topics previously listed can be packaged together. Consideration must be given to providing a varied programme and to introducing different speakers who have specific responsibilities that employees can relate to. Activities should be introduced at different times to break up the sessions rather than employees having lectures all morning and then spending the afternoon rushing around the establishment. It is usually worthwhile following up the programme with a session later in the week to sort out any problems and to explain further training that will take place in fire precautions and safety. During the second or third week of employment the new employee should have a private interview with the personnel department, for assessment purposes, to sort out individual needs and any problems that have arisen.

IMPERIAL HOTELS

PROGRAMME FOR INDUCTION COURSE

SUPREME HOTEL, LONDON AIRPORT. MONDAY 31 MARCH 19-5

LOCATION: DRAYTON ROOM

TIME	TOPIC
9.30	Personnel Introductions by Kim Bowden, Personnel Officer.
9.45	Welcome to company and talk on the hotel, its development, aims and objectives, by Alan Wills, General Manager.
10.15	Conditions of employment by Kim Bowden.
11.00	Coffee in the Drayton room.
11.15	Tour of hotel and facilities by Jerome Marcus, Chief Security Officer.
12.30	Training opportunities by Simon Francis, Training Officer
1.00	Lunch in the staff dining room.
2.00	Welfare and social facilities by Kim Bowden.
2.45	Safety and fire precautions by Jerome Marcus.
3.15	Introduction to department by departmental heads.
4.15	Tea in the staff dining room.
4.30	Customer and staff relations by Steven Flood, Deputy Manager
5.00	Questions and course appraisal by Kim Bowden, Simon Francis and Steven Flood.
5.30	End of course.

Fig. 24.   *Hotel induction programme.*

In smaller establishments there will not be the resources or need for such elaborate courses. However induction procedures must still be followed in order to introduce new employees to the establishment. This is often done initially by senior staff on a more informal and personal basis and followed up as and when necessary. Employees should not be thrown in at the deep end and left to find things out on the grapevine.

Their head of department and supervisor must be available when the employee starts work, and all staff informed of any part they have to play in the induction in order for it to be effectively carried out.

Part-time employees also need introduction to the workplace, even though it may not be economic to conduct a full programme. The relevant topics that apply to them should be made into a shorter programme or talk given by the personnel officer or head of department, supported by a fact sheet containing the information they need to know.

Induction is important. It can save a business organisation a lot of problems and money if it is properly organised and carried out.

HEALTH AND SAFETY TRAINING

The Health and Safety at Work etc. Act 1974 states that employers should supply adequate instruction and training to ensure the safety of the workplace and persons involved, both employees and outsiders. This is an important part of any training in an organisation and must be considered in all courses offered to employees. Most organisations include health, safety and fire training as part of their induction and job training programmes; in the example of an induction programme given in Fig. 24 it can be seen that health and safety at work are both covered. It will also be necessary from time to time to hold specific health and safety training courses for all levels of employees, e.g. hazard spotting, the use of safety equipment, health and hygiene, etc.

For fully-trained employees it is important that consideration is given to safety training when new equipment is purchased and installed.

It is important for records to be kept of health and safety training in order to make sure it is systematically covered and that employees are trained in specific areas concerning the work they are directly involved in.

Health and safety training is further considered in the next section on the planning of job training programmes.

JOB TRAINING

Job training can be described in general terms as the instruction of a person so that he can perform a task of skill to the required standard set down in the organisation's objectives.

It is obviously necessary for inexperienced staff to be trained in the methods and systems of their employer. Experienced staff who have been newly recruited will also need job training in the systems and standards required by their new employer as these may well differ from those of past employers. When planning a job training programme we must therefore consider the needs of both the employer and the employee, as discussed earlier in the chapter.

The first stage in planning any job training programme will be to look closely at the job specification; this will list the duties and skills involved. These duties and skills can then be broken down into tasks, if this has not already happened, and the training programme then planned around these tasks. It is best to arrange such tasks in a logical progression in order that they flow from one to another. In Fig. 17 the job specification is set out in a series of tasks. Each task should be analysed by what is known as task analysis, the purpose being to identify areas of difficulty and devise an appropriate method of training such that staff can subsequently perform the job. An example of task analysis is illustrated in Fig. 25, showing the detailed breakdown of the preparation of half a grapefruit to be served on a breakfast menu. Note that the trainee is simultaneously being taught quality control, portion control, hygiene and safety, as well as the practical skills involved.

PREPARATION OF HALF GRAPEFRUIT	
STAGE OF PREPARATION	PROCEDURE AND POINTS TO NOTE
1. Select grapefruit.	Grapefruit should be firm with a slightly moist skin.
2. Halve grapefruit.	Place on board. Using a vegetable knife cut in half horizontally from the stem.
3. Remove flesh from skin.	Take half grapefruit face up on palm of hand. Gently cut the flesh away from the peel with a vegetable knife all the way around.
4. Cut flesh into half segments.	Using a vegetable knife, cut away each segment from the membrane taking care not to damage flesh and that each individual segment is released.
5. Remove pith.	Using a vegetable knife, remove the central pith.
6. Preparing for service.	Place half grapefruit in coupe, making sure all segments are neatly arranged. Sprinkle with desert spoon of castor sugar and place half a cherry in the centre. Place dish containing grapefruit on a side plate with a doily.
7. Clear down.	Remove any waste, clean table and board. Wash knife to avoid staining by grapefruit.

Fig. 25. *Task analysis sheet.*

A common error when instructing staff in new skills is to take for granted their knowledge or ability to understand and carry out an instruction. In the illustrated analysis, the instructor must be able to show the trainee how to select a grapefruit and teach him or her the knowledge required to ascertain its quality. The use of the correct knife must be taught, emphasising the fact that it is sharp so as to avoid both accidents and damage to the grapefruit; the safety factors in using knives and boards are as important as the skill itself. It should also be important to show errors that can be made, to demonstrate how to rectify them and to make the trainee aware that wasted materials cost money if they cannot be utilised elsewhere.

Whenever possible trainees should participate in tasks when being instructed, and praise or encouragement should be given when appropriate. This helps build confidence as demonstrations can be confusing. If a trainee is being shown a skill on the job he should then be given the opportunity to practise what he has been taught under supervision before being left to carry on with the task on his own.

At all times during training the trainee's progress should be monitored and recorded on his training record. The trainee should be able to see his training record in order to monitor his progress and be aware of what stage he has reached. Some organisations provide trainees with their own log or record of achievement which is completed at the end of each stage. An example of a training record is illustrated in Fig. 26, showing a record of the tasks in which they have to be trained, to be signed by the trainer, and the date when each task is successfully completed. On completion of training the trainee should be formally informed and paid any bonuses or receive pay increases agreed by the organisation. Details should also be recorded on the employment record.

STAFF DEVELOPMENT

It is important for all organisations to have a staff development programme, the advantage of this being that it gives the organisation the opportunity to develop the skills of its staff to the maximum, thus furthering its business objectives. The organisation will also be better able to retain staff, as each employee will be motivated to pursue career objectives within the company. A staff development programme therefore needs careful planning in order to motivate and select the right employees for further training and promotion.

The first stage of this procedure, whether we are looking at the development of supervisors or managers, is drawing up a succession plan for the business from its organisational structure. A succession plan is basically a plan showing the most suitable replacements for positions

NAME OF TRAINEE	DATE	SIGNATURE OF TRAINER	NAME OF TRAINEE	DATE	SIGNATURE OF TRAINER
Signing in and signing out procedures. The collection and return of keys. The security of keys.			The use of equipment. The care of equipment, e.g. washing cloths, emptying hoovers, etc.		
The position of: the Housekeepers' office; floor linen room; stores; room service; ice machine.			Cleaning the bathroom. Replenishment of bathroom supplies, e.g. soap, towels, kleenex.		
The division of rooms for cleaning. Types of rooms and their position on the floors. The numbering of rooms.			Cleaning the bedroom. Vacuuming the carpet - moving the furniture. The positioning of furniture. Stationery - the contents of the folder and replenishments.		
The laying up of a trolley.			Checking of rooms - early morning and afternoon checks. Please make up my room / Do not disturb } cards		
The collection of stores.			Completion of worksheets. Reporting of any irregularities or out-of-order items.		
Entering a guest's room. Bed making - types of sheets. Changing of blankets, counterpanes, etc.			Sequence of servicing rooms. Checkouts and residents.		
The removal of rubbish. The removal of used linen. Cleaning of miscellaneous item, e.g. ashtrays, ice bowls, wastepaper bins. Removal of room service trays.			Procedure with regard to lost property and room keys left in doors. The handling of guests' property. The checking of rooms by Floor Housekeeper.		

Fig. 26. Training record of a chambermaid.

held within the organisation. Illustrated in Fig. 27 is a succession plan for a medium-sized industrial catering company with some 30 units, catering for an average of 1,000 meals in each unit and based in London and the home counties. This plan is drawn up from the organisation chart for the same company, shown in Fig. 28. When drawing up such a plan the existing management is compared with the future management needs of the organisation, due to promotion, unexpected departure or retirement.

Figures 29 and 30 show the succession plan and organisation chart for the front office of a 250-bed hotel to show how the system works at the supervisory level. Again the needs of the department have to be considered against existing staff currently working in the department.

It is worthwhile in the succession plan to show two persons who could succeed the existing jobholder, as first and second choices. This might be necessary because the first choice may be working on a specific project or problem which would be affected by his movement to another post. Some organisations just draw up a list of suitable persons for further selection in their succession plans and make their selection when the need arises.

There is a need, in any succession plan, for staff not to be aware that their name is definitely put against a certain post as this may lead to complacency or an attitude of one-upmanship towards colleagues who may also be aspiring towards the position, which in turn could lead to disillusionment. Naturally, holders of more senior positions should be aware of whom their successors or likely successors are so that they can make recommendations and help in their assessment. Such assessment of employees who are suitable for promotion is known as staff appraisal.

APPRAISAL

Appraisal of employees by their superiors takes place in some way or another throughout their employment. It is done by making considered judgments as to the employees' ability to perform their jobs, both from the technical and social point of view. The purpose of such appraisal is to improve the performance of an employee, and consequently the performance of his group or department and of the organisation as a whole, to assess employees' suitability for promotion and to prepare a succession plan as shown in the previous section of this chapter. By conducting staff appraisal it is also possible to identify the training needs of individuals, to eliminate any weaknesses they may have and to develop their qualities or skills.

Whilst appraisal may be continuous on an informal basis, when employees' work is assessed day by day either by looking at the quality

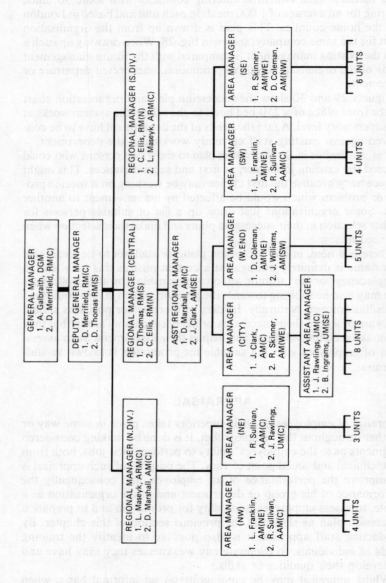

Fig. 27. Senior management succession plan for London and home counties catering company.

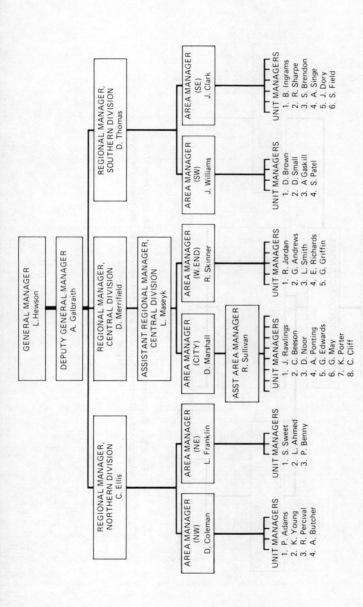

Fig. 28. *Organisation chart for London and home counties catering company.*

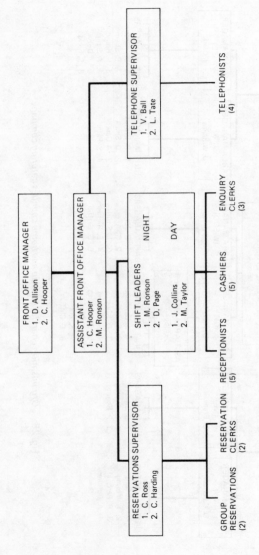

Fig. 29. *Succession plan for hotel front office of 350-bedded hotel. The telephonists and reservation staff are often regarded as autonomous in large hotels due to their specialist nature.*

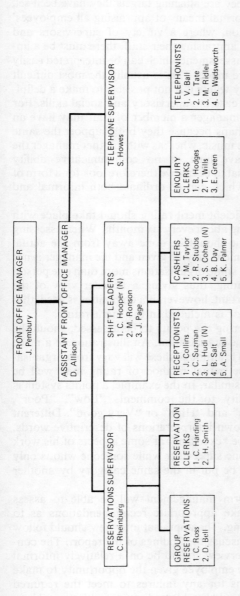

Fig. 30. *Organisation chart for front office of 250-bed hotel. N = night.*

of their work or at whether they are attaining targets they have been set, there must also be a more formal means of appraising all employees' work. In a large organisation, where a variety of supervisors and managers will be involved in appraising their staff, there must be a uniformity to their methods of assessment which can be interpreted easily when joint considerations are made. This is usually the most difficult aspect of appraisal, especially where it is not possible to make a definitive judgment, e.g. as in the case of supervisory and social skills. For example, in the eyes of one manager a member of staff may have an excellent social manner, perhaps because they both support the same football team or like the same music, whereas with another manager the employee may seem to have little or no communicative ability whatsoever. For staff appraisal to be fair we therefore look for a form of merit rating of employees which can co-ordinate both informal and formal assessments.

In order to be fair and efficient merit rating should take place with some regularity, the ideal being about every six months. When assessing an employee's merit rating it should be done away from the actual workplace so that a fair judgment may be given and the manager is not distracted by other events. In some organisations more than one person will be involved in merit rating, thus giving a broader view of the employee's ability. It is important, however, if a committee is used, that the employee's direct superior is included in the merit rating.

A merit rating form, covering the points to be assessed, should be devised that is suitable for the organisation. An illustration of a merit rating form is shown in Fig. 31; although these will vary from organisation to organisation and the actual method of rating may well be different, the content will be similar. In the example, a points system is used to give some flexibility to the comments "Low", "Poor", "Average", "Above average" and "High" or "Very good". Different supervisors may have their own interpretations of descriptive words, e.g. an employee who may be "excellent" at some aspects of his work can be given ten points by one supervisor while someone who is only "well above average" could be put in the same category by another person.

On completion of the form management will be able to assess employees' abilities and make appropriate recommendations as to promotion and further training. The appraisal interview should follow the merit rating in order to discuss the findings of the report. The conducting of the appraisal interview should be on a relatively informal basis and in private, with the employee given the opportunity to make suggestions and give reasons for any failures to meet the required standards. The interviewer should be able to discuss problems and how the employee's performance can be improved.

POINTS RATING	1-3	4-5	6-7	8-10	Points awarded	Remarks

GROSVENOR HOTEL BIRMINGHAM 6 DATE _____ **STAFF APPRAISAL MERIT RATING FORM**

NAME OF EMPLOYEE _____ AGE ____

DEPARTMENT _____ JOB TITLE _____

POINTS RATING	1-3	4-5	6-7	8-10	Points awarded	Remarks
All employees						
Work output	Low	Average	A. Average	High		
Work quality	Low	Average	A. Average	High		
Initiative	Poor	Average	A. Average	V. Good		
Staff relationships	Poor	Average	A. Average	V. Good		
Customer relationships	Poor	Average	A. Average	V. Good		
Total						
Supervisors and Management						
Organisational ability	Poor	Average	A. Average	V. Good		
Planning ability	Poor	Average	A. Average	V. Good		
Man-management	Poor	Average	A. Average	V. Good		
Inter-department cooperation	Poor	Average	A. Average	V. Good		
Communication	Poor	Average	A. Average	V. Good		
Recommendations				Total:		
Signed:				Personnel Dept. Supervisor/Manager		
Appraisal interview date:						

Fig. 31. *Merit rating form.*

What results are communicated to the employee will depend on the purpose of such merit rating. If it has only been used to analyse the ability of the assessors, then it would be a waste of time to keep the results from the employee. Employees have the right to be informed of their progress and shortcomings, but it is not necessary to give results in detail and in some cases this can actually be counterproductive. In the case of any promotion which may be planned, the employees should be informed where practical, as well as being told of any developments that are likely to take place that may affect them. Details of any development courses they may have to attend should be given and, where applicable, any adjustments in their remuneration fully explained.

MANAGEMENT DEVELOPMENT COURSES

Management development courses are basically split into three categories: for management trainees; for supervisory training; and for the training of management itself. Each category has different objectives.

Management trainees are usually recruited straight from college, although in some cases they are recruited direct from school, with a few more mature people deciding to enter the industry later in life. Trainee courses usually last two or three years, with the trainee working in the different departments of a hotel to a planned schedule and attending a local college to further his or her academic qualifications. The trainee should be given specific objectives to achieve and should be closely monitored by the training officer and departmental manager. Trainees are important to the company as they are tomorrow's managers and have the advantage of being trained to specific requirements. If a training course is not properly planned and organised the trainee quickly becomes disillusioned and may feel he is being used as cheap labour; this will obviously affect his attitude towards the company and its general image.

Supervisory training is provided for potential supervisors, the purpose being to make them appreciate the work and problems peculiar to their department, both in its own function and that related to others. Such training should also give them a complete understanding of methods used in controlling and supervising the work of their department. With these objectives in mind a course should be designed and potential supervisors asked to attend. An example of the programme for such a course is given in Fig. 32.

When planning such a course it is important to select members for the course from different departments within the organisation, in order to encourage interaction between departments on both a social and professional level. The use of case studies or key tasks should be used as a basis for team-working by the delegates as well as a means of evaluation. It is also important, when communicating a course of this nature, that all members of the course are informed and that other key staff in the organisation are aware it is taking place. An example of the type of communication to be used for the course programme in Fig. 32 is shown in Fig. 33. Note that the lecturers are also sent a list of course members' names.

The training of managers themselves is meant to broaden their knowledge of the company's operation and of general management. It should also be aimed at developing their intellectual skills and their use of modern techniques in decision-making and problem-solving. Management needs training in a variety of skills such as forecasting and

THE EXCELSIOR HOTEL, LONDON AIRPORT, 19-21 and 26-28 MARCH 19—4

DAY	TIME	SUBJECT	LECTURER
1	9.00 a.m.	Personnel introduction	P.G. Pratt
	9.45 a.m.	Coffee	
	10.15 a.m.	Introduction to course	F.L. Stokes
	10.45 a.m.	The supervisor's job	P.G. Pratt
	12.15 p.m.	Motivation	P.G. Pratt
	1.00 p.m.	Lunch	
	2.00 p.m.	Styles of management	P.G. Pratt
	2.45 p.m.	Training	Mrs S White
	3.30 p.m.	Tea	
	4.00 p.m.	Induction	Mrs S White
2	9.00 a.m.	The hotel's organisation structure	J.R. Desmond
	9.45 a.m.	Coffee	
	10.00 a.m.	Interviewing	J.R. Desmond
	10.45 a.m.	Administration	J.R. Desmond
	11.30 a.m.	Labour turnover	N. Edmonds
	12.15 p.m.	Communications	N. Edmonds
	1.00 p.m.	Lunch	
	2.00 p.m.	Organisation and profitability	M.J. Reid
	3.00 p.m.	Key tasks	M.J. Reid
	3.30 p.m.	Tea	
	4.00 p.m.	Key tasks	M.J. Reid
3	9.00 a.m.	Reporting back key tasks	M.J. Reid
	9.45 a.m.	Coffee	
	10.00 a.m.	Reporting back continued	M.J. Reid
	10.45 a.m.	Standards of performance	M.J. Reid
	1.00 p.m.	Lunch	
	2.00 p.m.	Summary and course assessment	P.G. Pratt
	3.30 p.m.	Tea	

Fig. 32.   *Programme for supervisors' course.*

budgetary controls, interviewing and selection techniques, marketing and promotion, instruction and aspects of planning; and the use of courses is the most common method of such training.

In general, the theory of management is taught by colleges and professional associations via a range of courses covering the broad base of subjects. However some businesses plan their own courses, which means that they can be tailor-made to their own needs both in the subject and content; projects can be based on "live" situations and the company can choose its own speakers. A criticism of such internal company courses is that they may become restricted because the attending delegates all have a similar background; consequently the course may become stereotyped, without the input from people working outside the company. However internal courses tend to be more competitive as delegates are aware that they are being watched or assessed

MEMORANDUM	SUPERVISORS' COURSES

Date:
10.3.—4

Ref:

SAR/SS

The supervisors' courses are to take place at the Excelsior Hotel from 19-21 March, and from 26-28 March. Staff to attend the courses are as follows:

From:
Mrs White

To:
All staff attending
the courses

c.c.
Mr Gieves
Mrs Roberts
Mr Grate
Mr Prowse
Mrs Owen
Mr Ryan
Mr Brian
Mr Edmonds
Mrs Reid
Mr Desmond

19-21 March	26-28 March
1. Mrs Gavin	1. Mrs Newton
2. Miss Timms	2. Mrs Louse
3. Mr Baker	3. Mr Wakefield
4. Mr Yardley	4. Mrs Fry
5. Mr Smith	5. Mr Bateman
6. Mr Balke	6. Mrs West
7. Mr Jones	7. Mr Beeson
8. Mr Wiseman	8. Mr Collins
9. Mr Franklin	9. Mr Atkins
10. Housekeeper	10. Mrs Cabouche
11. Mr Frost	11. Mr Tubb
12. Mr Clark	12. Miss Bragg

Please find a course programme attached to the memos for all staff attending a course.

I would be grateful if you could let me know as soon as possible if these arrangements will cause any inconvenience.

P.C. White

Mrs P.C. White

Fig. 33.   *Communication sent to staff regarding a supervisors' course.*

by their employers, although this can be counterproductive if it takes over the course (unless of course this is meant to happen). External courses have the advantages of independence when assessing results, of greater resources and of a mixture of delegates either from different industries or from different sectors within the one industry. This can give an added input to the course; it gives managers the opportunity to discuss ideas practised by others and to compare them with their own, thus broadening their outlook.

All aspects of management and supervisory training must be considered against the objectives of the organisation. Different levels of training will require the use of different internal and external training facilities, while the finance available may well be another influence on the type of training offered. In trainee and supervisory courses the number of employees who require training will make internal training worthwhile for larger organisations, whereas in specialist management training, where only individuals can be trained, the use of external courses is preferred, unless of course the company is part of a large group.

In the next chapter we look at the financing of training in greater detail and examine the role of the training boards and education.

SELF-ASSESSMENT QUESTIONS

1. Explain how training needs may be identified in a hotel and catering organisation.
2. Explain the methods of training that may be used.
3. Explain the purpose of a training plan.
4. List the important points that should be covered by an induction course.
5. Explain why induction training is necessary.
6. Draw up an induction programme for a group of new employees.
7. Explain the importance of health and safety training.
8. Explain the need for task analysis.
9. Draw up a task analysis sheet for a task that you are familiar with.
10. Explain the importance of a staff development programme to hotels and catering establishments.
11. Explain the purpose of succession plans in large-scale catering organisations.
12. Explain why staff appraisal is important.
13. List the areas in which staff should be appraised.
14. Explain the purposes behind management development programmes.

CHAPTER TWELVE

The Role of Training, Education, Welfare and Counselling

CHAPTER OBJECTIVES

After studying this chapter you should be able to:
* understand the role of the training board;
* know the structure of educational courses available to entrants to the industry;
* understand the role played by welfare and counselling in the personnel function.

INTRODUCTION

We have already examined the role played by the personnel function of an organisation in the provision of various personnel services. In this chapter we examine the role played by the Hotel and Catering Industry Training Board and the various educational institutions, as external bodies, in the provision of personnel services. Whilst they have been treated separately as external bodies, there is in fact consultation between them and the industry as to the roles they play and the courses they offer. Education must be regarded as training entrants to the industry in the knowledge and skills required; training, as administered by the Training Board, is more specific to the needs of the individual employer. However neither should be treated in total isolation.

The Training Board is made up of representatives from the government, the various sectors of the industry, educational establishments and the professional and examining bodies. All educational establishments have governing bodies and departmental advisory committees, again made up of representatives of the various sectors of the local industry, local government officials and area Training Board officials. Examining bodies make up their own syllabuses in consultation with industry, educationalists and Training Board representatives; in fact the examining bodies often use representatives from industry as examiners or moderators.

Training and education therefore take place in joint consultation with industry at all levels. In this chapter we look at the development of training and education in recent years to meet the ever-changing needs and demands of the industry.

Due to a heavy reliance by the catering industry on its workforce in the provision of service and customer relations, no personnel function, however large or small, can ignore the welfare of its staff. The morale of the workforce is therefore important to enable them to carry out their work effectively. Thus in this chapter we also consider welfare as an important contribution to staff morale, both in the provision of improved facilities and conditions of employment, as well as in the counselling function taken on by the employer.

THE ROLE OF THE TRAINING BOARD

In 1962 a government White Paper was published expressing concern about the unbalanced nature of training in the country, stating that it was inadequate and to a degree unsatisfactory. This led to the government passing the Industrial Training Act in 1964 which had three main objectives:

(a) to ensure an adequate supply of properly trained men and women at all levels of industry;
(b) to improve efficiency and the quality of training;
(c) to spread the cost of training between firms.

This Act led to the formation of the Hotel and Catering Industrial Training Board (HCITB) in November 1966, its main duty being to ensure that sufficient training was provided in the industry. It was also to publish recommendations on the nature, content and length of training for various occupations in the industry.

In 1970 the Board's activities were extended from the commercial sector of the industry to include employees in local authority, i.e. school meals, halls of residence etc., and institutional, i.e. hospitals etc., sectors.

The Act also specified how training and the training boards were to be financed, a levy being raised from employers in the industry both to meet the cost of the boards' operations and to provide grants to employers for specific training activities. This levy and grant system was seen as an incentive to encourage firms to participate in approved training. The system however was subsequently abused by some members of the hotel and catering industry when it was realised that grants could exceed the levy paid, and several dubious training schemes were started by firms on their own premises. In 1973 regulations were changed to eliminate this, and in 1976 the levy procedures were again changed to raise levies from the 1,500 largest employers in the industry (at 0.7 per cent of their payroll). Exemptions were granted to companies who offered satisfactory internal training whilst also offering grants to non-leviable employers who trained staff in key areas.

The HCITB offers a range of training advisory services to the industry, and has also linked up with the Manpower Services Commission in the provision of the Training Opportunities Scheme (TOPS) designed to combat unemployment by giving people new skills. As discussed in the previous chapter, the Board has set up its own training courses to train trainers for industry. Supervisors and other skilled staff can attend short five-day courses for on-the-job trainers and ten-day courses for off-the-job trainers. The courses involve trainers being instructed in methods of effective training; on completion of the course they are then qualified to train employees, entitling the employers to grants to cover the cost of the training.

The HCITB publishes a range of training aids and publications which have helped employers to plan and give more effective training. Supplementing its training role, the HCITB has also carried out research into the industrial supply of manpower, into the qualifications training staff have received, and into labour movements within the industry.

EDUCATION

Education within the hotel and catering industry first started in this country with the opening of a catering department at Westminster Technical College in 1910. Its concern was solely with the technical training of chefs, this mainly being geared to the needs of London's hotels and restaurants. The only formal education that was available for the industry until the late 1940s remained that of Westminster Technical College, plus that of the armed services and the Swiss Hotel School at Lausanne. However the Catering Wages Commission in the 1940s recommended the development of hotel and catering education as part of the rebuilding of British industry after the Second World War.

In the late 1940s and throughout the 1950s there appeared three influencing factors that helped in the development of the industry.

(a) The Hotel and Catering Institute (HCI) was founded in 1949 with the objectives of increasing professionalism in the industry and encouraging education in both technical and management areas. The Institutional Management Association (IMA), although formed before the HCI, also had similar objectives within its own sectors of the industry. The courses and examinations of these two bodies set standards for training and education necessary for management in the industry which are still highly regarded today.

(b) Recruitment by the industry itself, with a view to training entrants for management, became more apparent throughout the 1950s as it recognised the need for training within its own ranks.

(c) During this time catering diploma courses were developed by technical colleges for school leavers and employees already in the industry.

In order to look more closely at the development of hotel and catering education since the Second World War it is necessary to look at it in terms of management education and craft education.

Management education

By 1960 there were some 20 colleges throughout the country offering diploma courses in hotel and catering management. The Hotel and Catering Institute, via technical colleges, ran intermediate and final membership examinations for their professional qualification throughout the 1960s, on both a full- and part-time basis. In 1964 the University of Surrey set up its Bachelor of Science degree and the University of Strathclyde followed suit in 1965. The Higher and Ordinary National Diploma schemes were introduced in 1969 in polytechnics and colleges of further education, the purpose of these two levels of diploma being to provide management entry to the industry via the higher diploma and supervisory entry via the ordinary diploma. In 1971 the HCI and IMA amalgamated to form the HCIMA and revised its courses, the latest of which were introduced in 1984.

With the loss of mandatory grant awards for HCIMA courses most full-time sandwich-type courses are ceasing at colleges, although day-release courses will continue to cater for the needs of people working in industry who require the qualification for career development.

HCIMA examinations

The professional qualification is in two stages, part A and part B. Part A consists of the skills which are appropriate to all sectors of the industry, and is only available, through part-time or block-release study over two years, to students who have appropriate employment in the industry. The course comprises the following study areas:

(a) Business and Supervisory Studies   (90 hours);
(b) Food Studies   (120 hours);
(c) Liquor Studies   (90 hours);
(d) Accommodation Studies   (120 hours).

The second stage, Part B, consists of a compulsory core of management-orientated subjects which are divided into foundation and major studies, with elective study areas. These courses are available on a one-year full-time and two-year sandwich basis but will, as previously mentioned, be few in number due to non-availability of grants in most cases. A three-year part-time course of study is available for students who are employed in the industry.

Part B is structured as follows.

(a) Foundation Studies:

(i) Technical Operations	(60 hours);
(ii) The Industry	(60 hours);
(iii) Management	(120 hours);
(iv) Marketing I	(90 hours).

(b) Major Studies:

(i) Food and beverage Management	(120 hours);
(ii) Financial Management	(120 hours)
(iii) Manpower Studies	(120 hours).

(c) Elective Studies:

(i) Gastronomy;
(ii) Human Nutrition;
(iii) Food and Beverage Science and Technology;
(iv) Science and Technology of Accommodation;
(v) Accommodation Management;
(vi) Financial Management II;
(vii) Business Statistics;
(viii) Information Processing;
(ix) Tourism;
(x) Marketing II.

These courses are 90 hours each and students must take at least two.

The HCIMA allows students to prepare by means of correspondence courses, subject to certain requirements. Specific entry requirements are set out by the HCIMA for their courses and they grant exemptions from certain parts and studies of the course according to alternative qualifications, e.g. OND or BTEC diploma, and experience.

Degree courses

In 1977 the Council for National Academic Awards (CNAA) approved degree courses, some with specific sectors of the industry in mind, at four colleges in the UK. All the degree courses now available (see Table 2) contain technical, business, management, science and social science subjects. The structure, content and approach to the various disciplines varies from college to college, according to their expertise and the disciplines they have to offer. The length of courses are four years on a sandwich basis, with students spending at least a year in industry. In most cases entry requirements in general are GCE passes in five subjects, including at least two at A level, with minimum grades specified. Some institutions will accept a good OND/BTEC diploma pass or HCIMA qualifications as alternatives.

TABLE 2 COLLEGES OFFERING DEGREE COURSES IN HOTEL AND CATERING SUBJECTS

College	Course
Robert Gordons Institute of Technology, Aberdeen	BA in hotel catering and institutional administration (CNAA)
Ulster Polytechnic, Belfast	BSc in catering administration (CNAA)
University College, Cardiff	BSc (Hons) in institutional management
Napier College, Edinburgh	BA in catering and accommodation studies (CNAA)
University of Strathclyde, Glasgow	BA and BA (Hons) in hotel and catering management
University of Surrey, Guildford	BSc (Hons) in hotel and catering administration; BSc in hotel management
Huddersfield Polytechnic	BA in hotel and catering administration (CNAA); BSc (Hons) in catering science and applied nutrition (CNAA)
Leeds Polytechnic	BA in food and accommodation studies (CNAA)
Polytechnic of North London	BSc in institutional management (CNAA)
Manchester Polytechnic	BSc in hotel and catering studies (CNAA)
Oxford Polytechnic	BSc or BA or honours degree (CNAA modular) in catering or catering and food nutrition or catering and another study
Dorset Institute of Higher Education, Poole	BSc in catering administration (CNAA)
Portsmouth Polytechnic	BA or BSc in hotel and catering management (CNAA)
Sheffield City Polytechnic	BSc (Hons) in catering systems (CNAA)

Special one-year graduate-entry courses for a CNAA postgraduate diploma are offered by Leeds Poytechnic for holders of a degree in non-catering disciplines.

Technician Education Coucil (TEC)

The Technician Education Council was set up in the mid-1970s, together with its Scottish counterpart SCOTEC, with the aim of developing a unified system of technical education. TEC oversaw the introduction of new diploma and higher diploma courses to replace the traditional ordinary and higher national diplomas in colleges of further and higher education throughout the country. It merged with the Business Education Council in 1983 to form BTEC (the Business and Technician Education Council).

In England, Wales and Northern Ireland, colleges have been encouraged to design their own programmes within guidelines set down by BTEC to meet the needs of industry and specific occupations. In Scotland SCOTEC has worked with the colleges and industry to produce a national syllabus.

The courses run by BTEC are basically explained as follows, with examples of detailed course programmes from Westminster College Hotel School at the end of this section.

BTEC diploma

This is based on a modular programme, run over two years, by which students take a number of units which are built up into either a certificate or diploma. The purpose of the diploma is to equip students for a career in any sector of the industry, and it provides technical, business, social and personal skills as required. After appropriate experience the student will be able to undertake a supervisory position, e.g. head receptionist. Entry qualifications are at least three 0 level passes in GCE or four 0 grade passes in the Scottish Certificate of Education for SCOTEC.

Potential supervisors for the industry look to attain a BTEC/SCOTEC diploma. There are at present (1984) 3,700 students studying at some 116 institutions for these qualifications.

BTEC higher diploma

This is based on a modular programme, run over three years on a full-time sandwich course (or two years if a student has previously obtained a BTEC diploma in hotel and catering operations), during which time students take a number of units which build up into a diploma. The purpose of the course is to prepare students for a career as a manager in the provision of food and accommodation services in any sector of the industry. As such, a course is designed to provide the technical, business and management knowledge and skills. The potential first position on completion of the course would be at the level of junior management in an organisation, e.g. food and beverage assistant manager in a hotel.

Entry requirements for BTEC higher diplomas are for students to have studied at least two subjects at GCE A level and passed in one, as well as having passed at least three other subjects at O level.

The potential managers for the industry therefore look to attain either BTEC/SCOTEC higher diplomas, BA or BSc degrees or part B membership examinations of the HCIMA. The completion of such courses provides them with the technical, business and management knowledge and skills, together with personal and social skills demanded by the industry. On obtaining these skills they are able to apply for licentiate membership of the HCIMA and, after the appropriate experience, full corporate membership. There are at present (1984) 2,800 students studying at some 48 institutions for these qualifications.

Craft education

City and Guilds

We have already mentioned the introduction of catering craft education in this country at Westminster Technical College. A national approach to the training of chefs in trade cookery evolved during and after the Second World War, particularly through the introduction of syllabuses and examinations by the City and Guilds of London Institute. Both full-time and part-time City and Guilds courses were run at technical colleges for training young entrants and those already working in the industry. The National Joint Apprenticeship Council for the Hotel and Catering Industry was established in 1952, introducing an apprentice scheme lasting five years for cooks. This was reduced to three years in 1957, but introduced attendance at college on a day-release basis to study for City and Guilds examinations. When the Training Board was established in 1966 it took over the administration of apprenticeship training from the Council.

Career training in food preparation is based around three courses leading to qualifications offered by the City and Guilds of London Institute. City and Guilds certificate no 706 is in Cookery for the Catering Industry and is divided into three levels, while 706–2 is the advanced craft award and 706–3 is the most advanced craft award in two main specialisations, either kitchen and larder or pastry. The three courses provide a continuity in career development, integrating college training with industrial training and experience.

Food service training and education started between the wars at Westminster Technical College and was considered more as

TABLE 3 BTEC DIPLOMA IN HOTEL CATERING AND INSTITUTIONAL OPERATIONS, TWO-YEAR FULL-TIME COURSE AT WESTMINSTER COLLEGE

Unit	Level	Unit value
Year I		
Food commodities	I	0.5
Methods of food provision	I & II	2.0
Alcoholic beverages	I	0.5
Food sales and service	I & II	1.5
General science	I	1.0
Accom. and cleaning science	I	1.0
Premises and plant	II	1.0
Front office operations	II	0.5
Purchasing, costing and control	I	1.0
Accounts	II	1.0
Mathematics*	I	0.5
Human relations	I	0.5
Personnel practices and procedures	II	0.5
Economics	FS	0.5
General and commercial studies	FS	0.5
French	FS	1.0
Year II		
Alcoholic beverages	I	0.5
Food and drinks operation	III	1.5
Methods of food provision	II	1.5
Applied science	II	1.0
Applied science assignments	III	0.5
Accommodation operations	II	0.5
Materials and accom. operations	III	0.5
Premises and plant	III	1.0
Front office operations	III	1.0
Costing and control	II	1.0
Accounts	III	1.0
Health and safety at work	FS	0.5
Sales and marketing	FS	0.5
Human relations	II	0.5
Personnel practice and procedures	II	0.5
G&CS (English) or G&CS (French)	FS	1.0

BTEC Diploma = 26 units plus $3\frac{1}{2}$ practical units.
FS = freestanding.
* Only for students without an approved qualification in maths.

TABLE 4 BTEC HIGHER DIPLOMA IN HOTEL, CATERING AND INSTITUTIONAL MANAGEMENT, THREE-YEAR SANDWICH COURSE (BTEC DIPLOMA STUDENTS EXEMPTED FROM FIRST YEAR) AT WESTMINSTER COLLEGE

Unit	Level	Unit value
Year I		
Food and drinks operations	II	2.0
Food and drinks operations	III	3.0
Applied science	II	1.5
Materials and accom. operations*	II	1.0
Premises and plant	III	1.0
Front office operations	II	1.0
Costing and control	III	1.0
Accounts	III	1.0
Human relations	II	0.5
Personnel practices and procedures	II	1.0
G&CS French/Spanish	FS	1.0
Economics*	FS	0.5
Legislation*	FS	0.5

Most units in Year I are "bridging" units and, as such, the unit level reflects the ultimate level to be achieved and will not necessarily compare in content with units in the diploma.

Year II (17 weeks only)		
Food and drinks operations	IV	2.0
Food and materials science	III	0.5
Materials and accom. operations	III	0.5
Personnel practice and procedures	III	1.0
Management principles	III	0.5
Interpretation of accounts	IV	1.0
Structure and resources of industry	FS	0.5
Legislation	FS	0.5
French/Spanish	FS	1.0

Students also spend 6 months on approved industrial release during their second period.

Year III		
Food and drinks management	IV	2.0
Gastronomy	IV	2.0
Marketing	IV	1.0
Manpower studies	IV	1.0
Management techniques	IV	1.5

TABLE 4 CONTINUED

Unit	Level	Unit value
Premises and plant	IV	1.0
Accommodation management	IV	1.0
Financial management	IV	1.0
Options: Tourism, Consumer studies, Product quality, Management, French, Spanish	FS	2.0

BTEC higher diploma = 22 units including 2 units from the first (bridging) year.

*These units are part of the 22-unit higher diploma. The others in year I are "bridging" units.

preliminary training for higher positions in hotels and restaurants than as a training for waiters. The Hotel and Catering Institute introduced its waiting certificates in the 1950s but they were used not by people entering the industry as waiters but by students at colleges as part of a wider course in the industry.

In 1959 the National Joint Apprentice Council for the Hotel and Catering Industry introduced a three-year apprentice scheme; it was not a success as it was geared to the top end of the market, for which there was little demand. The HCITB discontinued the scheme in 1967 when it took over control.

Three courses, originally sponsored by the HCITB and the City and Guilds of London Institute and leading to certificates, were set up in the 1970s. Trainees could supplement their industrial experience with day-release courses at colleges, although students could also take them on a full-time basis. These courses are City and Guilds no. 707, Food and Beverage Certificate, of which part 1 is the basic award and part 2 is the advanced qualification, while City and Guilds no. 717 is the Certificate in Alcolholic Beverages which replaced the old 707–3 in providing students with the skills and knowledge required to sell and serve wines and other alcoholic drinks. As with chefs and cooks, these courses provide a career development path integrating college and industrial experience. Other courses in bar-work are run in conjunction with the training board and the National Trade Development Association.

Other areas of employment in the hotel and catering industry which are covered by City and Guilds of London Institute courses are no. 709, the Hotel Reception Certificate which replaced the former HCI Hotel Bookkeeping and Reception Certificate, and no. 708, which is the Certificate in Accommodation Services covering housekeeping activities in commercial and institutional establishments. Many colleges run City and Guilds no. 705, a one-year full-time general catering certificate, as an introduction to the industry. The syllabus covers aspects of food preparation, food service, science, accommodation operations and related business studies, and students then have the opportunity in the following year to specialise in food preparation and service, accommodation operations or hotel reception.

In 1980 City and Guilds pioneered a range of specific skill schemes for the hotel and catering industry and the licensed trade. The impetus for these schemes came from the industry itself and the schemes were developed in co-operation with the HCITB. The schemes cover the following areas of work:

(a) call order cook;
(b) room attendant;
(c) food service assistant;
(d) counter service assistant;
(e) bar service assistant; and
(f) bar/cellar-work staff.

Each scheme runs for six to eight weeks and involves theoretical and industrial training. At the end of such a scheme the student is awarded a certificate. These short schemes, concentrating on specific basic skills, can be an essential part of the Youth Training Scheme programme (YTS). Other elements of the YTS programme provided by City and Guilds include communications skills, numeracy, computer literacy and trainee profiles.

The role played by City and Guilds in catering craft education can be endorsed by the fact that in 1982 the institute received over 40,000 entries for the main level craft certificates we have discussed in this chapter (see Table 5). The progressive pattern of certificates, together with their recognition of practical skill achievement, can lead to the award of Licentiateship of the City and Guilds of London Institute, which corresponds in status to that of Master Craftsman in Europe.

BTEC certificates
In 1982 colleges of further and higher education which ran craft courses started to introduce modular programmes in which students take a number of units building up to a BTEC certificate. Colleges are in fact using City and Guilds courses as a foundation for the units required in the awarding of these certificates.

As with BTEC diploma programmes, colleges are able to structure these programmes to meet the specific needs of industry and employers. Examples of such courses, both full-time and part-time, are combinations of food and beverage operations or accommodation operations or

TABLE 5 PRINCIPAL COURSES FOR CRAFT EDUCATION RUN BY CITY AND GUILDS OF LONDON INSTITUTE

Title		Duration	
		Full-time	Part-time
CGLI 705	General catering	One year	
CGLI 706–1	Basic cookery for the catering industry	One year	Two years
CGLI 706–2	Cookery for the catering industry	One year	Two years
CGLI 706–3	Advanced cookery for the catering industry		
	Kitchen and larder		Two years
	Pastry		One year
CGLI 707–1	Food service	300 hours*	300 hours
CGLI 707–2	Advanced serving techniques	150 hours*	150 hours
CGLI 708	Accommodation services	300 hours*	300 hours
CGLI 709	Hotel reception	One year	30 weeks' block release
CGLI 717	Alcoholic beverages	150 hours*	150 hours

* Often included in other full-time courses.

a more general range of study over both areas. Entry qualifications for such courses are a minimum of three CSEs at not less than Grade C, including English language and a numeracy subject. Students are required to complete 16 units, although exemptions are granted for City and Guilds qualifications.

Summary

There are thus several paths open to would-be entrants to the hotel and catering industry. The type of course available depends on the level of education and background experience of the entrant. The three main paths which entrants can follow are:

(a) via nationally-operated government education schemes of the Technical Education Council or by undertaking a degree course at a polytechnic or university;

(b) via the professional examinations of HCIMA;

(c) via City and Guilds courses which form a foundation for BTEC courses.

WELFARE

Welfare may be best described as concern for staff well-being. As far as this section is concerned we take welfare as meaning a concern, and its practical demonstration, for the human needs of staff whilst they are at work.

It is difficult nowadays to distinguish between welfare benefits and fringe benefits. Often fringe benefits such as sick pay and pension schemes or staff meals and accommodation are regarded as welfare benefits. Strictly speaking they are not, as they make up part of the remuneration package offered to an employee. In contrast, welfare is the function controlling the provision of these benefits the drawing up of the conditions of employment, i.e. the quality of such provisions ought to be considered as the welfare function.

It is best to examine aspects of staff welfare in two areas: in an applied practical form, as examined in this section; and by way of counselling, which we look at in more detail in the next section. Applied welfare is the practical way in which concern for staff well-being may be expressed by the employer. Staff welfare is an important function of personnel management; in large organisations there if often a welfare officer who takes on this function, while in small establishments it is a role often taken by the manager or proprietor.

The provision of recreational and social facilities for employees, both past and present, may be regarded as the best example of a welfare facility. Large companies often organise and sponsor sports teams and pensioners' clubs and provide social activities such as bingo or discos for employees and their families. Smaller organisations do not have the resources to provide welfare facilities on such a scale, although they can easily take the opportunity to behave in a normal social manner, perhaps by using the hotel facilities for social activities for the staff.

Accommodation

Staff accommodation must be regarded as the employees' home and not merely the place where they live. Rooms should be warm, well maintained and furnished, and staff should be encouraged to give their own rooms a feeling of identity and security. Rest-rooms or dining rooms should be made as comfortable and as well-decorated as an average home; they should certainly not be spaces tucked away in the basement which staff are not encouraged to use. The provision of a television or other forms of recreation and entertainment for live-in staff or for those who work split-shifts shows a consideration for their welfare and encourages social interaction between them.

Meals

Staff meals are provided as part of an employee's remuneration, but they are often open to criticism from staff and abuse by employers. Whilst it is not practical to provide staff with the same meals that are sold to guests or customers, staff meals should not be regarded as a means of getting rid of waste or unsold food. The employer should be concerned as to the quality and quantity of the food and how it is presented. Considerations should be made as to the tastes of staff, with special regard to ethnic backgrounds, diets and, within reason, personal likes or dislikes.

Uniforms

Staff uniforms, which must be provided by law, are again a remuneration benefit, ensuring that employees do not have to wear out their own clothes whilst at work. A welfare concern would be the provision of uniforms that are comfortable to wear and do not cause the employee any embarrassment through being unstylish or ill-fitting.

Summary

The true concern for staff welfare will be indicated by the employer's attitude towards the employees and their needs. However, in addition to specific welfare requirements we must also examine the general welfare role of the provision of advisory or counselling facility for staff with regard to problems that they may have.

COUNSELLING

Before we examine the function of counselling within the workplace, it must be established that the attitude of the "counsellor" is of primary importance to its very existence. Employees must feel that they are able to approach their employer or "counsellor", should they feel the need to, and that any discussion they have will be confidential. The "counsellor" must establish the trust and respect of employees, without being paternal. We must also remember that counselling, although an applied form of welfare, cannot be considered a *practical* provision of welfare, in that it cannot be costed.

Counselling takes place either informally, both in groups and individually, or formally, usually at the request of the employee. (We examined informal groups and the role they play in an organisation in Chapter Seven.) Counselling should not merely be regarded as sorting out employees' problems; then it would take on a more formal meaning. Instead it should be considered more as helping staff to help themselves. It may simply involve providing whatever assistance or advice is possible with the best interests of the employee in mind, although in some cases this may be different from what the employee is asking for. For example, if an employee falls into debt and asks for a loan to repay it, the employer would do him a greater favour in the long run if advice was given as to how to re-arrange his personal budgeting and assistance was given in arranging terms for the repayment of the debt; hopefully this would help prevent a similar occurrence in the future. Another example could be that an employee has a legal problem and comes to his employer for help. Whilst it might be easy for the employer to sort the problem out and make the necessary arrangements, the employee will get a greater feeling of satisfaction if he is able to sort it out himself. This may involve the employer giving advice as to where or who to go to for assistance and possibly allowing the employee time off to do so.

There are certain simple rules to follow when dealing with staff concerns and problems. When a member of staff has a problem it will often take a lot of courage to approach his employer or "counsellor". Employees should therefore be seen as quickly as possible, before their courage disappears. Privacy is also important and should be made clear to the employee. However, if the counsellor feels a third party may be able to help he should inform the employee and ask his approval. Counsellors should be good listeners and should encourage staff to come forward with their grievances or problems, however small they may seem. Such problems may involve sickness, bereavement, financial difficulties and family or domestic problems. Counselling can also deal with situations directly concerning work, involving either the making of suggestions or the airing of grievances.

It must always be remembered that all the problems we have mentioned above affect staff at work. If counselling takes place effectively and helps staff with their problems, it will raise staff morale.

SELF-ASSESSMENT QUESTIONS

1. Explain the objectives of the Industrial Training Act 1964.
2. List the principal courses that are open to students wishing to enter the industry at a management or supervisory level.
3. Explain a career development programme and examinations that may be taken for a school leaver wishing to train as a chef.
4. List the specific skills schemes available through City and Guilds and the Youth Training Scheme.
5. Briefly explain the three paths which entrants to the industry may follow through attending colleges of further or higher education.
6. Explain how employee fringe benefits may also be considered as part of a staff welfare policy.
7. List activities that may be provided or organised by the employer as part of a staff welfare policy.
8. Explain the importance of counselling in the workplace.

CHAPTER THIRTEEN

The Legal Aspects of Employment

CHAPTER OBJECTIVES

After studying this chapter you should be able to:
* know the contents of a contract of employment, as required by law;
* understand the difference between fair and unfair dismissal;
* understand legislation that controls the payment of wages;
* understand legislation that controls the employment of different groups of people;
* understand legislation concerning industrial relations;
* understand the legislation to provide a safe workplace.

INTRODUCTION

There is a wealth of legislation, passed by various governments, protecting the rights of employers and employees. The earliest legislation—the Truck Acts—dates back to the nineteenth century. These Acts were concerned with the payment of wages to employees and were brought about by employers paying wages by means of tokens, which could only be spent in the employers' shops, or "payment in kind", i.e. by the provision of accommodation and food, etc. The Truck Acts stopped these activities by stipulating that employees must be paid in the coin of the realm. These Acts are still in existence today, although they have been modified to a degree to cope with modern innovations, e.g. payment by cheques or credit transfer. Whilst we have discussed in other chapters the effects of the wages councils on the industry, the Truck Acts are the main legislation controlling remuneration to employees.

In the post-war period up to the 1960s employees had a rough deal from employers with regard to job security and conditions of work. However with the development of mass media people became more aware of these bad practices and there was a demand for protection against them. The early 1960s therefore saw legislation formalising the terms of employment, the payment of wages and compensation in cases of redundancy.

The 1970s saw a great deal of legislation protecting the interests of the employee with regard to equality at work for all persons, industrial relations and rights to trade union membership. More recent legislation in the Employment Acts of 1980–2 modified what were regarded by some as the more extreme measures passed in the 1970s.

CONDITIONS OF EMPLOYMENT

A basic contract of employment may be verbal or written, although if the contract is verbal the employee must have confirmation in writing not more than 13 weeks after the commencement of employment.

The verbal offer of a job amounts to a contract of employment and is as legally binding in law as a written, signed contract. When the employee starts work it indicates that he has accepted the contract. The terms expressed in such an offer of employment cannot be changed by the employer unless the employee agrees. Statements made must be accurate, especially about salary, working hours, holiday entitlement and periods of notice, etc; the employer should ensure that these details are confirmed in writing in the letter of appointment. Informal verbal agreements between the employer and employee can amend a contract. The main disadvantage of any verbal agreement is that the interpretation of the terms relies on both parties recalling what was said and how they may interpret it.

A written contract, however, is signed by both employer and employee and indicates the terms by which they are bound during the course of employment. Changes by the employer must be agreed by the employee and, if necessary due notice of any changes must be given. Whilst some of the terms are explicit and specifically agreed by both parties, there may also be implied terms, i.e. terms which reflect normal practice at the place of work. Other examples of implied terms are primary rights and duties during the course of employment or statutory terms such as wages council regulations. The contract may also include the terms of a collective agreement made with trade unions.

Written statement of terms of service

A written statement of the terms of service is not necessarily a contract of employment. However, all employees who work for 16 hours or more per week must have in the first 13 weeks of their employment a written statement containing the following details:

(a) the parties to the agreement (employer and employee);
(b) date of commencement of employment;
(c) job title of employee;
(d) rate of pay, how pay is calculated, overtime rates;

(e) frequency and method of payment;

(f) hours of work, normal working hours and compulsory overtime;

(g) details of holiday entitlements regarding payments, bank holidays and termination;

(h) sickness procedures and sick pay;

(i) pension scheme details and contracting out details regarding state pension schemes;

(j) periods of notice required and given by the employer to end employment and any amendments to the contract;

(k) disciplinary rules and procedures and subsequent appeals procedure;

(l) grievance procedures and subsequent appeals procedure;

(m) the health and safety policy of the employer;

(n) references to employee relations policy to include membership agreement with trade unions;

(o) expiry date of contract if it is for a fixed period of time or seasonal employment with any relevant information;

(p) whether previous employment with other employers counts as continuous with the present employment with regard to payment and pay scales.

Whilst the above details must be contained in a written statement, employers may attatch documents or refer the employee to other documents for information.

Other specific clauses which may be contained in a contract of employment if the employer so wishes and the employee agrees are:

(a) restraints on employees in order to prevent them divulging trade secrets, setting up in competition or working for someone else;

(b) searching of employees and their property in the event of this being necessary or for periodic checks;

(c) deductions from wages in the event of shortages in tills or carelessness causing damage to equipment.

Whilst these clauses may sound sinister, they are accepted practice in the catering industry, protecting the employer against any actions by his employees that may be detrimental to his business. Employees should have details of such clauses, and any variations in them that may occur, thoroughly explained.

Time off

Employees are entitled to a reasonable amount of time off if they have certain responsibilities and duties, and employers should seek agreement as to how much time is reasonable. Paid time off should be granted in the following circumstances:

(a) for employees made redundant who have been employed for two years or more to seek other work or retraining;

(b) for employees who are trade union officials to be trained in and carry out industrial relations duties;

(c) for ante-natal care.

Unpaid time off is allowed for public duties, e.g. JPs, local councillors, school/college governors, members of other official bodies. Time off is allowed for trade union activities, including meetings, but not for strikes.

Termination of employment

The period of notice given by an employer to an employee must be as stated in the contract of employment or the statement of the terms of service. When an employee has worked for at least four weeks he or she is entitled to the following statutory minimum periods of notice:

(a) one week for employees who have worked continuously for less than two years;

(b) one week for every year of continuous employment between two and twelve years;

(c) twelve weeks for employees who have been employed continously for twelve years or more.

The notice required by the employer from employees who have worked for more than four weeks is one week and does not increase with time spent in continuous employment. Payments in lieu of notice by either side may be accepted to waive any rights. With regard to periods of employment for staff, a week is regarded as 16 hours or more. When an employee has been employed for five years or more a week is regarded as eight hours or more. Periods of notice do not apply in the cases of instant and summary dismissal, both of which are explained in the next section of this chapter.

An employee has certain rights during notice such as receiving normal pay for a normal working week.

DISMISSAL FROM EMPLOYMENT

A dismissal occurs when an employee's contract is terminated with or without notice, when a fixed term has expired or when the employee terminates the contract himself through being at fault regarding the terms contained in the agreement.

Fair dismissal

Reasons for fair dismissal by an employer are:

(*a*) lack of capability to do the job for which the employee was engaged;

(*b*) any misconduct by the employee;

(*c*) redundancy as defined by the relevant redundancy legislation;

(*d*) the employee being unable to carry out the job due to legal restrictions;

(*e*) some other substantial reason.

An employer may dismiss an employee instantly without giving notice or payment in lieu of notice in the following circumstances:

(*a*) serious or repeated negligence at work;

(*b*) serious or repeated disobedience at work;

(*c*) serious or repeated misconduct at work;

(*d*) drunkenness on duty;

(*e*) theft from employers, from other employees or of customers' property;

(*f*) accepting bribes or commissions;

(*g*) misconduct away from the workplace and outside working hours if it involves other employees or affects the employer's business.

In all cases the employer should dismiss the employee as soon as he is aware of the occurrence, giving the employee the reason for his action and witholding pay if there is a good reason, e.g. damage or theft.

Unfair dismissal

Employees are protected against unfair dismissal under the Employment Protection (Consolidation) Act 1978. Claims for unfair dismissal must be made within three months of the dismissal, after a Department of Employment conciliation officer has investigated the case to see if a settlement can be made without going to a tribunal.

In the case of a tribunal the employer must show reason for the dismissal and that he acted reasonably in treating it as sufficient cause. The employee must show that he was eligible to complain and that he was dismissed. The tribunal on reaching its findings can make recommendations. If dismissal is found to be fair then the employer's action stands. If unfair dismissal is found then the tribunal can recommend reinstatement of the employee or for compensation to be paid, the amount of compensation depending on the circumstances of the case and the employee concerned.

PAYMENT OF WAGES

The payment of wages by employers to employees must be stipulated in the contract of employment as to the amount and method of payment. Wages in the hotel and catering industry often include the provision of accommodation and meals whilst on duty. In this section we consider the relevant legislation which applies to the payment of wages.

Wages councils

The industry's wages councils superceded the Catering Wages Act and now fix minimum levels of pay, holidays and other terms and conditions of employment. Up-to-date regulations made by these councils must be displayed in the appropriate premises for all employees to see.

The wages councils which operate in the hotel and catering industry are for:

(a) licensed residential establishments and licensed restaurants;
(b) licensed non-residential establishments;
(c) unlicensed places of refreshment.

Payment of Wages Act 1960

This Act modified the Truck Acts (explained in the introduction to this chapter) by requiring that wages be paid in cash, although wages may now be paid by other methods if both parties agree, e.g. cheque or credit transfer. An employee can insist on cash payment or an employer can refuse to pay by any other method than cash.

Deductions from wages

Under the Attachments of Earnings Act 1971 employers must deduct tax payable and national insurance contributions payable on wages paid to all employees. An employer must also deduct any amounts which have been ordered by the courts in payment for fines, maintenance of dependants or the clearance of civil debts. All other deductions from wages must be agreed in writing or authorised by the employee. These deductions may be for accommodation and food, union fees, repayment of loans, pension schemes, save as you earn schemes, etc.

Pay statements

Employers are required to provide a pay statement containing the following details:

(a) the amount of gross pay;
(b) the amount of fixed and variable deductions and the purpose for which they are made;
(c) the amount of net pay.

Where parts of the net pay are made in different ways the employee must be informed of the amount and method of each part-payment. When deductions are fixed the relevant details need not be given on each pay statement, although they must be given at least once every year and whenever the fixed deduction is changed.

Statutory sick pay (SSP)

Employers must pay the approved rate of SSP to employees for up to eight weeks in any tax year or any single spell of absence, irrespective of their length of employment, provided an employee is not in an excluded category. The rate of SSP, which is reviewed annually, is calculated on the average gross pay during the previous eight weeks and it is subject to normal tax and insurance contributions. The rate is a flat rate, irrespective of dependants and marital status. The employer can reclaim SSP payments from his national insurance contributions and must keep adequate absence records.

Guarantee payments

If the employer does not have sufficient work for which an employee was specifically engaged, and the employee does not refuse alternative work offered, he is entitled to guarantee pay. The cessation of work, however, must not be connected with a trade dispute involving the employer. The maximum number of days in a quarter that an employee is entitled to receive guarantee pay is five.

Medical suspension

If an employee is suspended from work on medical grounds, either through statutory regulations or because of the Health and Safety at Work Act 1974, he or she is entitled to pay for up to 26 weeks, unless his is able to do alternative work.

Suspension

If an employee is suspended from work pending a disciplinary hearing he or she is entitled to normal pay unless it is otherwise stipulated in the contract of employment.

DISCRIMINATION AGAINST EMPLOYEES

There is a variety of legislation to prevent discrimination against people of different sexes and races.

Equal pay

The Equal Pay Act 1970 established the rights of men and women who are in full- or part-time employment to equal treatment in respect of their terms and conditions of employment when they are employed on the same or similar work.

Sex discrimination

The Sex Discrimination Act 1975 states that it is an offence to discriminate directly or indirectly against men or women in full- or part-time employment and in related matters. It is also unlawful to discriminate against married persons directly or indirectly.

Discrimination in the following employment areas is unlawful:

(a) advertising job vacancies;
(b) recruitment procedures;
(c) offering differential terms and conditions of employment;
(d) offering promotion, training, transfers and other benefits;
(e) refusing offers of employment.

The only exceptions which permit discrimination to occur are when it may be a genuine occupational qualification such as to preserve decency or privacy, e.g. cloakroom attendants, and reason of physiology, e.g. authenticity in drama. Additionally, a privately-owned establishment that employs less than five persons, including the proprietor and spouse if they are employed in the firm, is allowed to state whether they require a male or female employee. However if such an establishment is a public house owned by a brewery this exception is not permitted.

Race discrimination

The Race Relations Act 1976 makes it illegal to discriminate against any person because of his colour, race, religion, creed or ethnic background in the offer of employment or in the employment itself, either directly or indirectly.

SPECIFIC GROUPS OF EMPLOYEES

There is legislation which protects the interests of specific groups of employees with regard to their employment, whether their circumstances find them permanently or temporarily within these groups.

Maternity rights

The maternity rights and maternity pay for women are subject to a wide variety of conditions, providing they have worked for an employer continuously for at least two years. The Employment Protection (Consolidation) Act 1978 grants a woman maternity leave commencing 11 weeks before confinement and 26 weeks afterwards, with a right to return to work at that time. She need not be re-instated in her former job, but has to be offered alternative employment suitable to the circumstances, and her conditions of employment should not be substantially less favourable to her than those of her original job. She must be paid maternity pay for the first six weeks of her leave at nine-tenths of her normal pay, this being reclaimable by the employer.

The employee must notify her employer at least 21 days before starting maternity leave of her condition and that she intends to return to work at the end of her leave. Seven weeks after the confinement the employer can ask the employee whether or not she still intends to return to work, and at least three weeks before her return she must inform her employer that she is returning. In cases where an employee is not able to carry out her work because of pregnancy, and no suitable alternative work is available, she may be fairly dismissed and is entitled to maternity pay and her job back at the end of the maternity leave. Companies employing less than five persons are not obliged to allow the right to return to work if it is not reasonably practical for them to do so.

An employee is entitled to paid time off for ante-natal care however long she has worked for an employer, provided her medical advisers require it.

Disabled persons
The Disabled Persons (Employment) Acts 1944 and 1958 provide for the reservation of certain types of employment for persons who are registered as disabled. Employers with 20 or more employees are required to allocate a quota of jobs for the disabled. Exemptions may be granted by the Manpower Services Commission where their employment may be inappropriate due to the nature or location of the job.

Rehabilitation of offenders
The Rehabilitation of Offenders Act 1974 allows persons who have had convictions, with certain exceptions, to be rehabilitated and for the conviction to be treated as if it had never happened, these being known as "spent convictions". Prospective employers may ask about convictions but not "spent convictions", and employees are under no obligation to reveal them.

INDUSTRIAL RELATIONS

A wealth of legislation regarding industrial relations has been enacted since the mid-1970s, the most prominent being the Labour Relations Act 1974, the Employment Protection Act 1975 (Consolidation Act in 1978) and the Employment Acts 1980 and 1982. In this section we examine the present situation and the codes of practice that apply to employment in the industry.

The Employment Protection Act 1975 provided for the setting up of the Advisory, Conciliation and Arbitration Service (ACAS), making it a statutory independent body. ACAS is designed to help settle and avoid disputes through mediation and conciliation and it provides machinery for arbitration. Its objectives are to promote, improve and extend collective bargaining and it provides advisory services on industrial relations and related matters, with a view to improving industrial relations and employment policies and procedures.

Codes of practice

ACAS issues codes of practices which give practical guidance in order to promote good industrial relations. A code of practice is not legally binding, in that an employer cannot be prosecuted for not following it, but if a code of practice is not followed a tribunal would take this into consideration.

The existing codes of practice are as follows:

(a) disciplinary practices and procedures in employment—this describes the essential features of disciplinary and grievance procedures, their operation, records and appeals.

(b) disclosure of information to trade unions for collective bargaining purposes—this is for employers who recognise independent trade unions and provide them with information on pay and benefits, conditions of service, company performance and personnel policies.

(c) time off for trade union duties and activities—this covers trade union officials' duties concerned with industrial relations with the employer, as well as the training of such officials in industrial relations.

(d) picketing and the law—this deals with lawful picketing.

(e) closed shop agreements and arrangements—this deals with the scope and content of union agreements and the provision of ballots.

Trade unions

Independent trade unions must be certified as such by the certification officer who maintains the lists of employers' associations and trade unions. Recognised trade unions are those unions which the employer recognises for collective bargaining and consultation procedures. Union membership agreements (UMA), referred to as closed shops, require the approval of 80 per cent of the workforce for approval and the situation must be reviewed every five years. The law also states that an employer cannot insist on employees joining a union or prevent them doing so, nor victimise them for being a member or not being a member. An employer cannot prevent employees from taking part in union activities. The employer must allow the union the right to use his premises for meetings, although this is limited and it does not have to be in working hours.

Secret ballots may be held for union votes in certain cases, these being partly financed by the certification officer. The employer must however supply the facilities.

Redundancy

If for some reason the workload of a business ceases or diminishes it may be necessary to reduce staff levels through redundancies. On occasions this need can be avoided by bringing in early retirement or work sharing. Employers should have a redundancy selection policy which is made clear to employees in order to avoid claims for unfair dismissal. It may be unlawful direct discrimination for part-time employees to be made redundant first, and such actions may have to be justified according to the Redundancy Payments Act 1965.

Redundancy payments must be made to all employees who have more than two years service, so long as they are over 18 and under 65 for men or under 60 for women. The amount of redundancy pay is based on age, length of service and rate of pay of the employee, and the employer can claim 41 per cent of these payments back from the Department of Employment.

The procedures for handling redundancies are laid down in the Employment Protection Act 1975.

Employees' rights in insolvency

If an employer becomes insolvent the employee has rights to certain debts in respect of arrears of pay, accrued holiday pay, outstanding compensation awarded by an industrial tribunal, pay in lieu of notice and any pension considerations. The payment is made by the liquidator and has preference over other debts of the employer.

Transfer of undertakings regulations

When a business undertaking is transferrred from one owner to another the new owner must observe the terms and conditions of employment that applied before the transfer, with the exception of pension schemes. Dismissals arising from the transfer are unfair unless the new owner can prove organisational, economic or technical reasons. This applies to transfers due to the sale of a business or death of the owner if the owner is a sole trader, partnership or limited company. However it does not apply if the transfer is by share transfer.

HEALTH AND SAFETY AT WORK

The health, safety and welfare of both employees and guests is the responsibility of the employer. The obligations of the employer are set out in the Health and Safety at Work etc. Act 1974 and aim to protect employees and other persons who may be at risk as a result of the activities of people at work. The general obligations of the employer are as follows.

(a) To provide and maintain safe systems of work and plant which are practicable, safe and without risk to health.

(b) To ensure safety in connection with the use, storage, handling and transportation of anything.

(c) To provide information, supervision, instruction and training as necessary to ensure health and safety.

(d) To maintain the workplace in a safe and satisfactory condition, including safe access to and from it.

(e) To provide and maintain safe and satisfactory working conditions and facilities.

All employers with more than five employees must prepare a written statement of a general health and safety policy and bring it to the attention of all employees. Within the Health and Safety Commission's guideliness for safety policy this statement should contain the following details:

(a) the name of a senior manager who is responsible for safety;

(b) employees who are exposed to hazards should be made aware of them, the precautions to be taken and the reasons for controls;

(c) the procedures of notification and analysis of accidents;

(d) the arrangements for joint consultation, reviewing of safety measures and the monitoring of safety developments.

The Act also lays down general regulations on the appointment of safety representatives, the setting up of safety committees and time off for safety training and first aid.

The employee has statutory duties under the Act to take reasonable care of the health and safety of himself and others who may be affected by his actions at work. The employee must also co-operate with the employer as far as necessary to see that statutory duties are performed or complied with. This is best explained by an example; the employer has a duty to provide protective clothing free of charge to the employee but the employee has a duty to wear it.

The Health and Safety at Work etc. Act also re-enacted the Offices, Shops and Railway Premises Act 1963 which includes most catering establishments within its scope. This Act covers aspects of cleanliness, lighting, temperature, ventilation, overcrowding and sanitary arrangements for people at work.

Employers' liability insurance

The Employers' Liability (Compulsory Insurance) Act 1969 requires every employer to take out an insurance policy to cover any claim by employees for injuries or diseases sustained at work. A copy of the insurance certificate must be displayed in a prominent position at the workplace. Failure to do this is a criminal offence and punishable as such.

SELF-ASSESSMENT QUESTIONS

1. List the contents required by law of a contract of employment.
2. Explain the statutory periods of notice to terminate employment required of the employer and employee.
3. Give the reasons for fair dismissal by an employer.
4. What are the employee's rights in the event of unfair dismissal?
5. List the wages councils that set remuneration rates for employees in the hotel and catering industry.
6. Explain which deductions from an employee's pay are (a) compulsory, and (b) voluntary.
7. Explain the legislation passed to prevent discrimination in employment.
8. Explain the maternity rights of women in employment.
9. Explain the role of ACAS in industrial relations.
10. Explain which employees qualify for redundancy payments and what considerations are made in the calculation of payment.
11. Explain the general obligations of the employer to provide a safe workplace, as contained in the Health and Safety at Work Act 1974.
12. Explain the employee's obligations contained in the Health and Safety at Work etc. Act 1974.

CHAPTER FOURTEEN

Trade Associations, Professional Bodies and Trade Unions

CHAPTER OBJECTIVES

After studying this chapter you should be able to:
* understand the role of trade associations in the industry;
* understand the role of professional bodies in the industry.

INTRODUCTION

At a national level the employers in industry are represented by the Confederation of British Industry (CBI) and the employees are represented by the Trades Union Congress (TUC). Various sectors of the hotel and catering industry are represented by the CBI, and employees who are members of trade unions are represented by union executives of the TUC. However the hotel and catering industry is mainly made up of small units, spread throughout the country and employing small numbers of employees. Consequently representation of both parties in national decision-making organisations is not adequate. The industry has an estimated work force of 1,668,000 employees in 205,000 establishments, but because of the complexity of the industry there are no statistics available to show what proportion of employers and employees are represented.

In the first part of this chapter we examine the role of trade associations and the part they play in representing the various sectors of the industry. We then examine professional bodies and the role they play in representing senior employees and setting codes of practice and standards for the employees. The function of trade unions and the effects of unionisation are examined in the final part of this chapter.

TRADE ASSOCIATIONS

A trade association may be best described as a voluntary body of independent organisations formed to protect and advance their collective interests. They are both nationally and locally based. National organisations, e.g. the British Hotels and Restaurants Association, have local branches acting autonomously and, as a means of communication, local associations, e.g. the Torbay Hotels Association, act independently in their own area. In this section we look at both types of organisation in some detail.

As with all non-profit making organisations and associations, we must first establish a need for their existence. They were originally established to provide a collective voice in order to protect their own interests against competition or government legislation which could affect them either individually or collectively. The earliest trade association was the London Coffee, Restuarant and Dining Room Keepers' Trade Protection Society, founded in 1900 to fight the London County Council's plans to provide a catering service for the occupants of their lodging houses. As more legislation affecting the industry was passed by Parliament or local authorities, so the number of trade associations increased.

As well as a protective role, trade associations have developed a range of other services available to members, e.g. product and service information. The main method of communication is through journals and newsletters sent to all members.

Firstly let us look at the functions of the national trade associations. They make representations, on behalf of their specific trades, to official bodies such as government departments, e.g. the Department of Trade and Industry and the Department of Employment, on matters affecting proposed legislation, staff training, etc. They also negotiate with other official bodies such as tourist boards, on classification of membership and promotional activities, wages councils, as representatives of employers, and government economic development committees (EDCs), on the implications of any government policies that may affect the industry. As can be seen, although trade associations were formed to protect members, a lot of the work they do now is also of a constructive nature, e.g. helping to form policies in the best interests of the industry and the nation alike.

The British Hotel and Restaurants' Association (BHRA) was formed in 1948 as a result of the merger of Hotel and Restaurants' Association of Great Britain and The Residential Hotels' Association, both of which date back to the early 1900s. In 1972 it joined forces with the Caterers' Association of Great Britain to form the British Hotels', Restaurant and Caterers' Association (BHRCA) as it is known today. It has a membership of almost 10,000 catering organisations spread throughout the country, with some 80 local associations. The BHRCA approaches the government directly as a pressure group in its own right, as well as a member of the Hotel and Catering EDC. It undertakes other functions such as publicising the trade through its hotel guide, which is on public sale, and the promotion of meetings in which the industry can voice its opinions at both a national and local level. In the 1950s and 1960s, before the growth of our own labour force and our membership of the EEC, the BHRA organised the import of foreign workers and the obtaining of their work permits, thus easing the industry's labour problems. They have also been involved in the promotion of catering exhibitions, on both a local and regional level and nationally, e.g. Hotelympia.

The National Union of Licensed Victuallers was formed in 1976 as an amalgamation of various bodies with the Licensed Victuallers' Associations, whose earliest roots date back to the fifteenth century. The need for trade protection for publicans has been recognised for a long time due to ever-changing government legislation. The Union has several differing functions. It has a voice in government legislation through its parliamentary representative. It is involved in the negotiation of relationships between breweries and their tenants (this is further explained under the functions of tenants' associations later in the chapter). The third function is of a more charitable nature, in that they are affiliated to the Licensed Victuallers' National Homes which make provisions for licensees' children in the event of any misfortunes. The union also has its own school, with 200 boarding places for members' children should a need arise through death or illness.

Whilst the National Union of Licensed Victuallers has several roles to play in an official capacity, there is also the social role played by the local branches in arranging events at which their members can meet and discuss various aspects of their business. The Union, via its local branches, will also provide legal representatives of licensing courts to act on behalf of its members in any cases or applications presented. This may again be described as a "protective" but very necessary role due to the high cost of legal fees which individual licencees may not be able to afford. A good example of this would be an application for a new liquor licence to be granted which would compete with existing members' trade and affect their business. The Union's solicitor would oppose the application at all stages of the legal process.

Other trade associations are of a more specialist nature and consequently are smaller in their membership. A complete listing of trade associations, together with addresses, may be found in the current *HCIMA Reference Book.*

Whilst not linked to trade associations, there are trade publications that often take up causes which may affect the industry and provide a voice for their readership, whatever association they belong to. The most popular of these is the *Caterer and Hotelkeeper*, which is published weekly and has a wide readership at all levels of the trade. The licensing trade has its own newspaper, *The Morning Advertiser*, which is published daily and is solely owned by the National Union of

Licensed Victuallers, although its circulation is not limited to its membership.

Whilst we have considered the two main national trade associations, it ought to be apparent that they have strong local connections, with branches throughout the country. There is as great a need for local representation as for national representation, and therefore throughout the country there are also many small, independent locally-based associations that play a similar role to their national counterparts, only instead of dealing with government they deal with local or county councils. They usually take the form of local hotels' associations and, by the very nature of their size, location and common interests, often offer many services to their members. Often such local associations have representatives on local government and tourist boards. The associations can also be brought together by joint marketing schemes, such as local guides for holiday resorts, which may then be advertised nationally. Some local associations venture into more practical ways of assisting their members such as joint purchasing schemes, employee blacklists and passing on bookings to other members during peak periods of operation.

Restaurants and similar establishments are often members of local trade associations or chambers of commerce, all of which have similar objectives and provide similar services to their members. Licensed houses in many areas have tenants' associations in order to negotiate better terms with the breweries or to cope with distribution problems created by a draymen's strike. National brewery companies' tenants may also be organised into an association, with local branches around the country.

Trade associations are therefore made up of the managers, owners or tenants of a business, but it is the business that entitles them to membership, not the individual. Whilst the objectives and aims of trade associations and professional bodies may overlap, the difference between them is in their membership.

PROFESSIONAL BODIES

A professional body is an organisation of individuals who are engaged in a particular occupation and who have gained qualifications or experience in that occupation. The professional body will lay down standards by which members will have to qualify for membership; these standards will be based on knowledge, expertise and competence to carry out the occupation. The professional body will set up a code of conduct for its members to abide by in order to retain their membership.

Unlike trade associations, where the business organisation is the qualification for membership, a professional body will represent the individual, who will carry his membership from one position to another. Whilst some professional bodies demand academic qualifications to a specified level, either from some other examining body or in their own examinations, other bodies may demand experience at varying levels in order to qualify for membership. There are, in most professional bodies, differing levels of membership, ranging from student or associate to a fellowship, and it is usually possible to transfer from one level to another, subject to the requirements of the body.

All professional bodies have similar aims of furthering and maintaining standards within their membership and promoting research in their profession, as well as giving the opportunity for the exchange of information and contact between their members.

Professional associations in the hotel and catering industry

The hotel and catering industry has several professional associations which represent different sectors of the industry. The principal association is the Hotel Catering and Institutional Management Association (HCIMA) whose role in education in the industry was discussed fully in Chapter Twelve. The HCIMA was set up in 1971, as the result of a merger between the Hotel and Catering Institute, founded in 1949, and the Institutional Management Association, founded in 1938.

Whilst the Association is best known for its educational work, it has also set up a research register, updated annually, which provides a wealth of information for all participants in the industry. The Association also provides publications, advisory services, meetings, conferences and lectures to both the industry and its members. Because of the nature of its strict entry qualifications, there is a high regard for members of the association.

Student membership is available for all students studying hotel and catering courses, from BTEC diploma level upwards. On successful completion of OND, BTEC diploma or similar courses, students are eligible for intermediate membership. Students successfully completing the Association's membership examinations, HND, relevant degree courses or BTEC higher diploma are eligible for full corporate membership (MHCIMA) after two years' industrial experience. Fellowship (FHCIMA) is the most senior grade of membership and is awarded to members of at least ten years standing who have held a responsible post for five years, or the equivalent. There is also a grade of membership for senior personnel in the industry whose careers have been based on practical experience rather than academic qualifications; this is known as licentiate membership (LHCIMA).

The Association has approximately 21,000 members at different grades, a number which has been constant for the last ten years. Its membership principally comprises corporate members (8,500) and student members (6,092). In addition to this there are 1,720 fellow members and 4,660 licentiate members of different grades.

It is difficult to ascertain in which sectors of the industry the Association's members are employed due to the constant movement of personnel, this movement being created by the very nature of the industry and the flexibility of the qualifications.

Whilst the HCIMA, as a professional body, represents management employees in the industry, other associations are more difficult to define. These bodies tend to be more specialised, are linked to specific occupations and have more flexible membership qualifications. To describe them as professional bodies is open to question, as their membership qualifications are so flexible, while to call them trade unions would be incorrect as they only rarely negotiate with employers. The most common form of entry is for someone to be employed to a certain level in an occupation, either as a skilled employee or a manager. The prime functions of these associations are the exchange of information between members, the organisation of competitive and social events and the promotion of ideas for discussion in their particular trade or field of management.

The main craft-based associations are the Cookery and Foods Association for chefs, which has a high grade of membership, and the Craft Guild of Chefs, for members who have attained an even higher level of craftsmanship, usually having passed City and Guilds 706–3 examinations. Specialists in the service of alcoholic beverages may sit for qualifications for membership of the Guild of Sommeliers or the United Kingdom Bartenders' Guild. The Society of Golden Keys is an association of hall porters and uniformed staff and has great pride in its association and membership.

Management associations are self-explanatory and represent the interests and aims of their sector of industry. The longest established associations are the Catering Managers' Association, the Industrial Caterers' Association and the Hospital Caterers' Association. As more diverse management skills are used in the industry, new organisations have been formed for the interchange of ideas. Examples of these are the British Association of Hotel Accountants, the Hotel and Catering Personnel Training Association and the Hotel Purchasing Managers' Association. Teachers in hotel and catering colleges have formed the Catering Teachers' Association, giving them a say in course development and other matters concerning education for the industry. Members of these associations are usually qualified in their own profession or are members of the HCIMA and regard the specific management association they belong to as a source of information and communication between colleagues of a similar level and with similar problems.

Whilst a professional body is not regarded as a trade union, it is often consulted by employers with regard to conditions of employment, either for its own membership or for employees in their sector or specialism.

TRADE UNIONS

The effects of unionisation on the hotel and catering industry can only be viewed realistically by first making some comparisons with trade union membership in other industries. Trade union involvement in the hotel and catering industry has traditionally been low and on a very small scale in comparison with other industries. National average trade union membership for all workers is currently 52 per cent, while for hotel and catering workers the figure is approximately 5 per cent. Therefore in sheer numerical terms alone the effects of unionisation in the catering industry are considerably less than in other industries.

Many reasons have been proposed to explain the lack of trade union involvement in the catering industry and we need to consider these in turn in order to obtain a clearer picture of the overall effect of unionisation in the catering industry.

Reasons for low level of trade union involvement

The following factors may provide an indication as to why recruitment into trade unions has been relatively low in the hotel and catering industry.

The attitude of employers

There is evidence to suggest that employers in the hotel and catering industry have a general reluctance to accept or encourage trade union involvement within the industry.

For trade unions to be able to represent a labour force they have to obtain recognition by the employers in the industry concerned. Trust House Forte, for example, will not recognise or negotiate with trade unions unless they possess over 50 per cent membership of those working in any one unit. Trade union recognition then enables negotiation, discussion and consultation to take place between officially elected representatives of the labour force and the employers and their representatives in management. Therefore if a trade union is not recognised by an employer then, should any dispute arise, no framework for discussion will exist other than on an individual basis.

In 1946 the General and Municipal Workers' Union's London-based Catering no. 1 branch was involved in a dispute with the Savoy Hotel over the question of union recognition. This is generally regarded as being the first strike of its kind of any significance in the catering industry, and the fact that it was unsuccessful gives some indication of the difficulties experienced by trade unions in this field.

The reward system

If union recognition cannot be achieved, then the only contact between employee and employer is on an individual basis; indeed, within the catering industry much wage negotiation is carried on in this way. The very complex nature of the reward system within many catering establishments shows in turn how difficult the subject of industrial relations between employees and employers actually is.

Unlike many other industries there are numerous accepted means by which catering workers receive payment in addition to their basic declared weekly or monthly wage. For instance, many catering workers live in, making it difficult to estimate what they gain in real terms for their accommodation and food. In addition many catering workers receive considerable payments in the form of gratuities or tips; the relatively low wages of waitress staff, for example, are seen as being compensated by the tips the waitresses receive from customers at table. Management are also often aware that certain "fiddles" are taking place or that certain "backhanders" are being given. Providing these forms of pilferage do not become too excessive there is a tendency for management to turn a blind eye or look the other way when such unofficial forms of payment are taking place. Evidence for such practices may be difficult to produce, but anyone with experience in the catering industry will be well aware that they do take place.

The point of this analysis of the reward system in the catering industry is that although wages in some sectors of the industry are particularly low, and are therefore in need of improvement, it is unlikely that trade unions will be able to achieve these improvements because of the reluctance of catering workers to declare their "unofficial", and therefore non-taxed income.

Staff fragmentation

In large-scale catering organisations a clearly defined division of labour exists; our analysis of the formal organisation (see Chapter Three) shows just how clearly defined the various areas of work and responsibility can be. This in turn leads to an increasingly high degree of specialisation within these organisations, with little overlapping of duties and clear definitions of the various tasks to be carried out. In a large organisation this can often lead to a lack of communication between the various departments or selections, other then for the purposes of making the formal organisation function efficiently, e.g. the smooth efficient links that need to exist between food preparation and food service staff. This fragmentation of staff does not encourage any form of collective action, other than perhaps on a small-scale informal basis.

Staff fragmentation is also related to the attitude of employers to their employees on the one hand and the reward system for employees on the other. It is likely that if a trade union tried to organise this fragmented workforce, perhaps on the basis of improving low pay, management would resist such an action on the basis that it would undermine its authority and control. In addition, the workforce might resist such involvement because they might feel they have less to benefit financially from collective bargaining and the setting up of fixed rules and procedures for improving their pay, preferring instead the individual contracts they have negotiated, which might be supplemented by the addition of perks or unofficial untaxed payments.

The individual contract

Staff fragmentation on an organisational level tends to reduce the possibility of any collective activity such as unionisation taking place. Cynical observers might suggest that this situation is perpetuated by management, on the principle of "divide and rule". The popularity of the individual contract within the catering industry certainly gives support to this observation. Catering management can quite reasonably argue that the nature of the industry is such that formal personnel procedures can often be too rigid, inflexible and unsuitable for the constantly fluctuating customer demands and the generally changing nature of much of the industry. Certainly in catering establishments which operate on a seasonal basis, where banqueting and special functions occur frequently and which generally fluctuate to accommodate changing customer needs, the practicality of a rigid and general personnel policy can be questioned.

The individual contract is usually drawn up by management, acting in what is sometimes known as an ad hoc manner in response to the needs of a given situation, without strict reference to formally drawn up rules and procedures. An essential element of the individual contract is its secrecy; it is worked out between the two parties concerned and no one else. It may be formulated in such a way that the individual worker feels he is receiving preferential treatment, perhaps in the form of better wages or promotion possibilities than a comparable worker in the organisation. In addition, the individual contract may not be written down and might also involve a sense of obligation on the part of the worker to fulfill his duties and responsibilities.

It is clear to see that such practices do little to encourage any form of collective trade union activity. The worker feels that he is receiving special treatment from the manager with whom he has drawn up the individual contract, and at the same time the manager himself is aware that he is working to prevent any form of collective activity that might undermine his authority.

Labour turnover

The system of individual contracts contributes to the high level of labour turnover in a catering establishment, particularly when a change of management takes place. The new manager may not be aware of the individual contracts that have been created. Additionally he may either introduce his own individual contracts with staff members or perhaps introduce a more general set of rules and procedures to which staff have to adhere. Whatever the reasons, it is likely that the introduction of new management in this situation, will increase labour turnover. (In a situation where more formal and more generally accepted procedures have been worked out for the benefit of all staff, new management is less likely to cause disruption.)

If labour turnover is high in an industry or in any establishment within it, the feeling of a permanence amongst staff will be correspondingly low and consequently it is unlikely that they will want to enter into what is a relatively permanent commitment such as joining a trade union.

In addition to the problems related to the individual contract, discussed above, there are other reasons which account for high labour turnover in the catering industry. These can be classified into two principal categories:

(a) those occurring within a given organisation;
(b) those related to the nature of the industry itself.

Within the organisation the management technique may contribute to high labour turnover. For example, a manager with a laissez-faire approach might well overlook the needs of the workforce, which in turn could cause frustration and job dissatisfaction. This type of management may also be deficient in other areas, for example in not encouraging participation amongst staff members or not organising occasional staff meetings where points of view might be aired. Entry into the organisation can cause new employees to be apprehensive; management can easily work out an induction programme designed to reduce the tension the new recruit may well feel and welcome him into the organisation, but this is not always done. Tension is often caused because the catering worker is unsure of whom he is working for; on the one hand he receives a wage from his employer but at the same time he can also receive a substantial amount of his income, through tips, from the customer, creating an ambiguity in terms of whom he is actually responsible to. This ambiguity is much more prevalent in catering than in any other industry.

The catering industry itself imposes special demands upon the workforce which often contribute to the high rate of labour turnover. A large number of catering establishments operate on a seasonal basis, with a high demand for labour during the season but a low demand during the off-season period. Similarly, part-time or casual staff might only be needed during periods of high activity, e.g. a hotel or outside catering company might only employ part-time banqueting waitresses. This gives staff very little allegiance to an individual employer and therefore contributes to high labour turnover. A large portion of the catering workforce is therefore transitory, moving from one job to another as seasonal demands require, creating little feeling of need for trade union representation at any time.

Clearly then high labour turnover contributes to low trade union involvement. We next need to consider the type and variety of staff that catering attracts in order to assess if this is also relevant to our explanation of low trade union involvement in the catering industry.

Catering staff
Any form of general statement regarding the nature of the catering worker may turn out to be misleading and will certainly leave room for many exceptions which apparently contradict the general rule. However there are certain things we *can* say about the catering workforce as a whole which throw some light on their general reluctance to become involved in the activities of trade unions.

Many catering workers are women and, traditionally, in all industries women are found to be less inclined to join a trade union than men. This may partly be due to the fact that as women have only recently been employed on a large scale in many sectors of industry they have not developed an awareness or feeling of need for the representation by a trade union. Male workers, on the other hand, are more likely to be used to participating in various forms of joint or collective activity. In addition, much of the female catering workforce is employed on either a part-time or casual basis and this, combined with their domestic commitments of home and family, is also likely to contribute to low levels of union involvement.

Catering traditionally involves the employment of a high proportion of overseas workers, and this tends to contribute to low levels of unionisation in catering. Such workers may be migrant workers who only possess a short-term work permit, in which case they are unlikely to wish to join a union if they are only in the country for a short period of time. Secondly, there may be a language problem; they may not speak the language of the country they are working in, which will cause problems for them in working out the exact details of a trade union membership form. In addition, the branch official is unlikely to be able to converse with them in a common language, with the likelihood that he will not bother to encourage them to join the union. Thirdly, many foreign workers come from countries where either there is no tradition of trade unionism amongst the work force or membership of trade unions has been repressed or discouraged by the government. Many foreign workers in the catering industry also feel that a trade union will not represent them and their needs, being designed more for the indigenous or home-based workforce. Many, therefore, unite together in racially or ethnically identifiable groups in the hope that this will protect their interests more effectively.

The type of worker that the catering industry traditionally employs therefore tends to contribute to low levels of union involvement. Their interests or needs do not motivate them to become involved in trade union activity in any large numbers.

The size of the establishment

The size of the organisation also tends to contribute to the degree of unionisation. A large-scale industrial catering unit is much more likely to have a union represented workforce than a small seasonal hotel.

We have previously considered the way in which communication can take place in both formal and informal organisations. We saw that a small-scale unit with a relatively informal organisation and no clearly defined division of labour was likely to possess a close and direct relationship between the owners of the unit and the staff working within it. This close and direct relationship in turn enables a form of instant industrial relations to operate. In this kind of establishment the owner also acts as manager and therefore has direct contact with staff without having to communicate or go through an intermediary; complaint or grievances can thus be dealt with quickly and effectively without the need for representation by trade union officials.

The fact that the catering industry largely consists of small-scale organisations is another contributory factor to the relatively low level of trade union involvement in the industry. According to HCITB surveys, 31 per cent of the industry's labour force work in units employing less than nine people. In addition these small operational units are widely spread throughout the country, thus reducing the opportunity for creating links between the various units and providing trade union representation. When we consider the number of small hotels, guesthouses and restaurants spread between the tourist resorts of South West England and Scotland we realise the difficult task any trade union faces in trying to organise the workforce; any elected official, e.g. a branch representative, would have to travel fairly large distances to establish contact with potential membership.

In contrast, a larger operational unit will have a large workforce located on the same site, connected mainly by the formal organisation. There will be a more clearly worked out management structure designed to control the unit according to the demands of the owners, with less direct face-to-face contact between employer and employee. It is in this situation that trade union membership is more likely to occur. Industrial relations in a large-scale organisation tend to be formal, i.e. between employer representatives in the form of management and employee representatives in the form of trade unions.

It is possible that the growth of large-scale organisations, through expansion, centralisation and amalgamation, may well indirectly contribute to an increase in trade union membership in the industry. Overall, however, the predominance of a large number of small units employing a few staff and spread over a wide geographical area will continue to contribute to the relatively low level of trade union membership in the industry as a whole.

The unions

It has been argued that the lack of appropriate unions has been a major factor in contributing to the low membership amongst hotel and catering workers. We will now consider the various types of union it is possible for catering workers to join and examine the membership of some of these.

(a) craft unions

This is the type of union whose members are of one skill, trade or craft; in other words the trade union is set up to represent all the workers within a given occupational category, e.g. the National Association of Licensed House Managers (NALHM). Craft unions are not bounded by a particular industry so their membership may be derived from the workforce of a number of different industries.

(b) industrial unions

This is the type of union whose membership is drawn from one industry. It usually represents the manual workers in that particular industry. For example the National Union of Railwaymen represents members who are ticket collectors, porters, signalmen and, in growing numbers, catering workers. In works canteens, station restaurants and buffet and restaurant carriages, catering workers come into contact with manual workers from other trades within the industry, thus contributing to their affiliation to this particular union.

(c) general unions

This type of union recruits wherever the need for trade union representation is felt, regardless of industry or craft; for example the Transport and General Workers' Union (TGWU) and the General and Municipal Workers' Union (GMWU) are both unions which have made efforts to provide representation for catering workers. In fact the TGWU pressurised the Trades Union Congress (TUC) to set up a Hotel and Catering Industry Committee in 1972 to look into the low level of union recruitment of catering workers. The GMWU claims a membership of 25,000 catering workers throughout the industry, but this remains a small figure in relation to the total workforce of approximately 2,000,000.

Conclusion

There has been no tradition of trade union membership within the catering industry for reasons previously discussed, and it is only in recent years that general unions like the TGWU and GMWU and industrial unions like the NUR have made any real attempt to encourage recruitment of catering workers. In response to the argument that existing unions do not fully represent the collective needs of catering workers and that this is why they do not join them, in February 1980 the GMWU set up the Hotel and Catering Workers' Union designed to fulfill the union needs of the hotel and catering worker. It remains to be seen whether such a union can successfully represent workers in the hotel and catering industry, or whether in fact a demand exists for representation of individual crafts and sectors of the workforce by separate unions.

Whatever the case, the development of trade union representation for hotel and catering workers of all kinds will need to come to terms with all the factors outlined in this section before any success will be achieved.

SELF-ASSESSMENT QUESTIONS

1. Explain the role played by trade associations on a national basis.
2. Explain the role played by trade associations on a local basis.
3. Explain the influences that professional associations have had on the development of the industry.
4. List the professional associations that exist within the hotel and catering industry, briefly describing the category of employee they represent.
5. Describe the ways in which the reward system that operates in the hotel and catering industry works against unionisation.
6. Describe what you understand by the term staff fragmentation in relation to unionisation.
7. List the advantages and disadvantages of the individual contract.
8. List the main reasons for accounting for high labour turnover in the hotel and catering industry.
9. Describe the relationship between the degree of unionisation and the size of the establishment.
10. Distinguish between the various types of trade unions.

CHAPTER FIFTEEN
Job Security at Work

CHAPTER OBJECTIVES

After studying this chapter you should be able to:
* understand the role of the supervisor in job security procedures;
* understand the role of management in job security procedures;
* explain the essential features of disciplinary procedures;
* understand appeals and grievance procedures;
* list the employees' rights that are covered by industrial tribunals.

INTRODUCTION

In this chapter we will examine the job security of employees and the role that supervisors and management play in contributing to this. We have examined certain theoretical, practical and legal aspects of job security in previous chapters. In Chapters Five to Eight, on human relations in the workplace, we looked at individual differences in employees; by these very diferences we can establish that there are individual needs as regards job security. The role of groups, both formal and informal, is also regarded as a constituent part of job security, in that the individual who needs support, either formally or informally, will find security in the fact that he or she is part of a group. In Chapter Twelve we examined staff welfare, counselling, the provision of facilities and management's attitude towards staff, all of which give employees a feeling of belonging in the workplace and, again, contribute to job security.

External factors such as legislation relating to industrial relations, the setting up of bodies such as ACAS and the drafting of codes of practice also contribute to job security. Even though such codes of practice are, in the eyes of the law, only recommendations, industrial tribunals accept them as procedures for employers to follow and base their rulings on them. These recommendations are especially concerned with unfair dismissal, dealing not only with the cause of dismissal but also with the manner in which it was handled.

The setting up of procedures for dealing with disciplinary actions and grievances is therefore an important contribution to employees' job security, in as much as they will be aware that dismissal or disciplinary action is not at the whim of a supervisor or management.

THE ROLE OF MANAGEMENT

Management is responsible for maintaining discipline within its organisation and for ensuring that there are adequate disciplinary rules and procedures. As explained in Chapter Thirteen, the Employment Protection Act 1975 set up ACAS who, in 1977, produced a code of practice for disciplinary practice and procedures in employment. The document gives practical guidance for employers and management on how to draw up disciplinary rules and procedures and their effective operation, with the aim of helping employers, trade unions and employees. Management must be aware that such rules and procedures are necessary for promoting fairness and setting standards. Whilst it would not be reasonable to expect management to prepare a set of rules that can cover all circumstances, any rules should not be so general that they are meaningless. The rules therefore should specify, clearly and concisely, standards necessary for the safe and efficient performance of work and the maintenance of satisfactory relations within the workforce and between management and employees. Management should consult trade unions and supervisors in the drafting of these rules as well as in the drawing up of procedures to be followed if the rules are not observed. Considerations should also be made regarding the type of work, working conditions and the size of the establishment when drawing up such rules and procedures.

The rules of the organisation should be readily available and management should make every effort to ensure that employees know and understand them. The best method is to issue employees with their own copy of the rules and to back this up by having them verbally explained by the supervisor. For new employees it is best to include such an explanation in the induction programme. Employees should also be made aware of any penalties that will be imposed for breaking the rules; in particular those infringements that warrant instant dismissal should be emphasised.

THE ROLE OF THE SUPERVISOR

The supervisor has immediate responsibility for his subordinates, their activities and the workplace over which he is given formal authority. In the personnel function of his job he is responsible for his subordinates' morale, discipline, welfare, safety, induction and training, as well as being available for consultation with them. An employee will look to his supervisor to provide these functions as part of his job security, the supervisor being his link with the hierarchy of the organisation where he works; a lack of this supportive relationship will affect the employee in his feeling of security.

It is often the supervisor who instigates disciplinary proceedings against the employee, e.g. for constant lateness or lack of ability to do a job properly. The supervisor therefore needs a sound knowledge of the procedures and regulations concerning industrial relations in order to be effective in his role. Most situations that need disciplinary action or involve grievance procedures start in the workplace, for which the supervisor has responsibility. If such procedures are not carried out properly, or the employee feels the action is unfair, the case may go to a tribunal, in which case the supervisor must produce evidence to support his case. The supervisor should therefore participate with management when formulating new or revising existing rules and procedures and, if necessary, help in communicating them to the staff.

ESSENTIAL FEATURES OF DISCIPLINARY PROCEDURES

The attitude of management in the setting up of disciplinary procedures should not be seen as that of imposing sanctions but of emphasising and encouraging improvements in individual conduct.

Disciplinary procedures should be detailed in writing. It should be specified to whom they apply, the disciplinary actions which may be taken, which levels of management have the authority to take the various forms of disciplinary action and any communication between levels of management that must take place, e.g. between immediate supervisors and senior management in the case of dismissals.

The procedure should ensure that any disciplinary action is not taken until the case has been thoroughly investigated and that employees are not dismissed for a breach of discipline, except in the case of gross misconduct. There should be provision for employees to be informed of the complaints made against them, and they should be given the opportunity to state their case before any decision is made. The employee should have the right to be accompanied by a "friend" (either trade union representative or fellow employee) when stating his case. The procedure should ensure that employees are given an explanation of any penalties that can be imposed and told that there is an appeal mechanism.

However, an essential overriding feature of any disciplinary procedure is that matters involving them should be dealt with quickly.

The application of a disciplinary procedure
When a disciplinary matter arises, for example an employee is frequently late for work, the supervisor or manager must establish his facts—in this case they would include dates and times of recorded lateness—together with any evidence, e.g. witnesses, clock cards, etc.

The supervisor should issue the employee with an oral warning stating the facts of the lateness. In some cases a supervisor will make such a warning informal, with the purpose of giving the employee an opportunity to improve his record. However if a formal verbal warning is given, it is best to support it with a letter confirming the oral warning (see Fig. 34). The letter should contain details of the nature of the offence and the likely consequences of any further offences. The employee should be advised that the letter is part of the formal procedure.

---

7 April 198–

Dear Mr Barlow

I am writing to you to confirm that on 6 April 198– you were given a formal oral warning by myself regarding your poor timekeeping.

This has occurred on several occasions and you have provided no reasonable excuse for your lateness. I therefore formally warn you to improve in this matter. If this warning is not taken seriously and your timekeeping does not improve immediately you will be given an official written warning as set out in the company's disciplinary procedures.

Yours sincerely

Joanna Wills
Supervisor

I acknowledge receipt of this official warning.
Signature_____ Date_____
Name_____

Fig. 34. *Example of a letter confirming an oral warning.*

Any recurrence of the misconduct would warrant a final written warning (see Fig. 35) containing a statement that any further occurrence will lead to suspension or dismissal or some other penalty. A copy of the letter should be sent to the employee's representative or "friend", and another copy placed on file. In a case of poor timekeeping it would be unreasonable for a final warning to last for ever; in such cases a time limit is therefore usually a condition of the warning.

Continued misconduct would result in either disciplinary suspension

                                                              10 May 198-

Dear Mr Barlow

FINAL OFFICIAL WARNING

You received a formal oral warning from myself on the 6 April 198-,
which I confirmed in writing on the 7 April 198-, regarding your
poor timekeeping.

Unfortunately you seem to have ignored this warning and I am now
issuing you with a final official warning.

Your late arrival for duty on three occasions since 7 April 198-
have been noted without any reasonable excuse from yourself, these
occasions being:

14 April 198- – 20 minutes late;
29 April 198- – 15 minutes late;
 9 May   198- – 30 minutes late.

If you should be late on duty again in the next 6 months you will
be liable to dismissal from the company.

Yours sincerely

Joanna Wills

Supervisor

I acknowledge receipt of this final official warning.

Signature _____   Date _____

Name _____

A copy of this warning is lodged on your file.

Fig. 35. *Example of a letter of final written warning.*

without pay or dismissal, according to the nature of the employee's misconduct (these measures are only open to the employer if they are allowed for in the contract of employment, either by express or implied terms). Disciplinary suspension without pay needs special consideration and if imposed should not be for a prolonged period of time. In the example given the employee would face dismissal; on the final occurrence of the employee arriving late for duty he would be suspended from duty whilst his case was considered by the manager, who should seek advice from the personnel officer or other authoritative persons.

When determining the disciplinary action to be taken, the manager or supervisor should consider the need to satisfy the test of reasonableness in all the circumstances involved. Consideration should also be made of the employee's record and any other relevant factors. A letter should then be sent to the employee giving details of the disciplinary action taken (see Fig. 36) and, if requested by the employee, a copy should also be sent to his represetnative or "friend". The employee should be informed as to his rights of appeal, how to make an appeal and to whom.

In situations where an employee has been given a final warning for one type of misconduct, e.g. lateness, he cannot be dismissed for another form of misconduct, e.g. rudeness, if this occurs; in such a case a separate disciplinary procedure must be followed.

In more serious cases, e.g. serious negligence or pilfering, consideration should be given to suspending the employee whilst the case is being investigated, suspension in this case being with pay. It is important that the supervisor or manager establishes all the facts of the case promptly before recollections fade, and takes statements from any witnesses to the event. Before any decision is made regarding the penalty, the employee should be interviewed, giving him the opportunity to state his case. The employee should be advised of his rights under the procedure, including the right to be accompanied at any hearing by a representative or "friend".

In cases of dishonesty, when prosecution may be pending, an employee may be suspended without pay until the outcome of the court case. In cases where there is no conviction then the employee should be reinstated and paid for the period of suspension.

Should it be decided to dismiss without notice an employee who is guilty of serious misconduct, the employee should be informed and given the opportunity to reply. The employee should then be informed in writing (see Fig. 37) within 14 days of the dismissal; if the employee has requested them, reasons for the dismissal should be stated. Copies of all letters should be placed on the employee's file.

Appeals procedures

An appeals procedure for employees should be drawn up and made

27 May 198–

Dear Mr Barlow

NOTICE OF DISMISSAL

Following your suspension from employment with the company on
25 May 198–, we have examined the facts of your case, which are
that you continuously fail to report for duty on time.

You were given a formal verbal warning on 6 April 198–, which
was confirmed in writing on 7 April 198– and a final written
warning was sent to you on 10 May 198–. Despite these warnings
you have continued to report late for duty on occasions.

Your employment with the company is therefore terminated with
effect from 3 June 198–, which takes into account the week's
notice that is due to you on the grounds of misconduct.

According to your rights under the Employment Protection Act 1975
this letter is given to you at your request.

You have a right to appeal against your dismissal and a copy of
the company's appeal procedure is attached

Yours sincerely

Joanna Wills
Supervisor

Fig. 36. *Letter terminating employment with notice.*

available to them. Employees who have been dismissed from their
employment have a right to appeal to an industrial tribunal. However
some organisations have their own appeals procedure where dismissal
is concerned, especially if dismissal is made by supervisors or middle
management. Grievance procedures, which are explained more fully in
the next section of this chapter, are sometimes used for dealing with
disciplinary appeals. It is better to keep the appeals procedure separate,
though, because of the need to deal with appeals quickly.

In general appeals are best resolved within an organisation, although
independent arbitration may in some cases be the most appropriate
means of resolving disciplinary issues, and can constitute the final stage
of the procedure, providing both parties are in agreement. There should
definitely be a procedure within the organisation for employees in

                                            12 November 198–

Dear Mr Verity

NOTICE OF DISMISSAL

Following your suspension on the 9 November 198–, the company
has considered your case of taking a bottle of whisky without
payment from the hotel's bar on that date. You were made aware,
in the company's handbook which was issued to you on 3 August 198–,
that employees stealing company property would be liable to
immediate dismissal.

Your employment with the company is therefore terminated with
effect from today's date, without notice, on the grounds that
you stole company property.

In accordance with your rights under the Employment Protection Act
1975, this letter is given to you at your request.

You have a right to appeal against your dismissal and a copy of
the appeals procedure is attached.

Yours sincerely

M. F. Browne
General Manager

Fig. 37.   Letter of dismissal without notice.

higher management to appeal against warnings. Again speed is
important and employees should be given a time limit in order to
register an appeal, usually seven days. Employees should be made
aware of the scope of the procedure, i.e. what they may appeal against,
whether or not dismissal is included, to whom they should appeal and
how, and within what period of time.

GRIEVANCE PROCEDURES

The objective of having grievance procedures is to provide a congenial
working atmosphere and to maintain satisfactory relations among
employees. Employees should therefore be made aware that a procedure exists for them to air any dissatisfactions they may have regarding
their terms and conditions of employment, their working conditions,
methods of work and any other aspect of their employment.

The procedure should be organised in stages, involving higher levels of management at each stage. However it is best to settle all grievances as near to the point of origin as possible, indicating a need for supervisors and middle management to be trained in the handling of grievances. Often a grievance reflects discontentment which may have built up inside the employee out of all proportion to the original problem; therefore speed should be considered when planning a procedure, with time limits between each stage.

As in a disciplinary procedure, an employee has a right to be accompanied at all stages of the grievance procedure.

In a large hotel the procedure may be planned as follows.

(a) Stage 1—the complaint or grievance should be discussed with the employee's immediate supervisor, e.g. housekeeper. If the employee is dissatisfied with the outcome then he may proceed to stage 2.

(b) Stage 2—the employee should inform his supervisor that he wishes to discuss his grievance with the house/food and beverage manager. If the employee is dissatisfied with the outcome of his discussion with the house/food and beverage manager then he should inform him that he wishes to discuss the matter with the general manager.

(c) Stage 3—the employee is able to present his grievance to the general manager, whose decision is final.

In large organisations a final stage of a grievance procedure would be for the aggrieved party to present his case to a director of the company, again whose decision would be final. Some organisations may introduce external arbitration in the case of grievance procedures, although this is usually limited to local and national government bodies.

Often a decision on a grievance raised by an employee is limited by the authority of a supervisor or middle manager, as in the case of pay rises. In cases such as this the supervisor should refer the employee to the person who has control over such matters.

Details concerning all grievance procedures should be recorded and the case notes passed on to the person dealing with the next stage. Employees should be encouraged to go on to the next stage and to use the procedure without any fears of retribution. When a decision has been agreed on a grievance a statement of the details should be prepared, to avoid any future misunderstandings.

INDUSTRIAL TRIBUNALS

All employees may bring a claim before an industrial tribunal on their rights to:

(a) fair dismissal, or compensation in cases of unfair dismissal;

(*b*) written reasons in the case of dismissal;
(*c*) protection against discrimination because of sex, race or marital reasons;
(*d*) redundancy consultation protective awards;
(*e*) redundancy and insolvency payments;
(*f*) equal pay for equal work;
(*g*) protection against discrimination because of trade union membership or activities, including interim relief if dismissed for these activities and, if they are union officials, entitlement to time off with pay for union duties and training;
(*h*) written statements of employment terms and itemised pay statements;
(*i*) paid time off to seek employment if they are made redundant;
(*j*) guarantee or medical suspension payments;
(*k*) time off for public duties.

Women employees may also bring a claim before an industrial tribunal on their rights to:

(*a*) paid time off for antenatal care;
(*b*) protection from dismissal for pregnancy and to be able to return to work following the birth;
(*c*) suitable alternative work if available during pregnancy;
(*d*) maternity pay.

An employee who wishes to bring a claim to an industrial tribunal must make an application to the secretary of the tribunals. The secretary will issue an application form and suitable guidance booklets to cover the application. Providing the applicant satisfies the qualifying periods and time limits, and the case merits the tribunal sitting, a hearing will be held and judgment passed if the employer intends to resist the claim.

Employees' representatives
In all procedures relating to the job security, employees have a right to representation in some form or another, although naturally this will depend on the seriousness of the disciplinary or grievance procedure. For internal cases the representative is usually a fellow employee; if the employee is a member of a recognised trade union, it is usual for a union official to take this role. In cases which involve arbitration or industrial tribunals the representative may be a trade union official, a member of the appropriate commission in the cases of equal pay, sex or racial discrimination, or a solicitor who specialises in cases involving labour disputes.

As a result of the Employment Protection Act 1978 and the setting up of ACAS to provide relevant codes of practice and offer advice in matters concerning job security, employees now have protection against unfair practices by employers. ACAS, as well as protecting the individual employee against such practices, also arbitrates between the trade unions and employers on a national basis in the negotiation of conditions of employment, making its judgments after hearing cases put by both sides. In general these judgments have been accepted as a fair interpretation by both sides.

SELF-ASSESSMENT QUESTIONS

1. Explain the role played by supervisors in job security procedures.
2. Explain the role played by management in job security procedures.
3. Draw up a disciplinary procedure for an organisation.
4. Prepare a handout for employees, explaining the disciplinary procedure drawn up in question 3.
5. Draw up an appeals procedure for an organisation.
6. Draw up a grievance procedure for an organisation.
7. Prepare a handout for employees explaining the grievance procedure for an organisation.
8. List the employee's rights that are covered by industrial tribunals.
9. Explain the role of ACAS in job security.

CHAPTER SIXTEEN

Economics of Government

INTRODUCTION

An analysis of any industry must at some stage take into account the context in which that industry exists. In more specific terms it is important to examine the relationship of that industry to the government of the nation in which it functions. Government policy will determine many of the directions the industry will take and will also have an effect on the relationship of the industry to other industries in that nation. In this chapter we therefore intend to examine all aspects of government involvement in the economy and to relate this involvement to the hotel and catering industry. This approach should then enable us to predict the changes that the industry may experience as a consequence of a change of government. This in turn will enable us at a later stage to examine in detail, and place into context, the economics and operation of an individual business enterprise.

Our approach will therefore first of all take into consideration the different ways in which a government may become involved in the economy in a general sense. We will then examine the specific ways in which this may affect the hotel and catering industry, taking into account such areas as staff training, planning and development. We will consider the different forms of government income and expenditure and how the government controls the balance between these two items. Finally, we will explain the central economic concepts and terms necessary to an understanding of the relationship between the government and the hotel and catering industry.

GOVERNMENT INVOLVEMENT IN THE ECONOMY

In any society the government will have some degree of involvement in the economy; indeed the degree of government involvement greatly influences the nature of the nation's economy. We will begin by broadly classifying government involvement into three types.

The laissez-faire approach

The laissez-faire approach is adopted by a government that believes that any interference with the various economic forces of production and exchange should be kept to a minimum. Such a government would encourage free enterprise and competition in the belief that this will generate increased endeavour, raise profits and thus create economic growth.

The advantages of the laissez-faire approach are that industry has to be streamlined and efficient in order to compete and that this competition tends to keep prices down. The disadvantages of such an approach are that in any competitive situation there are winners and losers, and for every successful business there will be an unsuccessful business. This in turn leads to high levels of unemployment.

State control

This approach is in direct contrast to the laissez-faire approach. It involves complete government control of the economy, with all aspects of trade, finance and production either directly or indirectly under the authority of the government. When such an approach is adopted no private ownership of business will exist, the state owning and controlling all aspects of industry and commerce.

The advantages of this approach are that the needs of the community as a whole are more likely to be met and levels of unemployment are unlikely to be as high as with the laissez-faire approach. The disadvantages of such an approach are, however, that inefficiency often occurs because of centralisation and lack of incentives for the workforce.

The mixed economy

This situation represents a compromise between the two previous approaches. The mixed economy is quite simply a mixture of the two types; it will contain elements both of private enterprise and business and of government involvement. In Britain, for example, where a mixed economy operates, we see some industries functioning with very low levels of government involvement, the catering industry being a good example. Other industries—the railways and communications, for example—operate with a high degree of government involvement; these we call nationalised industries.

In reality most economies in the world allow for some degree of compromise between laissez-faire and state control, this varying according to the views of the dominant political group at the time. We may demonstrate this by further reference to the economic structure of Britain in recent years. The Labour party has always been in favour of some degree of state control, and so after its election victory in 1945 it introduced the nationalisation of many industries such as shipbuilding and transport. In contrast, the Conservative party has traditionally favoured private ownership and the minimum amount of direct government control; as an example, the 1983 Conservative government denationalised a number of concerns.

In a democratic society the passing of various forms of legislation by a governing party invariably means that some degree of government involvement in the economy exists. The aims of such involvement may be to control inflation, maintain acceptable levels of employment, create development areas, maintain the balance of payments, encourage economic growth, etc. In addition the government will also be involved in a diverse range of activities, e.g. training programmes, such as the Manpower Services Commission Youth Training Scheme, health and safety, with specific reference to the 1974 Health and Safety at Work Act, and other areas such as public welfare and consumer protection.

GOVERNMENT INVOLVEMENT IN THE HOTEL AND CATERING INDUSTRY

To demonstrate the nature and degree of government involvement in the economy we will briefly examine the hotel and catering industry. This will also show how a particular industry is affected by government involvement.

Liquor licensing

All catering establishments wishing to sell alcoholic liquor have first of all to apply to the licensing justices to obtain a licence to do so. The kind of licence obtained will determine the hours during which liquor may be sold and to whom, it may specify what type of alcoholic liquor may be sold and may also specify the special occasions when it may be sold for an extended period, e.g. bank holidays or weddings.

Liquor licensing is therefore a government control over the consumption of alcohol, specifying the exact way in which liquor sales may be carried out in hotels, public houses, restaurants, etc. To demonstrate this point further we may contrast liquor licensing in Britain with, say, France or Italy, where the licensing laws are quite different.

Staff training

In recent years the government has become involved in a variety of forms of staff training; the major development in this area in the hotel and catering industry was the setting up of the Hotel and Catering Industry Training Board (HCITB) in 1966. We have dealt in detail with this form of involvement in Chapter Eleven, but in short the government is closely involved in this aspect of the industry as it ensures an improvement in the supply of adequately trained staff.

The setting up of the HCITB not only benefits the industry, by providing a *framework* for staff training, but it also improves the overall *standard* of staffing in terms of skills and abilities, which in turn has a beneficial effect on the industry as a whole. Furthermore, if the catering industry is efficient this will benefit the economy of the nation.

Government economic policy

The Development of Tourism Act 1969 further demonstrates this point. Tourism during the 1950s and 1960s increased in line with the relative prosperity of the times and in turn made a substantial contribution to the balance of payments. By introducing an Act designed to exercise some control over tourism, it was felt that the government could further improve the contribution of tourism to the balance of payments. One of the ways this was attempted was by setting up the Hotel Development Incentive Scheme (HDIS) which provided grants, loans and assistance for hotel development.

Thus government economic policy can influence the catering industry, although this occurs mainly in areas where it may gain overall economic benefits such as foreign currency earnings and reducing levels of unemployment.

Industrial relations

We have dealt in some detail in Chapters Thirteen to Fifteen with industrial relations in the catering industry. We may add here that government industrial relations policy is generally applied to all industries, with the exception of the Catering Wages Act of 1943. The passing of this Act was largely carried out to compensate for the fact that catering wages and conditions of employment lagged far behind other industries. If a government is committed to ensuring certain standards amongst the workforce then it is also committed to intervene if these standards are not reached.

Local authority planning

Government involvement in the economy occurs both at national and local level, and local authority planning represents an area of local government that affects the hotel and catering industry considerably. Quite simply, the industry cannot develop unless it has permission from the local authority planning office.

Various Town and Country Planning Acts have been passed to ensure the careful development of local areas with regard to economic, social and environmental issues. The Acts were designed to ensure that a community develops in such a way as to maintain and preserve the existing environment and so that the area might benefit in the future. Thus, for example, they have the power to grant planning permission for the development of a new holiday camp; this will include acceptance of the site and consideration of the dimensions and appearance of the buildings and of available services and facilities.

Local authority planning reduces ad hoc or random development and ensures that the attraction and natural beauty of a tourist destination is not decimated.

Consumer protection

Finally we will consider the consumer and the way in which he is protected by the government. An acceptance of the importance of consumer rights has meant that various forms of government legislation have been introduced to ensure that these rights are protected. For example, in 1968 the government passed the Trades Description Act protecting the consumer from the purchase of ill-defined and inferior goods. This Act and the Fair Trading Act 1973 protect the consumer's rights generally; other forms of legislation relate specifically to catering establishments.

The Fire Precautions Act of 1971 specifies the need for hotels, guest-houses and boarding houses above a certain size to apply to the fire authorities for a fire certificate. This Act is designed to ensure that the consumer—in this case the hotel guest—is adequately protected in the eventuality of a fire breaking out in the hotel.

The Tourism (Sleeping Accommodation Price Display) Order 1977 demands that all hotels, guest-houses, etc., display information about the accommodation that they provide and the tariffs charged. In addition the Act attempted to set up a system of hotel grading and classification, but this has so far been resisted by the various hotel organisations.

Summary

The extent of government involvement in any one industry and in the economy in general will vary considerably from time to time and from one country to another. It is evident that recent government interest in the hotel and catering industry has created mutual benefits. On the one hand, because the industry is relatively labour intensive, it is able to provide employment at a time when other industries find this increasingly difficult. On the other hand, the increasing contribution that tourism makes to the balance of payments has encouraged the government to become involved and to provide organisational and financial assistance to the industry; for example in 1976–7 the government provided a £20 million grant to help the tourist boards.

We can conclude this section by pointing out that the degree of government involvement in a mixed economy might vary considerably, but for an industry to be efficient and for the government to benefit from this efficiency a close working relationship between the two must always exist.

GOVERNMENT INCOME

The major part of government income is raised by direct taxation on income and capital and by indirect taxation on consumer spending and national insurance contributions.

Direct taxes

Direct taxes are collected by the Inland Revenue. Income tax is a tax on personal income and is progressive, i.e. the more that is earned the greater the proportion of tax that is paid. Corporation tax is charged on the profits of limited companies and is a proportional tax, i.e. a flat rate is charged.

Unearned income—dividends and interest—is taxed heavily, which can be argued as having a detrimental effect on savings and therefore on the capital market. Increases in taxation will affect the amount of disposable income and spending, while decreases will have the opposite effect. The more progressive the taxation structure, the more the demand for luxury goods and services will be affected, although the extent of this effect is open to argument.

Capital gains tax was introduced to make sure that gains from transactions involving capital, especially speculative gains, are not exempt of tax. Capital transfer tax is a tax on the transfer of wealth from one person to another; it superseded death duties.

National insurance

National insurance contributions are not strictly taxes, although they have the same effect. They are now effectively a progressive form of taxation based on an individual's gross income and payable by the employer and employee. Formerly the contributions were deducted at a flat rate on all employees; they thus hit the small-income earner more heavily and were said to be a regressive tax.

Indirect taxation

These are taxes on spending as opposed to on income.

Customs and excise duty

These are taxes on spending collected by HM Customs and Excise. Customs duty is collected on goods entering the country and excise duty on good produced in this country, e.g. customs duty is collected on French wine and excise duty on Scotch whisky. The duties are paid by the importer or manufacturer and passed on to the purchaser by way of price increases. The main areas of government income from this method of taxation are hydrocarbon oils (petrol), tobacco, wines, spirits and beer.

Value added tax

This is a tax on spending on goods and services. As the tax is regressive, certain essential goods and services are exempt, e.g. food, heating and cooking equipment, and fuels. VAT is an effective taxation tool as it is easily and quickly adjusted, can affect market demand and the burden of collection is placed on the firm.

Rates

These are levied on the notional value of occupied property. They are used to finance expenditure by local authorities and are a significant contribution to a firm's costs.

Other forms of indirect taxation are motor vehicle licences, various stamp duties and licences and protective duties on foreign goods.

GOVERNMENT EXPENDITURE

The major proportion of government expenditure is on the provision of public services and goods, although expenditure on areas such as defence, social services and international commitments have to be weighed against economic circumstances prevalent at the time.

The government needs to plan its expenditure over a number of years. It has to be remembered that capital expenditure on any project will involve future spending on upkeep and running of the project; for example, £40 million spent on a hospital might require ongoing current expenditure of £20 million a year for the upkeep of the hospital, staff salaries, etc. The government is therefore faced with the dual problem of predicting future spending requirements as well as controlling government and local authority spending. This latter control is often used as a tool for short-term management of the economy; a controversial method of controlling such expenditure introduced in recent years has been the setting of fixed cash limits for government departments and local authorities.

An increase in government expenditure on services and goods will mean an increase in total demand, which in turn will create inflation, unless the effects are offset by a cut in consumer spending and investment or expansion of the gross national product. This is further explained at the end of this chapter.

Monetary policy

Monetary policy may be best defined as the measures adopted by the government to influence the supply of money circulating within the country. It also means the control of interest rates by the government either to make money more readily available or to restrict its availability to prospective borrowers.

Such policies may be used to achieve the overall government aims of controlling inflation, maintaining full employment or achieving a satisfactory balance of payments with foreign countries. The problems faced by the government at any time will influence the policies which it adopts in order to achieve these aims.

Supply of money

The supply of money is regulated by the Bank of England, which ensures that all financial institutions observe a minimum assets ratio. The Bank of England can also control the supply of money by adjusting the base lending rate, altering cash deposits and, if necessary, asking for special deposits from the clearing banks should they be lending too much.

These actions of the Bank of England indicate whether there is a tightening or slackening of monetary controls, and should be closely watched by businessmen, especially if they rely on credit for the existence of their business. The tightening of the supply of money can have a two-fold effect on a business; firstly it makes borrowing more expensive with regard to loans or overdrafts, and thus cuts back on profitability; secondly it can cut back on customer spending due to restrictions affecting them and their spending power. An increase in the supply of money, through the slackening of monetary controls, will have the opposite effect, although the increased spending can lead to increased demand and then increased prices, thus introducing the spiralling effect of inflation. In short, restrictions on the supply of money through high interest rates will lead to business organisations cutting back on production, manpower and stock levels; when restrictions are lifted or eased, consumer demand is created which the supplier may not be able to cope with, and prices rise.

Fiscal policy

Fiscal policy may be defined as changes in the method or amount of government income, i.e. taxation, in relation to changes in the extent or amount of government expenditure. The effects of fiscal policy will depend on whether the economy is being stimulated or deflated, which in turn will depend on the size of the budget deficit or surplus.

By balancing income and expenditure policies and controls on incomes and prices, a government seeks to arrive at a balanced allocation of national resources or achieve political or social ends.

Prices and incomes policies

A variety of government policies have been introduced from time to time to encourage economic stability and control inflation. They have been used when fiscal and monetary policies have not controlled inflation satisfactorily.

Incomes policies and their effectiveness will depend on:

(*a*) how rigid the policy is and whether there is any flexibility with regard to productivity or to flat-rate increases across the board to improve the position of lower-paid workers and reduce differentials;

(*b*) any linking with price controls and controls on company profits or dividends paid to shareholders;

(*c*) whether or not they are voluntary or statutory.

Any policies should be negotiated with the CBI and TUC, as was the social contract of 1975–6 introduced by the Labour government of the time, giving a £6 a week limit on wage increases. Policies in the early 1980s were controlled by the public sector to a certain extent as the government offered their employees pay increases of only 3 – 4 per cent. The CBI backed the government by offering similar increases, but this policy did nothing to reduce differentials between the high and low paid.

Price controls were introduced in 1973 with the setting up of the Price Commission, who enforced a price code by checking price rises of the large companies who tended to be price leaders. The aims were to control profit margins by only allowing price rises if material or production costs increased or when productivity improved.

GROSS NATIONAL PRODUCT

The gross national product (GNP) may be defined as the sum of all goods and services available for consumption or for addition to wealth (see Fig. 38 and Table 6). It is also described by some writers as the national income.

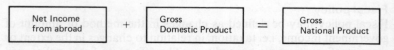

Fig. 38. *Calculation of the GNP.*

TABLE 6 SUMMARY OF GROSS NATIONAL PRODUCT FOR 1982

Income	£bn	Expenditure	£bn
Domestic output	248.4	Consumption of goods and services	206.2
Property income from abroad	1.0	Fixed investment and stocks	35.2
		Transfers abroad (net)	2.0
Total income (GNP market prices)	£249.4	Total expenditure	£243.4
Balance of payments current surplus in			6.0

Different governments, by their political bias and policies, will affect the proportion of the GNP spent by the government (see Table 7). During the 1960s and 1970s there was an enormous movement of resources, especially in manpower, into the public sector, until government departments were spending almost 60 per cent of the GNP. It is expected that during the 1980s this trend will be reversed.

TABLE 7 INCOME AND EXPENDITURE OF CENTRAL AND LOCAL GOVERNMENT FOR 1982

Selected items of income	£bn	Selected items of expenditure	£bn
Income tax	22.7	Defence	12.8
Corporation tax	4.2	Education	13.7
VAT	13.7	Health and welfare	16.4
Other customs and excise revenue	12.8	Social security	27.4
Motor vehicle duties	1.5	Housing	5.8
NI contributions, etc.	16.0	Roads	2.5
Local authority rates	10.4	Trade and industry	8.0
Borrowing	11.2		

To further explain GNP we must examine the meaning of consumption, production and additions to wealth.

Consumption
Consumption means any process by which goods and services are used up; it involves either the immediate destruction or use of the goods or services, or their gradual wearing out.

Consumer services such as hairdressing, travel, entertainment and leisure activities are an important element of our society's standard of living. It must also be appreciated that some goods are bought and sold that have an element of service attached to them, e.g. restaurant meals, cars or household equipment with free maintenance, and goods delivered to a customer's house. Consumer goods are described as consumable as their lifespan will be shortened every time they are used, e.g. televisions, furniture, etc.

To calculate consumption the total purchase price of all new consumer durables and services purchased during the year are included in GNP calculations. Houses are not classified in this category because they have a long lifespan and are treated as investment.

Production
This is a term which refers not only to the assembling of goods but also includes the costs involved in transportation, marketing and all other business services which get the product to the user or consumer when it is required.

Additions to wealth
Additions to wealth may be split into two categories, capital assets and services and addition to stocks.

Capital assets and services
Capital assets are:

(*a*) business capital, owned by business organisations and used for their own production;

(*b*) social capital, owned by the government including hospitals, schools, roads, houses, etc.

(*c*) private capital, which is regarded as owner-occupied houses.

Capital services may be regarded as the cost involved in producing physical goods, e.g. research, surveys, exploratory work, etc.

Additions to stocks
Additions to stocks are made up of stocks in raw materials, work in progress and finished products. Changes in stock levels are an indicator of growth in the economy as they will indicate if production is increasing ahead of consumption or vice versa. They can also be manipulated according to demand or seasonal changes; a country can maintain its standard of living by using up existing stocks.

CONCLUSION

In this chapter we have examined the economics of government in its broad context as it affects the economy as a whole. The hotel and catering industry, being the fourth largest industry in this country, is naturally affected by any economic policy, whether monetary or fiscal, that the government may introduce. The industry's contribution to the gross national product is approximately 8 per cent and it is said to employ in its various sectors 1 – 2 million people. Relying as it does on capital investment and its labour force for its very existence, it is more vulnerable than most other industries; changes in the economy therefore have an effect on capital available and customer spending which in turn affect the profits generated by the industry and the size of the workforce. Different governments and their respective policies have helped develop the industry over the last 40 years; when the economy has been in growth it has in turn been reflected by growth in the industry, when in recession it has affected the industry likewise.

SELF-ASSESSMENT QUESTIONS

1. Explain the different approaches a government may have towards its economy.
2. Explain how the government is involved in the hotel and catering industry.
3. List the sources of government income.
4. Explain the considerations the government makes in planning its expenditure.
5. Explain monetary policy and how the Bank of England controls the supply of money.
6. Explain fiscal policy.
7. Explain how the gross national product is calculated.
8. Explain how production may be calculated.

CHAPTER SEVENTEEN

Economics of the Firm

CHAPTER OBJECTIVES

After studying this chapter you should be able to:
* understand the meaning of supply and demand and their influencing factors;
* know the factors of production;
* understand the meaning of and difference between the industry, the firm and the unit;
* understand economies of scale;
* explain the concepts of division of labour and specialisation.

INTRODUCTION

We have considered the way in which the economics of government operate and the way in which it affects society in general. Such an approach is called macroeconomics, in which economic behaviour is analysed in broad theoretical terms. We now need to consider the way in which economic behaviour occurs on a smaller scale, with reference to small organisations and individual situations. This is called a microeconomic approach.

In adopting this approach we have to consider the way in which the economic law of supply and demand can be applied to an industry and to particular examples. We will distinguish between the various factors of production and describe the interrelationships that exist between them. We need to understand the relationship of the firm to the industry as a whole as well as the relationships between the various units that go to make up the industry as a whole.

Our approach also requires an analysis of the various economies of scale that exist within the industry, as well as the effect of a change from one economy of scale to another. The scale and size of a firm's operation naturally leads us into a consideration of the tasks carried out within the firm, the way in which the labour force is divided up and the effects of specialisation on the final product.

Finally, we will take into account the position of the firm within the market, which in turn will provide us with a means of appraising the position of the firm within the industry as a whole.

SUPPLY AND DEMAND

When we attempt to define supply and demand we find it is not possible to consider the supply or demand of goods and services without stating or giving an indication of the price; it must always be stated as supply or demand at a certain price.

Demand

Demand for any goods or services is the amount that will be bought at any given price. Factors which influence the demand for goods or services are as follows.

(a) For each price, demand will be different. In normal circumstances the lower the price, the lower the demand.

(b) The prices of other commodities and services which compete for the buyer's limited spending income will affect demand.

(c) The choice that the buyer has with regard to goods and services in direct competition will affect demand. This may be determined by individual likes and dislikes or preferences.

(d) The incomes of buyers and their individual needs will affect demand.

(e) If goods and services are wanted or give satisfaction it is said they possess utility in economic terms. Satisfaction or utility increases as the quantity increases. However the utility gained from each extra unit of goods or services will become progressively less. This is known as the law of diminishing marginal utility.

Joint demand is when two or more goods are required together at the same time, e.g. eggs, sugar and cream for making ice cream. Derived demand is the demand for one good or service as the result of the demand for another, e.g. the demand for bread creates a demand for flour. Composite demand is the total demand for goods or services that occurs when they are required for different purposes, e.g. oil for heating, motor vehicles, etc.

Considerations relating to the demand for hotel and catering services are discussed more fully in Chapter 18.

Supply

Supply is the amount of goods or services that is offered for sale at any given price. Factors which influence the supply of goods or services may be described as follows.

(a) For each price the supply will be different. As far as the supplier is concerned, the higher the price the greater the supply.

(b) The supply of goods can be held back by producers, e.g. by warehousing and storage, in order to create demands and thus price increases. This is known as the "market mechanism".

(c) The price of a commodity is related to its scarcity or availability, e.g. seasonal fruits and vegetables.

(d) Composite supply satisfies varying demands of customers, e.g. the supply of beverages is made up of the demand for tea, coffee, milk, etc.

(e) When commodities are supplied together, e.g. lamb and wool, a demand for lamb creates an increased supply of wool, causing the price of wool to fall, and vice versa. This is known as joint demand.

(f) Adjustments in production costs caused by new technology, new market sources and changes in the cost of the factors of production affect supply.

FACTORS OF PRODUCTION

The demand for goods and services determines the factors of production necessary to provide the goods or services. In economic terms there are four factors of production: capital, natural resources or land, labour and entrepreneurial skills. In this section we examine these factors and their interrelationship as applicable to the hotel and catering industry.

Capital

Capital means the provision of finance to purchase the assets necessary to produce accommodation, food and drink, etc. Capital is also necessary to purchase raw materials, other resources and to pay labour. Capital may therefore be split into two categories: capital for the acquisition of assets and working capital. The acquisition of capital is further explained in Chapter Nineteen when we examine financial institutions and sources of finance.

Natural resources and land

Natural resources and land in economic thinking originally meant wealth. Natural resources are an essential factor in all business operations; without them we would be unable to exist. Examples of natural resources particularly relevant to the hotel and catering industry and its suppliers are water, fuel and basic food commodities. Land in its own right is essential in as much as a business organisation needs land to build on and for access.

Labour

Labour is required in all aspects of hotel and catering operations for the very reason that it is a labour-intensive industry. The degree of intensity will vary according to the individual operation and the service it provides to the customer, the type of service or product it sells, the layout and design of the establishment, the use of labour-saving equipment and the type of raw materials used. Labour must be regarded as all human effort, whether mental or physical, necessary to achieve the aims and objectives of the organisation.

Entrepreneurial skills

Entrepreneurial skills are an essential factor of production in as much as the entrepreneur provides the capital, organises the other factors of production and makes the decision of how and what has to be done in the setting up and operation of the business. It also needs to be said that no person in a business organisation is the entrepreneur, this function being shared throughout the operation. This may be illustrated by the fact that shareholders provide capital, managers and supervisors organise and make decisions, as, to a lesser degree, do employees.

Factors of production in the hotel and catering industry

The hotel and catering industry and the firms that make it up require all the factors of production we have identified. No one factor is more important than another as they are all interrelated according to the needs of the operation; these factors cannot exist independently of each other. It is possible to be less dependent on one factor than another, but this will probably have the effect of making an organisation overly reliant on another factor. An example of this might be the use of convenience food in an establishment; this would decrease labour costs involved in food preparation, and hence the reliance on increased working capital to provide greater food stocks. Another example might be the purchase of new equipment in a bakery, involving capital expenditure and having the effect of reducing the reliance on labour to knead dough, etc.

As a business grows its capital expenditure will vary, varying the reliance on other factors of production in different proportions. For example if a hotel decides to improve its facilities by installing private toilets and bathrooms en suite, it will need capital to provide these facilities; it will also increase the labour factor of the hotel, as these rooms will have to be cleaned. The provision of such facilities will need entrepreneurial skills to acquire and deploy the capital, organise the labour and sell the new service to customers. It will also increase the reliance on natural resources via the increased use of water, fuel and cleaning materials.

A final example will illustrate all the factors of production working together. To build an extension we need land to build on, capital to buy the land, labour to build on the land, capital to pay for labour and materials and natural resources for materials, all of this being co-ordinated and organised by the entrepreneur.

Reward

It may be argued that reward is a factor of production. It is most certainly an incentive.

Reward is regarded as a return on human effort, whether mental or physical. Investors of capital in a business organisation expect reward by way of interest payments, a share of the profits or dividends. Providers of labour expect reward by payment of wages or salaries. Entrepreneurial skills are rewarded by profits and/or wages and salaries. Owners of land or natural resources are rewarded by payment, either of rents or of the freehold value. It can therefore be said that reward is an incentive for the supply of such factors.

THE INDUSTRY, THE FIRM AND THE UNIT

In order to understand the economics of the hotel and catering industry we need to be able to define not only the industry itself but also the various operational elements that comprise it. To begin we may quote Medlik, who suggests that the term "hotel and catering industry" is one which "embraces the economic activity of undertakings which aim to satisfy the demand for accommodation, food and drink away from home".

Having provided a basic definition we need to describe the industry before we can fully understand its economic operation. This in itself is a very difficult task because the industry covers a wide range of different activities and includes many "economic undertakings" which are very small. The hotel and catering industry is best described by the Standard Industrial Classification issued in 1968. According to this classification the hotel and catering industry is made up of the following economic undertakings or types of establishment:

(a) hotels;
(b) motels;
(c) holiday camps;
(d) boarding houses;
(e) guest-houses;
(f) restaurants;
(g) cafes;
(h) snack bars;
(i) clubs;
(j) catering contractors.

Without making too detailed an analysis we can see that the list provided by the Standard Industrial Classification does not provide us with a complete list of hotel and catering establishments. It is designed to include establishments that are in existence for purely commercial purposes; there are of course many other types of hotel and catering establishments we cannot classify in this way. For example, under the broad heading of industrial and welfare catering, we can include the following establishments:

(a) works canteens;
(b) educational catering (school meals);
(c) transport catering;
(d) armed forces catering;
(e) hospital and general welfare catering, e.g. meals on wheels.

The above description has enabled us therefore to distinguish broadly between hotel and catering establishments that are primarily concerned with making a profit, i.e. the commercial sector, and those that provide a service within a given budget and which may operate on certain subsidies, i.e. the industrial and welfare catering sectors. This latter category includes establishments whose hotel and catering functions provide a service to organisations that have other primary objectives, e.g. manufacturing industry, health care and the treatment of the sick.

We next need to consider the exact nature of what individual establishments or undertakings are involved in as part of their economic sphere of activity.

Ownership and control

The concepts of ownership and control are of primary importance to our understanding of the economic operation of any hotel and catering establishment.

Within the industry there will be a number of firms. We may again quote Medlik who defines the firm as follows: "The more or less independent unit in which final decisions are made and ultimate control is exercised is the firm, which raises capital, and employs and organises productive resources; it is the ultimate unit of accountability and profitability." This definition shows us that our understanding of the firm must therefore also embrace an understanding of ownership and control. Ownership clearly involves the raising of capital to invest in the firm and therefore also finally involves "accountability and profitability". Between the raising of capital and profitability, however, is placed the whole question of control; investment and various resources have to be controlled to ensure that the owners obtain a good return on their initial investment.

As we have already seen, the hotel and catering industry is made up of a number of different types of establishments which can all vary greatly in terms of size. Ownership of these establishments will vary, from the small privately owned and operated high street coffee shop to the large local authority-owned and operated school meals service. This should serve to illustrate the fact that the nature of control in one type of establishment may vary considerably from that in another.

We will now examine the way in which control of hotel and catering establishments takes place.

Types of control

The simple fact that one firm may operate more than one type of establishment should indicate that control will vary a great deal from one firm to another. In our discussion of control and the formal organisation in Chapter Three we saw that it is necessary to distinguish between two types of control. For our purposes we can distinguish here between operative control and allocative control.

Operational control

Operational control is that form of control which takes place within the organisation at a variety of different levels. It will be concerned with the day-to-day running of the organisation—the delegation of responsibilities, the coordination of duties, the issuing of instructions, and so on.

Allocative control

Allocative control is what Medlik referred to as "ultimate control" in the earlier definition. It describes the control that can be exercised over the running of the organisation. In other words, if operational control is seen to be malfunctioning in any way, allocative control may be exercised to attempt to remedy the problem. In this situation a form of allocative control might be the employment of new managerial staff or a re-investment of finance.

The size of the firm

The size of the firm will dictate the nature of control and also define the relationship between ownership and control. In a small firm it will normally be the case that control, both operational and allocative, will be in the hands of the owner. In a large firm, however, the owner will delegate operational control to appointed members of staff, for example a management team. In other words the scale of the operation has increased to such an extent that the owner is no longer able to exercise operational control over each individual element of the operation.

The growth of large-scale organisational units is linked with the growth of management—what James Burnham refers to as "the managerial revolution". This general growth of large-scale organisational units is not reflected in the structure and composition of the hotel and catering industry as a whole, though. This fact is demonstrated by the 1977 HCITB statistics, showing that the percentage of hotel and catering establishments employing ten people or less was 70.8 per cent. In contrast, only 2.5 per cent of hotel and catering establishments employed 50 or more staff. This provides a clear indication that in the majority of establishments there is more likely to be a close link between ownership and control. This is because the demand for managerial or operational control only increases when the number of employees in an establishment increases.

The firm and the unit

At this stage we must distinguish clearly between the firm and the unit. We have now seen that the size of the firm can vary considerably, from a very large corporation such as Trust House Forte or Grand Metropolitan to a small family, or even one-man, business. This variety of size determines the nature and extent of control.

However it is possible for one firm to operate more than one establishment. Thus, in theory a firm may represent a unit in terms of ownership and investment, but in practical terms, within the hotel and catering industry, an individual establishment may be seen to represent a unit of operation. Grand Metropolitan, for example, represents a unit in terms of its ownership, investment and sales, but its various hotels, restaurants, entertainments, public houses and so on will represent units of operation. Grand Metropolitan will have given each of these units of operation some degree of operational control, some degree of autonomy; in other words each will possess a certain independence of function, individual managers being able to influence and control the operation of the unit they are responsible for. Allocative control will be exerted from time to time to ensure that the firm's investment and assets are not being wasted and that efficiency is being maintained.

Although ownership may allow individual operations to be autonomous and to be run almost as separate units, as Medlik points out, "ultimate control" rests with the firm which is responsible for raising capital, employing and organising productive resources and is therefore "the ultimate unit of accountability and profitability".

ECONOMIES OF SCALE

Economies of scale may be described as the reduction in unit costs as production increases; for example, in a catering establishment the more meals produced the less the individual cost per meal. In this section we want to look at reductions in costs caused by increasing the volume of production, and compare them with any diseconomies.

Large-scale hotel and catering companies have great advantages in reducing costs, simply because of the volume of business they create for themselves. Bulk buying reduces unit costs, whether it be for capital assets such as furniture, china, glass and cutlery, or for consumable materials such as food, liquor and cleaning materials. Management skills in sales and marketing may be utilised to the maximum advantage in large-scale operations, e.g. a centralised reservation office for a hotel company can pass sales from one unit to another. Similarly, because of the security of using the well publicised name of a large organisation, finance is easy to raise, either by using financial institutions or issuing share capital.

Whilst it is easy to appreciate that in a large hotel and catering company many economies of scale may be practised in order to reduce unit costs, it must be remembered that the small independent unit has obvious *dis*advantages unless it is able to join joint marketing or purchasing schemes. Managers have to be "jacks of all trades" rather than having specialised skills, although, being independent, their motivation may be greater and their decision-making process much quicker than those of a large organisation.

The small unit, whether it be part of a large or an independent company, may also find itself in a situation whereby diseconomies of scale are created. For example, by reorganising the layout of a restaurant a small unit may be able to increase the number of covers served from 40 to 46, thus increasing sales by six covers per sitting. However the waiting staff of two may only be able to cope with 20 covers each, thus necessitating the employment of an extra waiter. The labour force is therefore increased by 50 per cent whilst sales revenue only increases by 15 per cent. This will obviously have an adverse effect on profitability and force the management to make decisions regarding the organisation and deployment of its labour force in order to maintain standards and profit margins.

Franchise chains

Franchise chains are a system whereby small independently-owned units become part of a national organisation on payment of fees, both on setting up and annually; examples of such chains are Wimpy's, Kentucky Fried Chicken, Dayvilles and Bake 'n' Take. By being part of a franchise chain the unit has the advantages of the economies of scale of a large organisation, e.g. group purchasing, national advertising and product recognition and the use of the franchisor's management skills and back-up organisation.

Tied public houses

Another example of individual units which have the benefits and economies of scale of nationally-recognised companies, although not to such a great extent as that of franchising, is tied public houses. Whilst the tenants do not own the freehold of the property and are restricted in the products they sell, they have the benefit of the breweries' marketing and management controls procedures, as well as being able to keep their profits in a similar way to franchising.

DIVISION OF LABOUR AND SPECIALISATION

We have seen that the size of the unit is particularly important in enabling us to understand aspects of control. As the size of the operational unit increases, operational control tends to pass into the hands of management. A more detailed analysis of a large-scale organisation shows us that the workforce is distinguishable in terms of a number of different occupational sectors. Chapter Three showed us, for example, that communication through the formal organisation is the means by which individuals in different occupational categories are connected. It is the task of management first of all to decide upon the most suitable form of organisation, co-ordinate the various departments and sections within them and then delegate authority by creating areas of responsibility within the organisation. In this way, through the processes of line management, each individual member of staff, whatever his occupation and at whatever level he is working within the organisation, should know exactly what his duties are and his area of responsibility, who his immediate boss or supervisor is and what other departments, stations or individuals he must communicate and work with.

In such a situation, therefore, it is essential that the minimum amount of overlapping occurs. If the organisation is to operate efficiently, the labour force should be divided into skill areas according to the organisation plan. In other words, in a large-scale organisation specialisations are closely linked so that we cannot talk about one without the other.

The importance of the division of labour for modern industrial society is best emphasised by a quotation from Adam Smith: "The greatest improvement in the production powers of labour, and the greater part of the skill, dexterity, and judgement with which it is anywhere directed, or applied, seem to have been the efforts of the division of labour."

We must bear in mind that the division of labour into specialised occupational categories is of importance mainly in terms of large-scale organisations. As the catering industry is made up mainly of small units, nearly 20 per cent employing less than 20 staff, we must view its relevance accordingly. The smallest operational unit will, however, require some degree of specialisation even though overlapping of skills in some areas may occur, e.g. a waitress may prepare her own sweets, ice creams and coffees.

Bar and cellar staff
The hotel and catering industry embraces a wide range of operational units and a vast range of occupations and skills. Analysis of one

occupational sector, bar and cellar staff, will demonstrate the way in which the labour force may be divided.

The staff are first of all divided into part-time and full-time, male and female workers, and are spread across a number of different operational units, mainly in hotels, restaurants, pubs and clubs. The main skill areas can be classified into the following occupational categories:

(a) head barman/maids;
(b) barmen/maids (general);
(c) barmen/maids (dispense);
(d) lounge waiters/waitresses;
(e) cellarmen;
(f) food service at bar;
(g) supervisors;
(h) other staff.

Each of these occupational categories will entail a degree of specialisation which the others will not have. The cellarmen, for example, will be skilled in regulating a stock rotation, ensuring that the correct amount of liquor is maintained in the cellar, maintaining the quality of the product (particularly important with the current trend towards traditional beers) and so on. In contrast, a cocktail barman, will need to have numerical skills in order to calculate quickly the varying costs of drinks; he will need to possess a broad range of knowledge regarding the composition of various mixed drinks and will need to possess social skills which will enable him to communicate effectively with a range of different customers.

This form of specialisation allows for a high level of skill to be developed in a particular area, improving the standard of service given to the customer at all levels. Without this division of labour, highly specialised skills are less likely to be developed.

THE MARKET SITUATION

The value of specialised skills will vary according to the demands of the labour market. For example, the value of the skills of the cellarman diminished during the 1960s because of the widespread introduction by breweries of keg beers requiring little or no care and attention. If we have a high degree of specialisation in a particular skill, then there is a likelihood that the value of these skills will change according to technological developments, i.e. the market value of certain specialised skills can change quite considerably. We may thus apply the law of supply and demand, discussed earlier, to the changing need for particular skills. For example, the possession of a highly developed specialised skill may be in short supply; this will increase the demand for this skill and hence increase its market value, allowing those in possession of the skill to demand high wages as a reward.

Alienation

We have so far considered the advantages of the division of labour in an industrial situation. We have seen the way in which the specialisation of skills can increase the quality of the product and also lead to an increase in production. However it has been argued that the division of labour can have some disadvantageous effects.

Richard Blauner in a study entitled *Alienation and Freedom* argued that alienation is a state of mind that can develop in an individual worker when he feels that he has no sense of purpose in his work, when he does not feel integrated into the industrial community and when his work does not contain any form of self-expression.

It is possible that the division of labour may produce such a feeling of alienation, of being a "stranger" in the workplace. Blauner argues that alienation has four dimensions: powerlessness, meaninglessness, isolation and self-estrangement.

Powerlessness

The alienated worker will feel powerless because he has little control over his work situation. If the demand for his skill diminishes, perhaps with the introduction of automation, then he will have little chance of controlling his future employment in this area.

Meaninglessness

If the specialisation in a particular task is such that the individual worker cannot relate what he is doing to the overall productive process, then it is possible that his work might seem meaningless to him. We might take the example of a commis chef working in the vegetable corner of a large hotel kitchen, whose sole task is to peel and prepare vegetables to be used as part of a garnish or a sauce. He may feel that his task is somewhat meaningless because for him it is far removed from the final product; for him it represents only a tiny part of a product he may not even see.

Isolation

Isolation comes about when the worker feels no sense of belonging to the firm, is unable to identify with the goals of the firm and feels that he does not fit into its organisation. This is more likely to occur in a large-scale organisation, perhaps where informal channels of communication and informal groups have not fully developed. Specialisation may thus isolate the individual worker from all but a few of the workforce.

Self-estrangement

Self-estrangement is when the individual worker feels no satisfaction in what he is doing; he does not feel in any way involved or engrossed in his job and probably experiences boredom because of what he sees as being a monotonous routine. He probably carries out the particular task only because he is getting paid for it, and feels little or no relationship with his work or the goals which he is meant to achieve.

Conclusion

Blauner's four dimensions of alienation require detailed application to the work environment to enable us to assess their value. Such an exercise will demonstrate first of all, considerable differences between one workplace and another and, perhaps, more importantly, will help us understand some of the reasons for dissatisfaction within the workplace. We have seen the way in which the division of labour and the specialisation it incorporates can benefit the productive process in the hotel and catering industry as well as in manufacturing industry. However management and supervisory staff must also be aware of the problems that can be created when such a system of working is implemented.

SELF-ASSESSMENT QUESTIONS

1. Describe the factors which influence the demand for goods or services.
2. Describe the factors which influence the supply of goods or services.
3. Explain the factors of production.
4. Discuss reward as an incentive.
5. List the types of undertakings that make up the hotel and catering industry.
6. Define the firm.
7. Distinguish between allocative control and operational control.
8. Distinguish between the firm and the unit.
9. Explain what is meant by economies of scale.
10. List the advantages of purchasing a franchise.
11. Define the division of labour.
12. Define specialisation.
13. Explain the meaning of the term market situation.

CHAPTER EIGHTEEN

The Customer

CHAPTER OBJECTIVES

After studying this chapter you should be able to:
* describe the different forms of customer demand, distinguishing clearly between each;
* distinguish between customer demand and customer profile;
* explain the importance of drawing up a customer profile;
* explain the various factors that contribute to the socio-economic grouping of customers.

INTRODUCTION

We have referred on a number of occasions to a basic principle underlying all commercial considerations in the catering industry, the product is ultimately customer satisfaction. Without creating an acceptable level of customer satisfaction, any given catering establishment will eventually lose customers and ultimately lose profits.

Having restated this basic principle we now have to establish how it can be put into practice. This is clearly a more difficult proposition. Our first difficulty arises from the simple fact that the "customer" is a continually changing and ever-different creature; to provide a service satisfactory to one customer may well cause dissatisfaction to another. Therefore the success of a commercially-viable catering establishment will first of all depend upon an awareness of the type of customer likely to use that establishment

The growth of the catering industry, the development of tourism and the increased amount of leisure time available to most people in the advanced industrialised nations means that today every individual is a potential customer of a catering establishment of some kind or another. Our analysis of customer satisfaction and profitability in different catering units must therefore be based upon a clear understanding of the customer. We will therefore consider some of the ways in which we can differentiate between customers, which should in turn enable us to cater for their differing needs.

THE CHANGING PATTERN OF DEMAND

Changing customer needs have changed the nature of the service the catering industry provides. If we begin by assessing the changing pattern of customer demand, a clearer picture of the exact nature of the customer should emerge.

The overall pattern of demand for catering services has increased in recent years. If we take the Second World War as a starting point we can see that in subsequent years Britain experienced a period of economic growth. General prosperity and standards of living improved during this period, including such things as income, education and health. Table 8 demonstrates how this increased prosperity was reflected in an increasing demand for holidays.

TABLE 8 HOLIDAYS IN BRITAIN (NUMBER OF TRIPS IN MILLIONS)

Year	Trips by British in Britain	Trips by British overseas	Trips to Britain by overseas residents
1951	25	0.8 (est.)	0.6
1956	27	2.2	1.1
1962	32	4.25	2.0
1966	31	5.1	3.2
1972	132	10.5	7.5
1973	132	11.5	8.1
1974	114	10.4	8.5
1975	117	11.6	9.5
1976	121	11.1	10.8
1977	121	11.0	12.2

Sources: BTA British Home Tourism Survey, National Catering Inquiry 1966, International Passenger Survey

We can see from these statistics, however, that trips by British holidaymakers at home and overseas peaked in the early 1970s and began to drop in subsequent years. The economic climate of the nation was largely responsible for this fluctuation; after the prosperity of the 1950s and the 1960s, the 1970s was a period of recession, rising unemployment and inflation levels reaching 20 per cent. Economic restraint was exercised and the population clearly reduced the number of holiday trips taken in this period.

In contrast, overseas tourism to Britain steadily increased over the period shown in the table. This could have been due to advanced marketing techniques or to the status of the pound against foreign currency.

Economic considerations therefore play an important part in enabling us to assess the demand for the services provided by the hotel and catering industry.

DOMESTIC AND OVERSEAS DEMAND

The increasing overseas demand for hotel and catering services in Britain on the one hand provides a valuable source of foreign exchange, but on the other hand presents difficulties not normally experienced when catering for the needs of the domestic tourist. A high proportion of overseas visitors use hotel accommodation, for example, and therefore the hotel has to be able to cope with such things as foreign languages, currency exchange, and cultural differences in terms of food, behaviour patterns and attitudes. The presence of foreign tourists in hotels may incidentally provide the hotel with additional income. We have already mentioned foreign currency exchange, which will inevitably take place at a rate favourable to the hotel, but the hotel may also obtain income from such things as commission on car hire, theatre tickets or the services of a travel agency. In catering for customer demand the hotel is also obtaining additional income.

In assessing the differences between overseas and domestic demand we should point out that in general overseas tourists tend to be more dependent on the facilities offered by the accommodation sector they are using. For example, because approximately 25 per cent of overseas tourists stay in hotel accommodation, it is important that this sector focuses a proportionate amount of its attention on catering for this type of customer. In contrast, domestic tourism traditionally involves visiting friends and relations and, more recently, self-catering holidays, camping, caravanning, etc. However, overall demand for various forms of tourist accommodation in Britain is domestic, accounting for approximately 80 per cent of the total market. It is this area, therefore, that should concern us most.

BUSINESS AND NON-BUSINESS DEMAND

We may further categorise customers into business and non-business, or holiday, demand. The business customer, as an employee of a company, is travelling in the course of his work and requires various accommodation and catering services away from home during his working week. The kind of need can vary from the casual accommodation needed by company representatives and transport drivers, perhaps on a one-nightly basis, to the slightly longer accommodation and catering needs of business people visiting trade-fairs, exhibitions, conferences and meetings. We can generalise by saying that this type of customer demand is usually directed toward hotels in urban areas, and tends to be less sensitive to price fluctuations than other forms of demand. Finally, business demand is usually non-seasonal; in fact in many cases it is purposely designed to be off-seasonal, particularly in the case of conferences and trade exhibitions.

Non-business demand, on the other hand, tends to be resort-orientated, seasonal and may well fluctuate according to price variations. We have already seen, for example, that the economic climate can determine changes in the nature of non-business demand. On average, non-business customers tend to stay in accommodation for a longer period of time than business customers, indicating perhaps a difference in customer demand. It is likely that the non-business customer, for example the holidaymaker, who is staying in tourist accommodation will be looking for a more complete "leisure package" than the business customer, who may require his accommodation to fulfill only a very temporary need—an overnight stay, for example. The demands placed upon hotels and guest-houses where there is a greater length of stay might include reduced rates, a more personal service, a "family" atmosphere, perhaps, and on-site entertainment.

The length of stay, however, is not always a primary consideration. The British Home Tourism Survey of 1977 shows us that although 77 per cent of all visits in all forms of accommodation were from the domestic non-business sector, this sector accounted for only 43 per cent of all expenditure. We may conclude from these figures that business and overseas customers spend more in accommodation than domestic customers.

THE BALANCE OF DEMAND

We pointed out in the previous section that business demand is less sensitive to price fluctuations, which may partially contribute to the differences in expenditure found by the British Home Tourism Survey. However, this concentration of business demand in fairly short stays in urban areas and, in addition, its relatively small numbers in relation to domestic non-business demand requires us to look in a little more detail at the latter category. Table 9 emphasises the substantial differences in customer demand for accommodation between the categories we have so far discussed.

The table shows us the way in which customer demand for accommodation has varied over this period and, more importantly, that the overall balance of customer demand is weighed heavily toward the non-business sector, and in particular the domestic non-business sector.

DOMESTIC NON-BUSINESS CUSTOMER DEMAND

If we classify different types of customer this should enable us to classify their different demands. In general terms we have already seen the different demands posed by, for example, business and non-business customers. However, because the domestic, non-business sector

TABLE 9 DEMAND FOR ACCOMMODATION IN THE UNITED KINGDOM, 1972–77
(MILLION BED-NIGHTS)

| Year | Domestic | | Overseas | | Total |
	Non-business	Business	Non-business	Business	
1972	560	45	95	10	710
1973	545	45	98	12	700
1974	490	45	98	12	645
1975	505	45	108	12	670
1976	500	45	112	13	670
1977	495	50	126	14	685

Sources: British Home Tourism Survey 1972–77 and International Passenger Survey 1972–77

represents the biggest group of customers we need to break this group down, if possible, into a number of component parts.

We may begin by stating that the bulk of domestic non-business demand for accommodation and catering services will be from those on holiday. Further reference to the British Home Tourism Survey of 1977 shows us that the demand for accommodation and catering services from the domestic non-business sector fluctuates according to the seasons. We see from Table 10 that the percentage of visits taken by this group of customers is much greater in the second or third quarters of the year, amounting to approximately two-thirds of all visits. In addition, the 103 million visits by the domestic non-business group far exceeded the 19 million taken by the domestic business group, further stressing the importance of analysing its composition in order to assess customer demand clearly.

Before analysing customer demand in greater detail, it should be pointed out that the decline in popularity of the traditional British holiday in a small seaside guest-house, in favour of a similarly priced overseas package holiday, has been reflected in an overall decrease in demand for accommodation, as Table 9 demonstrates. Criticism has been directed at these traditional providers of holiday accommodation, i.e. the small seaside hotels and guest-houses, for not responding to changing demands, although they do face severe competition from low-priced package holidays which can ensure such things as hotel accommodation with private bathrooms, warm seas and climate, entertainment and so on. This lack of response is further reflected by the fact that although only approximately a quarter of domestic non-business customers stay in hotels when on holiday in Britain, nearly two-thirds do so when taking holidays abroad. If we add to this the growth in

TABLE 10 SEASONAL PATTERN OF VISITS IN THE UNITED KINGDOM

Quarter of the year	Domestic		Overseas		Total (%)
	Non-business (%)	Business (%)	Non-business (%)	Business (%)	
1	15	23	15	22	16
2	26	31	25	25	28
3	40	21	42	25	37
4	20	25	18	28	20
Total	100	100	100	100	100
Total (millions)	103	19	9	2	133

Source: British Home Tourism and International Passenger Survey 1977

Britain of self-catering, independent holidays, the increasing popularity of farm holidays and, what in some circles is regarded as restrictive liquor licensing laws, then it is not difficult to see why the decline of the traditional domestic British holiday has occurred and why many small seaside hotels and guest-houses may be forced to close down.

CUSTOMER PROFILE

We have seen that the declining demand for accommodation in Britain is due partly to the lack of response by the providers of accommodation to the changing demands of customers. Clearly if these changing demands can be anticipated then it is possible that losses may be reduced. As previously stated, customer demand can only be assessed on the basis of customer analysis, so we will attempt to indicate some of the factors which enable us to classify and differentiate customers.

Careful consideration of the market and its demands should also be an essential exercise before any catering operation is set up and established. No sensible businessman will launch a commercial venture unless he has carefully considered whether or not that venture has a chance of survival and of making profits. We have already considered the differences in demand between the business and non-business sector and the domestic and overseas sector; from this analysis we saw that the greatest domestic demand was from the non-business sector. In addition, a large proportion of the domestic non-business sector uses accommodation and catering services on a local or "non-visiting" basis. Our profile therefore will be of this category of customer.

Socio-economic grouping of customers

Our analysis in Chapter Five showed us that many differences exist between individuals. Clearly it will be very difficult to cater for all customer peculiarities, but an analysis of the social and economic differences that exist may enable us to establish some viable group differences.

Our task would be much more simple had the dramatic social and economic changes which have occurred in the last century not taken place. The development of international communications, the large-scale migration between nations, and the increasing standard of living of most advanced industrialised nations has meant that catering now has to satisfy and fulfill a wide range of differing needs. We can no longer talk about societies as being homogeneous, i.e. made up of people from one origin or background; the above factors have produced societies that are hetrogeneous, i.e. made up of people from a variety of different origins and backgrounds.

On this basis, therefore, we will examine the various means by which we can distinguish between customers. We will concentrate on the major socioeconomic factors which contribute to this, under the following headings:

(a) wealth;
(b) income;
(c) occupation and occupational prestige;
(d) educational achievement;
(e) area of residence;
(f) cultural factors.

We will consider the relevance of each of these in turn as, without such an analysis, an awareness of the different markets available to hotel and catering establishments will be limited. Having carried out this analysis we will not only be able to assess these markets but also predict future trends and the way in which the markets may change. Without such a customer profile the need for an awareness of the market will not be fulfilled.

Wealth

The way in which wealth is distributed in our society is always seen as a controversial issue; it has been argued that the way in which wealth is distributed in a society is a major cause of inequality. It is therefore an important topic for us to consider in drawing up our customer profile.

We firstly need to define wealth. In most cases wealth refers to the fixed assets an individual may possess, e.g. the ownership of land, shares, buildings, possessions such as valuable jewellery, antiques, paintings, etc. We will see later that wealth is quite different from earned income.

With this definition established we next need to consider who the wealthy are and the way in which wealth in Britain is distributed. The government publication *Social Trends 1975* provides us with the following information regarding the distribution of wealth. In Britain 92.8 per cent of personal wealth is owned by 25 per cent of the population or, put another way, 75 per cent of the population owns only 7.2 per cent of personal wealth. This shows that wealth in Britain is clearly unequally distributed. Statistics published by the Inland Revenue in 1973 lend support to the figures shown in *Social Trends*. In a publication entitled *The Estimated Wealth of Individuals in Great Britain 1973* the following information can be found.

(a) Out of 19 million taxpayers in Britain, 14.7 million own wealth of less than £10,000.

(b) In contrast, 4.4 million taxpayers own wealth of over £10,000. Thus 22.9 per cent own 70.1 per cent of all personal wealth in Britain, totalling £114,866 million.

(c) The remaining 77.1 per cent of taxpayers own the remaining £49,006 million.

Our analysis of these statistics should take into consideration two other important factors. Firstly, the figures quoted are from 1975 in one case and 1973 in the other; these are likely to have changed in the intervening years. Secondly, the "taxpayer" category quoted above refers to married couples or single earners and not the total adult population. The wealthy sector of the population therefore amounts to an even smaller proportion of the total.

So far we have only referred to relatively recent statistics. If we can show that a redistribution of wealth is perhaps taking place throughout the population, then a more balanced picture may appear. Table 11, covering the distribution of wealth from 1911 to 1960, shows in fact that some redistribution has occurred, although massive inequalities still exist.

Therefore, despite certain changes that have occurred in the distribution of wealth, we can see from the above that an important market exists for certain types of hotel and catering establishments. The potential customers within this market own a considerable amount of wealth, of which an appreciable proportion we can assume to be disposable. Their demand for accommodation, catering services, etc., will be for the most expensive type, and therefore the setting up and operating of exclusive hotels and catering establishments will need to concentrate upon the demands of the wealthy category. This demand will exist on an international as well as a domestic basis and will expect a range of operations providing an intensive service to the customer. The luxury cruise liner, for example, will have to provide for total customer

TABLE 11 GROUPS WITHIN ADULT POPULATION OWNING WEALTH, ESTIMATED
PROPORTION OF TOTAL PERSONAL WEALTH

Groups within adult population owning proportions of wealth	1911–13 (%)	1924–30 (%)	1936–8 (%)	1954 (%)	1960 (%)
Richest 1% owned	69	62	56	43	42
Richest 5% owned	87	84	79	71	75
Richest 10% owned	92	91	88	79	83
Richest 1% owned	69	62	56	43	42
Next 2–5%	18	22	23	28	33
Next 6–10%	5	7	9	8	8
95% owned	13	16	21	29	25
90% owned	8	9	12	21	17

Source: Westergaard and Rester, Class in a Capitalist Society, *1975*

demand, including accommodation, food, entertainment and other
services of the highest quality. Luxury hotels will also have to be able to
provide a range of exclusive services for the wealthy customer. Other
specific services may be provided by individual operations. Exclusive
top-class restaurants, for example, will need to meet a demand for
expensive top-quality catering services only affordable on a regular
basis by the very rich; in order to maintain this demand the quality of
the food and service provided will have to be of the highest standard.
The provision of such quality should not be inhibited by the cost of
dishes as it is likely that such customers will be less restricted by high
costs.

We can see therefore that a market exists for the right type of hotel
and catering establishment. Although some redistribution of wealth has
occurred in society, the very wealthy still constitute an identifiable
customer category who have specific needs to be catered for.

Income
Whereas wealth is the possession of capital, income is the flow of
disposable or spendable money which an individual receives. Income
usually comes as a reward for work carried out, although some income
actually derives from wealth. Thus, for example, individuals who
possess wealth in the form of property or shares, may obtain income
simply through the possession of this wealth, i.e. through dividends and
interest.

A breakdown of income distribution will indicate the relative spending
power of different groups in the population, this being based on the

assumption that the highest income group is likely to have the greatest amount of disposable income and therefore the greatest amount of spending power.

As with wealth, a redistribution of income seems to have occurred in Britain; this has certainly occurred since the end of the Second World War. In fact, the top 10 per cent of the population now receive a proportionately smaller amount of total incomes than they did at the end of the Second World War. Many of the changes that have occurred in British society since the War have led to an overall improvement in income levels and therefore in standards of living. This has been partly reflected in the increasing demand for hotel and catering services during this period. Many inequalities in income levels continue to exist, however, particularly between men and women and between the manual and non-manual sectors of the working population. The latter distinction may be particularly significant in relation to demand for hotel and catering services. It is estimated, for example, that approximately 14 per cent of manual workers' incomes come from overtime payments, whereas only 3 per cent of non-manual workers receive their income from this source. Manual workers in metal manufacturing and mining, for example, receive as much as 30 per cent of their income from overtime payments. The fact that more hours have to be worked in order to receive overtime payment clearly imposes some limitation on the length of leisure time available to this category of worker, and therefore on the type of hotel and catering establishment he might use. In contrast non-manual workers may receive additional income in the form of fringe benefits such as loan facilities, a company car or luncheon vouchers. Potentially, therefore, the spending power of these two groups is quite different, as will be the possible use they make of hotel and catering services.

An assessment of the market in a particular area would therefore need to take into consideration the income levels of the customer group and also the way in which that income might be disposed. In this way a more complete appraisal of possible customer demand can be made.

Occupation and occupational prestige
The job that a person does is particularly important in assessing the socioeconomic position of that person. We have already considered differences in income levels and the way in which incomes are earned in two broad occupational categories, i.e. manual and non-manual workers. The occupation that someone has is thus clearly important in relation to the income he or she can obtain. In addition however, we also need to consider the prestige or status that a particular occupation holds in order to gain a clear impression of someone's position is society. We may illustrate this distinction between occupation and prestige attached

to it by reference to a simple example. Although nurses and many hospital staff have a high status in the eyes of society, their income and the conditions of employment they work in are inferior to the incomes and conditions of workers in other occupations of comparable status.

Occupation is thus taken as an important measure of someone's social position; indeed a number of attempts have been made to grade members of society in terms of their occupation. The most important gradings of these is compiled by the Registrar General, who places the population into six groups according to occupational classification. Table 12 shows various occupations and their respective social grades based upon the Registrar General's classification and compiled by the Institute of Practitioners in Advertising (IPA).

TABLE 12 IPA CLASSIFICATION OF SOCIAL GRADES

Social grade	Social status	Head of household's occupation
A	Upper-middle class	Higher managerial, administrator or professional
B	Middle class	Intermediate managerial, administrative or professional
C1	Lower-middle class	Clerical, supervisory and lower managerial and professional
C2	Skilled working class	Skilled manual
D	Working class	Semi-skilled and unskilled manual
E	Those at the lowest level of subsistence	State pensioners or widows (no other earner), casual or lowest grade worker

This classification can be used to group any occupation; the following represents examples of some of the occupational gradings that can be made:

(a) grade A—company directors, judges, university professors;
(b) grade B—small business owners, teachers, managerial grades;
(c) grade C1—foremen, supervisors, clerical officers, junior managers, typists;
(d) grade C2—technicians, fitters, skilled craftsmen;
(e) grade D—semi-skilled: machine operators, drivers, bus conductors;
(f) grade D—unskilled: labourers, refuse collectors, messengers;
(g) grade E—casual or part-time workers, the unemployed.

The relevance of this is that the owner or manager of a catering operation, in being aware of such an occupational classification, may well be able to assess the likely demand from potential customers. Thus, for example, the owner of a small bistro-type restaurant near the commercial centre of a large city may well adapt his lunchtime or early evening tariff to accommodate what he considers to be the needs of white-collar workers, i.e. clerks, typists and administrators in the C1 grouping.

More generally, the various grades of hotel may be seen to correlate with the occupational classification given above. A luxury or top-quality hotel may well attract customers from the grade A group, medium-quality hotels customers from grade B, economy hotels customers from grade C, and so on. It must be remembered, though, that such a correlation as this clearly simplifies the relationship between occupational grouping and type of accommodation used; for example, a junior manager from social grade C visiting a city for a conference may well stay in a medium-quality or luxury hotel because his accommodation is being paid for by the company's expense account. Another example where customers may be placed "up market" in this way is when an airline negotiates a discount booking to enable air hostesses and air crew to stay in a hotel during flight stopovers or whilst awaiting a return flight. The negotiated discount may then allow these staff to stay in accommodation which they may not personally be able to afford.

We can see from the above that our customer profile is aided considerably by reference to an individual's occupation, although we must also be aware that we are talking in general terms and our profile will only be complete when we have considered a wide range of factors.

Educational achievement

Levels of educational achievement across the whole of the population have increased quite dramatically since the 1870 Education Act laid the foundations for providing basic literacy and numeracy. Evidence shows that some sections of the population have gained in this respect more than others.

The achievement of educational qualifications is a means by which people in society can become socially mobile, i.e. they can improve their social position. For example, the expansion of further and higher education that occurred as a consequence of the 1963 Robbins Report meant that, through education, many young people achieved social mobility which would otherwise not have been possible. We use the term intergenerational social mobility to explain the movement of an individual up the social ladder from the social position "inherited" from his father; for example, someone whose father is a bricklayer in social grade C2 might obtain a university degree and become a computer programmer in social grade B.

In general terms, improvements in educational standards have a tendency to raise the level of demand in a wide range of hotel and catering establishments. Education increases the range of social contacts across socioeconomic boundaries and generally makes people more aware of various aspects of culture, e.g. different types of food, with which they may not otherwise have come into contact.

Area of residence

Our assessment of customer demand will need to consider where the customer lives in order to obtain a complete profile. A simple example will illustrate this point. The siting of a fast food outlet in a select residential area of a city, where demand for this type of establishment is limited, is not going to bring as high a level of profitability as if it was sited near the business or entertainment area of the city.

The fact that the population of Britain is geographically mobile, i.e. that it is able to move from one place of residence to another quite easily, has to a certain extent made the analysis of a customer's area of residence more difficult to assess. Despite this, a general picture can be obtained which will be an important feature in the overall development of the customer profile.

Cultural factors

The culture of any society is, in simple terms, the way of life of that society; we can recognise the culture of any society by the way people do things, by what is accepted behaviour and what is not, by the various beliefs and morals that are valued in that society, and so on. Thus British culture might be recognised in terms of such things as "a sense of fair play", Christian morality, a democratic system, etc. Culture is also recognisable in terms of more obvious and clear-cut features; the musical traditions of a country and, perhaps more relevant to our present study, what they eat tell us a great deal about the people and their way of life.

The study of gastronomy shows us that a very important aspect of a society's culture is food, to the extent that we often refer to "the national dish" of a particular society. Thus when we travel to a particular country we have a clear idea of what food and what type of dishes we are likely to encounter in that country, whether it be paellas in Spain or pastas in Italy.

Earlier in the chapter we referred to the increasing heterogeneity of advanced industrialised societies. Britain, for example, is a society which contains people from a wide range of different origins. Ease of travel and freedom of movement across borders has meant that the composition of British society is less uniform than it once was. The cultural background of potential customers is therefore a necessary feature of our overall customer profile. The wide range of food outlets with different cultural origins found in all British cities is an indication of the need to cater for the needs of a population drawn from a number of different cultural backgrounds. It is also interesting to note that the establishment of culturally different catering outlets attracts customers other than those of the cultural origin in question. The Indian or Chinese restaurant, for example, has today become as much a part of the British way of life as many other forms of catering establishment. An important additional factor is also the changing demands of customers; cheap holiday travel abroad brings tourists into contact with food from a variety of different nations, which in turn may encourage them to be less conservative in their tastes when they return to the home country. We can see, then, that over a period of time people of one culture will accept and even adopt food from the culture of another, the British habit of tea-drinking providing us with another excellent illustration of this point. Thus it is probable that the original demand for the food offered by Indian restaurants in Britain was from the newly arrived immigrants from India during the 1950s and the 1960s, but that over a period of time many other sections of the British population adopted this type of food and food service.

Consideration of the cultural backgrounds of customers then is particularly important. An industrial catering operation, for example, would need to provide a range of different types of food if the workforce was racially or culturally mixed.

So far we have seen the way in which the broad cultural background of a customer can influence his demand for various types of food, and how in some cases this can influence the demand from other sectors of the population. We should also point out that religion, an important aspect of any culture, can often stipulate very strict rules regarding the eating habits of those who uphold that religion; we may point to the sacred status of the cow in the Hindu religion or the rules against eating pork embodied in the Jewish or Islamic faiths as illustrations of this point. Therefore, religious background may also need to be considered when assessing the demands of customers.

Conclusion

We should be able to see from the foregoing that the potential customer of any hotel and catering establishment is not an easy individual to isolate or pin down. Many factors contribute to his make-up and therefore to the demands he is likely to make. However the success of any catering establishment will, of necessity, have to take into consideration at least some, if not all, of the above factors if acceptable profits are to be achieved. The nature of this demand will vary from the specific, in the case of an exclusive restaurant catering for the needs of a wealthy customer group, to the general, in the case of an industrial catering operation catering for a wide spectrum of occupational groups, for different income categories or for workers from different racial or cultural backgrounds.

In order to be successful, ownership and management must therefore be able to accommodate customer demand as it exists at present and, equally important, be able to predict the way in which it is likely to change in the future.

SELF-ASSESSMENT QUESTIONS

1. Distinguish clearly between overseas and domestic customer demand.

2. Distinguish clearly between business and non-business customer demand.

3. Describe the balance of demand.

4. Distinguish between wealth and income.

5. Explain the changing distribution of wealth.

6. Explain the difference between occupation and occupational prestige.

7. Explain the relevance of cultural background to the making of a customer profile.

CHAPTER NINETEEN

Financial Sources

CHAPTER OBJECTIVES

After studying this chapter you should be able to:
* explain the functions of the financial institutions;
* understand how bank credit is created;
* know the sources of finance;
* list the services offered by a bank to its customers.

INTRODUCTION

The provision of finance and financial services for government, the firm and the individual has grown throughout modern history.

We have discussed in previous chapters the economics of government and the firm and have been made aware of their need for finance in order to exist. In this chapter we examine the financial institutions and how they create finance in order to provide for the demands which are put upon them. It is described by some as a merry go ground; the provision of investment in order to provide loans in order to make profits, which are then invested to provide loans, and so on.

Britain is regarded as one of the financial centres of the world; indeed it was *the* financial centre in the nineteenth century and the early part of this century. Our financial institutions are part of the heritage and history of this country and are regarded by most as the best and most reliable in the world. In this chapter, we look at the role the Bank of England plays in the economy and in managing the government's finances, and how it controls the clearing banks and other financial institutions in their provision of finance for industry. The sources of finance for industry are considered, as well as the contribution these sources make to the growth and development of firms that constitute the industry. We also examine how a firm can develop finance from within its own organisation by skilfully managing its own resources and capital.

Nowadays the majority of employees are paid via bank accounts, so we examine the services that banks provide for their customers, both individuals and business organisations. Banking is now big business, with high profits to be made, and this has led the banks to compete with each other in the range of services and facilities they offer in order to attract more customers. This has resulted in their becoming more and more concerned with their marketing and the image they give in their attempts to attract customers from the cradle to the grave.

FINANCIAL INSTITUTIONS

The Bank of England

The Bank of England is Britain's central bank, and as such it has three main functions. Firstly, although it is under government control, it acts as banker to the government. This also gives rise to its second function, which is to act as agent of the government's monetary policy with regard to the clearing banks.

The basic function of acting as banker to the government falls into four roles.

(a) It maintains the accounts of government departments, transfers monies between them, receives taxes and other income and makes payments on behalf of them, as required by any large organisation.

(b) It administers the government debt by way of overdrafts, Treasury bills and bonds, paying interest and arranging transfers and repayments when due.

(c) It issues banknotes in circulation, which are backed by securities authorised by the government. It must be noted that this is only a small proportion of the total supply of money in circulation.

(d) It controls the rate of exchange between sterling and foreign currencies in accordance with agreements. The bank will intercept and buy sterling should its value be in danger of falling below the official minimum, and sell when the price rises.

The third role of the Bank of England is to act as banker to the clearing banks. Their indebtedness to each other at the end of each day's business is resolved by making the necessary adjustments to their accounts at the Bank of England. The Bank also acts as a means of communication between the government and the clearing banks, who in turn have members on the controlling board of the Bank.

The London clearing banks

The London clearing banks are important for the efficient working of the monetary system and may be defined as any organisation whose debts are widely acceptable as a means of payment. The four main clearing banks as we know them today are Barclays, Lloyds, National Westminster and Midland, these accounting for some 80 per cent of the total business.

Their main functions are the receipt of money and making payments on behalf of customers; from these stem the further important functions of granting loans and making advances to customers. They have a duty to safeguard their customers' money and repay it on demand or at short notice. Consequently they prefer to make loans for short periods, against securities which can be sold for cash.

Banking services are further explained later in the chapter when we look at personal banking and the expansion of credit in greater detail.

Merchant banks

Merchant banks specialise in arranging loans, managing credit services and providing financial advice. There are a variety of different types of merchant bank, which are briefly explained below, although leading organisations will combine some or all of these functions.

Investment and industrial banks

Investment banks are involved in the management and investment of unit trust funds, pension funds and the investments of charities.

Industrial banks lend capital to industry for longer periods of time than the clearing banks and are more flexible in their requirements of prospective borrowers.

Finance and issuing houses

Finance houses make credit available to consumers via hire purchase contracts.

Issuing houses specialise in arranging the issue of loan stock or shares, to be dealt in through the Stock Exchange, thus providing a link between short-term loans and the long-term finance market. When a company makes a public share issue, either when it is formed or when it wants to raise money, the issuing houses can provide guarantees, purchasing shares not wanted by the stock market. Consequently they are also involved in the setting up of a public company, surveying the company's activities, its management and preparing its prospectus to comply with legislation and Stock Exchange procedure.

Accepting houses

Accepting houses specialise in guaranteeing payments on bills of exchange, having satisfied themselves that the customer is able to ensure that he has sufficient funds to settle the debt when the bill matures.

CREATION OF BANK CREDIT

When a bank grants a loan or extends an overdraft to a customer it expands the amount of money in circulation in the country. The reason for this is that banks retain only 8 per cent of their deposits in cash, either on their premises or with the Bank of England. This is better shown in a very simplified bank's balance sheet.

Customer accounts	£100,000	Cash	£8,000
		Loans	92,000
	£100,000		£100,000

The balance sheet shows that the bank's customers' accounts hold £100,000, of which £8,000 is held in cash and £92,000 has been lent to other customers.

When a customer of the bank deposits a further £10,000 with the bank in cash, the balance sheet will then show:

Customer accounts	£110,000	Cash	£18,000
		Loans	92,000
	£110,000		£110,000

However as the bank is required to keep only 8 per cent of its deposits in cash, i.e. £8,800, it is able to lend a further £9,200 to other customers who may wish to borrow. When this takes place the balance sheet will show:

Customer accounts	£110,000	Cash	£8,800
		Loans	101,200
	£110,000		£110,000

This then has the effect of increasing the amount of money in circulation by £9,200, the borrowers having this amount of cash which in fact belongs to the depositors at the bank.

Therefore, should the government wish to control the supply of money for some reason or other, it asks the bank to make a special deposit with the Bank of England. If, for example, it asked for a special deposit of £5,000, this would leave only £4,200 to lend to other borrowers, and the balance sheet would read:

Customer accounts	£110,000	Cash:	£8,800
		Special deposit	5,000
		Loans	96,200
	£110,000		£110,000

It must be appreciated that in this example small simple figures have been used; in reality the figures dealt with are in the hundreds of millions. We must also appreciate why the flow of money between the clearing banks and their customers must be controlled. When money is borrowed from one bank and paid into another bank, the second bank has an increase in cash, allowing it to increase its lending. There is thus a multiplying effect.

When a customer withdraws a deposit from the bank then the opposite happens to that explained in the example, and the bank would have to reduce its lending by $12\frac{1}{2}$ times the amount withdrawn in order to maintain an 8 per cent holding to cover its other deposits.

Banks do not only deal in cash, so that the creation of credit does not actually reach the level mentioned. A great proportion of the banks' assets are tied up in Treasury and commercial bills, in other forms of investment and in buildings, etc.

A bank's balance sheet

Figure 39 shows a simplified form of a bank balance sheet, with the proportions shown as percentages. This indicates that the true figure of the bank's lending is in the region of 50 per cent of its customers' deposits.

BALANCE SHEET OF NATIONAL MIDLAND BANK PLC AS AT 31 DECEMBER 19–

Liabilities	£m	%	Assets	£m	%
Share capital and reserves	180	5.7	Cash in hand	245	7.7
			Short call loans	155	4.9
			Treasury bills	360	11.3
Customers' current and deposit accounts	3,000	94.3	Commercial bills	120	3.8
			Investment and subsidiaries	510	16.0
			Loans and advances	1,580	49.7
			Premises and equipment	180	5.7
			Special deposit with Bank of England	30	0.9
	£3,180	100.00		£3,180	100.00

A bank's liabilities

Share capital and reserves are owned by the shareholders in the bank, the share capital being capital invested in the bank at its true value, i.e. nominal, while reserves are monies set aside by the bank for further taxation, for dividends or for other purposes. It should be noted that, unlike many other business operations, the share capital represents a very small proportion of the bank's liabilities.

Customer accounts are liabilities because the bank is liable to repay to customers any money deposited with them. These accounts take two forms:

(a) deposit accounts, on which the bank pays interest of 2 per cent below the Bank of England's base lending rate and which usually require seven days' notice of withdrawal of funds from them; and

(b) current accounts, which are customers' working accounts, on which no interest is paid, charges being levied against account-holders for the use of the accounts.

Short term assets
Cash in hand should amount to 8 per cent of customers' accounts, as previously explained, and is made up of cash held in the banks' branches and at the Bank of England. In Fig. 39 you will note that cash in hand represents 7 per cent of total liabilities and 8.2 per cent of customers' accounts, i.e. £245m/£3,000m x 100 per cent. This figure is referred to as the cash ratio.

Short call loans are monies lent to discount houses for short periods of time in order to finance short-term government loans. Discount houses are merchant banks highly skilled in dealing with bills of exchange from the government and international traders. Short call loans are an efficient way of ensuring that a bank's working balances are fully employed.

Treasury bills are short-term fixed-interest securities issued to finance government borrowing and held by the bank until they mature.

Commercial bills are similar to Treasury bills. They are also referred to as gilt-edged securities.

The assets we have so far referred to are all short-term or liquid assets, meaning that a bank can quickly raise cash by manipulating these as and when necessary. Treasury and commercial bills are issued for a fixed time, and a bank will purchase them on a daily or weekly basis. This means that they have a constantly maturing stock of bills. Should the need arise for an increase in cash, then purchasing can be adjusted accordingly. The proportion of liquid assets is maintained at approximately 28 per cent of customers' accounts; in Fig. 39 the subtotal shown for liquid assets is 27.6 per cent of total liabilities and 29.3 per cent of customers' accounts, i.e. £880m/£3,000m x 100 per cent. This is known as the banks' liquidity ratio.

Long term assets
Investments and subsidiaries are government securities which are

usually repayable in less than ten years. Their purchase is arranged so that they are constantly maturing; this assists the bank in that, should the need arise, it does not have to sell investments at an unfavourable price. Other investments a bank may make, either in finance houses or smaller banks, may also come into this category, e.g. Barclaycard.

Loans and advances have already been discussed in this chapter; they form the main source of a bank's profits. Such loans and advances are generally made to industry and individuals, although loans to exporters and foreign industry, which often have government guarantees, would also be included in this category. Loan interest rates in this category are usually $1 - 3$ per cent above the Bank of England's base lending rate, according to the amounts and risks involved.

Premises and equipment belonging to the bank are always shown at cost and not at the appreciated price due to increases in property prices. The difference in the value between the cost and the true value may be described as another form of reserve which is not shown in the accounts.

Special deposits with the Bank of England have already been discussed. They are part of the government's monetary controls designed to restrict banks' lending when necessary by taking cash out of the system.

Building societies

The main concern of building societies is with the provision of finance for private house purchases, but they are allowed to lend to private businesses providing such loans do not exceed 10 per cent of their total lending. The maximum loan is £15,000, which limits them to lending to small businesses such as restaurants and guest-houses. Their finance comes from individuals and business organisations investing money in the societies, who in turn lend it at a higher rate of interest to their customers in order to purchase property.

Insurance and pension companies

These companies are concerned with long-term investments that yield a sufficient return to meet the requirements of their investors and of the insurance claims that are made. They are largely concerned with the purchase of stocks, shares and debentures.

Council for Small Industries in Rural Areas (COSIRA)

COSIRA makes loans in specific rural areas to small businesses, sometimes in conjunction with other financial institutions. The maximum loan it can make is £35,000 for up to 85 per cent of the purchase price of premises, allowing up to 20 years for repayment. A special feature of this type of loan is that interest payments are not demanded at the outset, thus allowing the business to establish itself. They also make loans for up to seven years for the purchase of equipment.

Industrial and Commercial Finance Corporation (ICFC)
ICFC makes loans to industry of between £5,000 and £500,000 for up to 20 years. It has recently been increasing its interest in the catering industry.

Government organisations
The government set up the tourist boards (1969) and the National Enterprise Board (1975) to make grants to industry, the former being more applicable to the hotel and catering industry. The most notable contribution the government has made to the industry has been the Hotel Development Incentive Loan and Grant Scheme in 1966. It also makes loans to hostels and guest-houses to help them comply with the Fire Precautions Act (1971).

At present grants are available through the tourist boards, although they tend to be made for tourist developments. The European Economic Community (EEC) also makes grants for tourism projects through its Common Market Regional Aid Fund.

Breweries
Breweries will lend to an operation for 5 – 10 years at low interest rates, in exchange for which the operation has to buy their products. This is commonly known as "tie". The borrower will have to guarantee to purchase a certain amount from the brewery according to the sum borrowed, this sum being calculated by "barrelage", i.e. the volume of liquor purchased.

SOURCES OF FINANCE WITHIN A BUSINESS

We have examined the financial institutions that provide sources of finance for the development of industry. Now we must examine other methods by which finance can be raised.

Financial institutions provide what we call the external sources of finance. However businesses must look to their own operations as internal sources of finance; by making economies and manipulating their assets firms can effectively raise their own finance, and then use external sources to provide additional money.

Sale and leaseback
A business may sell its assets, e.g. its premises, to a finance company who then leases the asset back to the original owner who pays rent. This method is used when other methods of borrowing fail and the business is

perhaps in financial difficulties caused by inadequate cashflow. The business should ascertain that the income received from the sale of the asset, by way of profit, is higher than the rent paid for the use of it.

Leasing and renting assets

If it is not possible to purchase outright it is always possible to lease or rent equipment from suppliers, e.g. televisions, microwave ovens, etc. Many suppliers of food and drink will often lend, free of charge, equipment for the sale of their products, e.g. deep-freezers and chillers for drinks.

Leasing and renting is usually backed up by maintenance agreements. Care should be taken, however, regarding costs and ties involved in any agreements, as they can prove very expensive in the long run.

Trade creditors

The manipulation of trade creditors in order to increase finance is regarded by some as a dangerous practice; however if it is included as an integral part of managing a firm's working capital it can be effective.

The nature of the hotel and catering industry means that the majority of sales in most businesses are for cash. It is therefore possible to buy stocks of food and drink on credit and sell them for cash in order to settle the creditors' accounts at a later date. The disadvantages of using trade creditors are twofold: goods purchased on credit are often more expensive than those purchased for cash, and discounts are lost if accounts are not settled promptly.

Trade debtors

Any operation which gives credit to customers must keep a tight check as to who is given credit, in order to minimise bad debts. Systems and incentives should be installed to encourage quick and prompt payment, with regular monitoring.

Stocks

Stocks tie up the working capital of a business. There should therefore be a strict system of stock control in order to minimise the holding of unnecessarily large stocks. Suppliers should be chosen who offer regular delivery services to keep stocks to a minimum, and stocks should be rotated to eliminate waste, with maximum and minimum stock levels ascertained. High stock levels produce a low turnover, tying up capital which could be working more effectively elsewhere.

Cash

A business should avoid having large cash balances in its current account for long periods of time, as it will tie up business capital. If such a situation arises, cash in excess of normal day-to-day requirements should be transferred to a deposit account where it can at least gain interest.

BANKING SERVICES

We have considered, earlier in the chapter, the financial services the clearing banks offer with regard to deposit accounts and their involvement in the creation of bank credit. However the clearing banks themselves are commercial organisations, in competition with each other, and with shareholders to satisfy by way of dividend payments. An ever-increasing number of services are therefore being offered by the banks in order to attract the business of the man in the street as well as of large and small businesses. A range of the services offered by the different banks to their customers is explained below.

Current accounts

A current account allows an account-holder to move money from one place to another without having to handle any cash. The account-holder can be paid by cheque, can pay other people or organisations by cheque, and can use a cheque to withdraw cash from the bank for personal use and small day-to-day transactions. The bank issues account-holders with personal cheque books and paying-in books to use with their accounts.

Another feature of a current account is that the bank will make regular payments on behalf of its customers for such transactions as mortgage or hire purchase payments, subject to the customer's instructions. These are known as standing orders; the bank transfers fixed amounts of money from the customer's account to the account of the payee at the required intervals requested by the customer.

A similar service, known as direct-debiting, is also available. Again on the instruction of the account-holder the bank will transfer money from the account at the request of the person or organisation requiring payment, i.e. the payee. This procedure is used when regular payments have to be made but the amount varies from time to time, e.g. subscriptions to associations, etc.

The bank will send regular statements to its customers showing the transactions which have been made, both in and out of the account, and the final balance, which shows the amount currently held in the account.

Bank charges on the use of the account are made by the bank according to the number and type of transaction made by the account-holder, although most banks will forgo charges if the account-holder keeps a balance of more than £100 in the account at all times.

Cheque cards

Bank cheque cards are issued by the bank to customers at the manager's discretion. The purpose of such a card is to guarantee the payment of cheques by the bank. Providing the cheques are written for less than £50 and the shop, hotel or other bank follows a simple procedure when accepting the cheque, the issuing bank will honour the cheque. These cards were introduced some years ago when many shops and hotels started refusing cheques, there being no guarantee that a bank would honour them; this was due to abuse by many account-holders who had insufficient funds in their accounts to cover cheques written.

Barclays Bank do not issue a cheque card, cheques written by their account-holders being guaranteed by using Barclaycards as a dual purpose credit and cheque card.

Cash cards

Because of the increasing demand for banking services, coupled with the fact that banks are only open from 9.30 a.m. to 3.30 p.m. on Monday to Friday in most cases, the main clearing banks have introduced 24-hour service tills. Cash card-holders may obtain varying amounts of cash, subject to certain limits, from these tills at any time. The tills are secure for both the customer and the bank; the customer has a secret identity number which can only be used in conjuction with the card, while the bank has security as all transactions through its machines are controlled by one centrally-based computer which refuses to accept the card in the event of a customer exceeding his arrangement with the bank or if the card falls into the wrong hands and the wrong code number is used.

Other services offered by these machines vary from bank to bank, but they will usually issue customer balances and can be used for cheque-book requests in most cases.

Credit cards

The main clearing banks now issue their own credit cards which can be used for obtaining cash, goods and services in some 200,000 retail outlets throughout the country. Credit card-holders can then either pay for these services after receiving their monthly statement or defer payments over a period of time, subject to credit limits. For credit card-holders who defer payments, interest is charged on their outstanding balance each month. Retail outlets who accept credit cards have to pay a small commission, usually 2 – 3 per cent, to the card company, but in return have guaranteed payment.

The two credit cards that are linked to the clearing banks in this country are Barclaycard, available to customers of Barclays Bank and

Trustee Savings Bank, and Access, available to the customers of the other clearing banks, i.e. National Westminster, Midland, Lloyds, etc. Diners Club, although owned by the Midland Bank, is a different type of credit card in as much as holders have to pay an annual subscription and are not allowed to defer payment. However there is no financial limit applied to use of the card.

Foreign currency
Most banks now have a financial travel service for their customers, providing foreign currency, travellers cheques and cheque guarantee cards in the form of Eurocheque cards. Due to the increase in foreign travel, both into and out of this country, the banks have rapidly increased this service, with many smaller branches now having foreign exchange tills.

Budget accounts
Budget accounts in some form or other are now available from all banks. These accounts allow customers to group regular and irregular payments, made throughout the year, into a single monthly payment from their current account.

All payments for such expenditure as mortgages, rates, fuel bills, insurance and subscriptions are totalled into an annual amount divided into 12 monthly payments. The bank sets up a separate budget account for this purpose, making a small charge for the facility. This allows the customer to plan his or her monthly income and expenditure, knowing that essential payments are budgeted for and thus avoiding any worry and inconvenience.

Loans
The banks have a variety of lending services available to their customers, ranging from mortgages for house purchase to cash loans for the purchase of motor vehicles, furniture, electrical equipment, etc. These loans are subject to varying interest rates according to the amount and period of borrowing. To support these services the banks provide consulting facilities to their customers, offering financial planning according to the type of loan they require.

Investment services
The banks have their own investment companies to advise on their customers' savings and suggest how they may be invested to gain maximum interest and capital appreciation. They have a wide choice of schemes to suit different types of investor, ranging from savings schemes to unit trust schemes and stockbroking services.

Insurance services

The banks can provide different types of insurance, either through their own insurance subsidiaries or via links with national insurance companies. In some cases the banks require insurance as a security for the loans they grant, or they may suggest an insurance scheme as a method of saving. Other types of insurance advice and cover on offer include household and house contents insurance, personal accident cover, motor vehicle and boat insurance and life assurance.

Other services

Other services that banks offer include:

(a) taxation advice with regard to income tax, capital gains tax, capital transfer tax, etc.;

(b) advice regarding the making of wills, as well as acting as executors of their customers' estates through their trustee departments;

(c) safe deposit facilities through which customers can deposit valuables, e.g. legal documents, jewellery, etc., in the banks' vaults.

Business services

Whilst all businesses require the use of the banking services mentioned above, the banks also offer other services of varying forms to business customers.

Financial advice and the negotiating of loans, either through their own departments or in conjunction with other institutions and government departments is their primary activity, as explained in detail earlier in the chapter. The banks obviously play a prominent role in this because of their knowledge of the business and of the locality in which it operates. They are also able to assist and provide advice in overseas operations, foreign exchange, transfer of funds abroad and exchange controls between different countries throughout the world. Some banks offer computer services to businesses, e.g. in the provision of ledger services for sales and purchases, credit accounting, payroll calculation and transactions, pensions, cashflow controls, etc.

It is naturally in the banks' best interests to provide such services for their customers as it allows profitable utilisation of their resources and generates further use of bank services by both the business and employees alike.

SELF-ASSESSMENT QUESTIONS

1. Explain the functions of the Bank of England.
2. Explain the functions of the clearing banks.
3. Explain the functions of the other financial institutions.

4. Explain how banks create credit.

5. List the external sources of finance available to the catering industry.

6. List the internal sources of finance that are available to the unit.

7. List the services offered by the banks to their customers.

CHAPTER TWENTY

The Industry and Change

THE EFFECTS OF SOCIAL CHANGE

Concluding remarks invariably take stock of what has been said as well as making careful projections about possible future developments. In making our concluding remarks, then, we will attempt to assess the effects of social changes and observe the way in which the hotel and catering industry is responding to the various changes that are occurring.

We have seen throughout the preceding chapters the way in which various forms of social change have affected the catering industry. Our understanding of the industry today, or indeed at any time, will require an analysis of events leading up to and affecting the conditions of that time; if a given trend has led to the present state of affairs, it will be valid to predict the future on the basis of the continuation of this trend. A simple example will serve to illustrate this point. A hotel manager, in budgeting for the year ahead, may notice that in recent years there has been an increasing demand in his hotel from the business sector from Monday to Friday. In anticipation of this trend continuing in the future he may provide services and facilities, e.g. convenient telephone access, conference facilities, business luches, etc. not only to accommodate this demand but possibly to increase it in the future.

The realisation that social change is continuous, and in many areas accelerating, should prepare us for certain future projections. An awareness of these changes will also enable us to recognise that customer demand is constantly changing, and this in turn will enable us to keep abreast of it. As service and accommodation provisions adapt to cater for ever-changing customer demand, it should also be possible for innovative and alert management to think ahead, preparing for these new demands in advance and perhaps even creating new demands on their own initiative.

THE DIMENSIONS OF CHANGE

We have so far referred to social change in rather broad terms. In order to consider fully the effects of change on the industry we must carefully examine the dimensions of change. These are various, and we will examine each of them briefly in turn, bearing in mind that the changes that affect the industry will be of two basic kinds. The first will be changes which occur in response to changes in the wider environment, e.g. changing customer demand. The second will be changes occurring within the industry itself; these are generated by the industry but may create changes outside the industry. An example might be a purpose-designed speciality restaurant with changing six-monthly or yearly themes; this would have the effect of generating its own eating-out trends amongst customers rather than simply responding to their demands.

With an awareness of these different effects of change we will now consider the different dimensions of change and give some indication of likely future trends.

Economic changes

Economic considerations are of primary importance to an analysis of any industry. By adopting macro- and micro-economic perspectives we have already considered some of the more important economic aspects of unit operation and of the industry itself. From these considerations we ought to be aware that certain changes are likely to occur in the economic environment which will have the effect of bringing about changes within the industry.

International trends

On an international scale, levels of affluence are apparently increasing as developing countries industrialise and become more "advanced". This has the effect of generating fluctuating levels of surplus money amongst the population of these countries, much of which will be attracted to a developing leisure industry. The development of international travel and tourism is a reflection of these increasing levels of international affluence. The hotel and catering industry clearly needs to respond to this by attracting tourists from these developing countries and opening up markets for new customer demand.

The United States is one of the most popular tourist destinations in the world; in the 1970s the influx of visitors to the USA increased by 75 per cent. Clearly, many factors are responsible for this growth but the overall economic effects are large; remember that tourism makes a considerable contribution to the balance of payments of any nation. Thus the hotel and catering industry is provided with a potential growth area producing increased income if only it can exploit this sort of expanding market.

Traditionally, international tourist demand in Britain has originated in the European and American markets, although it is only in recent years that the British hotel and catering industry has fully begun to exploit the potential for attracting tourists. However there is still a need for the British industry to use advanced marketing techniques to attract tourists from a wider range of countries; international tourism to Britain still tends to be characterised by the American or German tourist "doing" the "tourist triangle" of Edinburgh, Stratford and London. The setting up of the regional tourist boards had the effect of introducing tourists to a wider range of places of interest and resorts and, as this trend continues, hotel and catering establishments throughout the country will need to respond to new and developing consumer needs.

The decline of the traditional British resort holiday and the growing trend for Britons to take cheap package holidays abroad illustrates clearly the effect of not being aware of changing demands and outside competition. The survival of any industry depends not only on its ability to compete in the domestic markets but also in the international market. The hotel and catering industry is no exception.

Domestic trends

The success of hotel and catering establishments is obviously not wholly dependent upon their ability to respond to the international market; the same set of rules detailed above applies equally to the domestic market. Put simply, keeping abreast of domestic demand is vital if an establishment is to remain economically viable. The decline of the traditional British seaside holiday, as previously stated, is an illustration of the need for the industry in general, and the various units of operation in particular, to respond to the changes that may be occurring.

Population changes

Population changes will always influence demand. In Britain the population at present is relatively stable; the birth rate is showing a declining trend while the life expectancy of the population is increasing. This the economists refer to as an increasing dependency ratio; quite simply, the proportion of the overall population who depend upon the working population for their livelihood is increasing. In 1951 there were 6.8 million people aged 65 and over in Britain; by 1983 this figure had reached 9.6 million. If we add to this statistic the fact that the retirement age is now dropping to 60 or 55 in some industries, then the number of dependents is clearly seen to be increasing.

The significance of this trend for the hotel and catering industry is broad ranging. The population's dependence upon the state will inevitably increase, so the demands upon certain forms of welfare catering will increase also. Hospital catering, the development of residential homes for the aged and the possible expansion of the voluntary welfare sector, including such services as meals on wheels, are all areas that the industry needs to pay attention to. From the point of view of the commercial sector, an ageing, dependent population, which remains relatively active and affluent, represents a possible growth market. Many resorts on the Mediterranean coast of France and Spain, and the holiday islands of Mallorca and Ibiza, already cater for this more elderly market and as a result are now busy throughout the year rather than just during the short summer season. Holiday companies offer cheap package holidays to these resorts, often at rates that make it cheaper than staying at home in Britain. The benefits are many; for the holiday company, for the tourists themselves, who may not normally be able to afford a Mediterranean holiday, and for the tourist destination, which is able to extend its holiday season. An additional factor here is that, unlike younger customers, the elderly customer is essentially a dependent customer, requiring the complete resources of the hotel, not only for accommodation but also for catering, entertainment and other general services.

Some holiday companies have responded to this by attempting to exploit the possible holiday needs of the relatively affluent elderly person who does not wish to travel abroad. Holiday camps may offer reduced off-season rates, while other companies may make use of university accommodation which would normally be empty for the long summer vacation, enabling tourists to visit historic university towns such as Edinburgh or Canterbury.

Another significant population trend which needs to be considered is the gradual depopulation of some inner urban areas. The growth of new towns and the development of suburban areas has reversed the major trend of urbanisation that occurred through the nineteenth and early twentieth centuries. This trend has meant that inner urban areas of many major cities are increasingly becoming commercial and industrial zones. This places a demand on the industry to cater for a working population rather than for those holidaying or on visits. The growth of highly efficient fast food outlets is a response to the customer need for a quick, wholesome and relatively inexpensive meal. The fast food outlet also appeals to the shopper who only enters the commercial centre of a city for a short period of time and who requires a quick meal as part of the shopping trip.

This development of the fast food outlet, meeting the demands of the busy urban worker or shopper, has partly been associated with the growth of franchising in Britain. This trend has enabled independent operators to establish a business for themselves with all the assistance that the franchise organisation can offer. For a small investment the individual operator receives national or international advertising, staff training facilities, tried and tested marketing techniques and all the advantages that a large successful franchise organisation can offer. The advantages of the system accrue to the franchising organisations as well, who have an individual investor developing an establishment instead of a unit manager who may not be so highly motivated, not having made any financial investment. The customer will also recognise certain advantages whenever he visits, say, a Wimpy fast food outlet or a Holiday Inn hotel; he will know that the food product, the service, the decor and the price of what he is buying will be of a certain standard and, providing this standard reaches his requirements, then he is likely to return to this type of establishment on a number of occasions. The franchising system, which originated in the United States in the 1950s, is playing an increasingly influential part in the development of hotel and catering establishments in Britain.

The final point we should consider in relation to the population of Britain is the possibility of a population of whom a certain percentage may be permanently unemployed. Many economists have argued that high levels of unemployment may become a fact of life in our society, and a number of recent trends tend to support this view, e.g. the decreasing labour intensity of industry linked to increasing automation and computerisation and the current laissez-faire nature of the British economy which seems to operate successfully with high levels of unemployment. The likelihood of a section of the population being permanently unemployed, at least for some part of their lives, is increasing as the twentieth century passes.

This unemployment may take a number of forms. We have already seen that early retirement is being introduced in some industries; other possibilities include job sharing and a shorter working week. Whatever form this unemployment takes it is likely that, as a result, we shall see a further growth in the leisure industries; in simple terms a four-day working week means a three-day non-working week.

The increasing length and number of holidays taken by British working people will invariably be linked to an increasing demand on the hotel and catering establishments and on the leisure and recreational industries. This may be seen both on a small scale, e.g. the development of family public houses or keep fit centres, and on a large scale, e.g. the building of leisure complexes incorporating a complete range of facilities such as restaurants, shops, sports facilities, entertainments, etc.

Changes in the composition, movement and distribution of the population require consideration from a national and international perspective. As many more countries throughout the world begin to generate tourism, the competition for tourist markets will increase, further emphasising the need for the providers of accommodation and catering services to keep abreast of all new developments. Tourism no longer represents a random set of unrelated phenomena which can be exploited in a relatively relaxed manner; it is now an all-embracing industry which has become increasingly competitive and market-orientated.

Technological innovation

The twentieth century has seen an ever-increasing acceleration in the development of ideas and improvements in all technological fields. To keep abreast of all these developments would represent an impossible task, but we must consider here some of the technological innovations that are likely to affect the hotel and catering industry in the immediate future.

We have already looked at the way in which automated systems, by reducing labour intensity in manufacturing industry, have indirectly sent more customers in the direction of the leisure industry in general and the hotel and catering industry in particular. These automated systems have increased productivity and leisure time; it is to be expected that such systems will also be developed to improve the quality of the service that hotel and catering establishments can provide. Until recently, many operations have argued that to install an automated system into a food production unit or a computer system into a hotel would have been too costly. However, the relative diminishing cost of installing hotel computer systems means that many hotels are now implementing such sophisticated systems. It is envisaged that as the cost of computer systems continues to decline their use will be implemented in smaller-scale operations as well as in the large-scale operations that use them at present.

The effects of this are numerous. It is expected that the installation and smooth operation of such systems will improve the overall quality of service. Reductions in manpower will inevitably result and the relative labour intensity of the hotel and catering industry will decline as a result, representing a long-term financial saving for employers. In the initial stages at least, increased staff training, both on and off the job, will have to be carried out to ensure that the new computerised systems operate efficiently. This will be supplemented by periodic in-service training courses to ensure that staff operating these systems are continually aware of and able to cope with the rapid developments that will inevitably take place in this field.

Revolutionary forms of computer technology will inevitably spearhead many changes in all industries in the coming years, but we should particularly focus upon the many labour-saving devices from which the catering industry will also benefit. Among these we may point to the following as being most significant. The implementation of sophisticated electronic security systems represents a saving in manpower and, it is likely, an improvement in efficiency. Many hotels are now implementing automatic room service systems, which again dispense with manpower and considerably improve the convenience of the service. Automatic cash registers are increasingly being used, allowing smoother customer flow and more efficient cash calculations to take place.

The growth of obsolescence will mean that many items used in hotel and catering establishments will be disposable. By removing the high cost of maintenance and repair, replacement costs for such things as linen, uniforms, carpets, furnishings, etc., will be more easily met. Once again staffing will be affected, albeit to a lesser degree. The use of paper tablecloths and napkins, for example, represents a substantial saving in laundering costs.

In other areas we can see technological advances being made from which the catering industry can only benefit. A good illustration is the development of high quality, prefabricated building materials, enabling new buildings, extensions, etc., to be built in shorter and shorter periods of time. All these developments, and others, create benefits for the hotel and catering industry as a whole, although in certain areas disadvantages can be seen.

Changes in manpower

Developments in manpower in the hotel and catering industry will inevitably take place as a consequence of technological innovation. The most obvious effect will be a reduction in manpower within the industry, so that the labour-intensive nature of the industry may well begin to change. Many routine tasks such as account tabulation and stocktaking will become computerised, reducing man-hours appreciably and eliminating the element of human error, which in itself can often increase the amount of time taken to do a particular task.

The hotel and catering industry is not one in which we can envisage the reduction of human influence to such minimal levels as may be possible in some areas of manufacturing industry. In providing a service, various hotel and catering establishments specifically require the human element to ensure the personal touch, which in turn tends to enhance customer satisfaction. However a likely trend in staffing which could occur as a consequence of automation is the increasing specialisation of staff. As previously mentioned, many of the routine elements will be taken away from hotel and catering operations, leaving the field open for an increasingly specialised labour market. Such staff may share their specialist skills between a number of units or perhaps work on a consultancy basis, providing highly professional advice and instruction to a number of affiliated units.

These kinds of manpower developments pave the way for an elimination of many of the unskilled areas of the industry, while at the same time allowing for the growth and exploitation of specialist skills and knowledge. This development will only take place as long as customer satisfaction is maintained and indeed improved. The personal quality of the successful hotel and catering establishment will therefore have to be maintained by ensuring that staff are trained in the human skills and are able to continue to provide the personal service that customers demand.

Technological innovations and developments might also have a detrimental effect on the hotel and catering industry. Many traditional forms of entertainment such as bingo halls and cinemas have declined due to the growth of "private" forms of entertainment, starting with television, continuing with the video explosion of the 1980s and possibly being continued with the advent of cable television.

Declining family size and the geographical mobility of these small families often creates isolation from the rest of the family and from other social contacts. This trend can also be linked with the growth of home-centred entertainments, as outlined above, and suggests that many traditional forms of public entertainment may further decline. If this is the case then it may be the responsibility of the various branches of the leisure industry to regenerate an interest in less private forms of recreation and entertainment.

Education and training

In many respects the future of the catering industry lies in the appropriate skills and knowledge being obtained by young people as they enter the industry. This acquisition of skills and knowledge should also incorporate a broader understanding of the various factors that contribute to change so that, not only will all areas of education and training respond to the various changes occurring throughout the industry, but they will also go on to generate these changes within the industry. We may demonstrate this by the use of two simple examples.

The growth of computer technology and its introduction into many areas of the hotel and catering industry has meant that colleges, examining bodies, training boards, etc., have had to respond to the growing demand from the industry for staff able to use the various forms of computer technology being implemented.

Many catering departments of colleges of further education are now introducing a Business and Technician Education Council (BTEC) certificate course as part of traditional City and Guilds 706/1/2 general catering courses. This innovative scheme enables general catering students, if they are so motivated, to obtain BTEC certification, which in turn will improve their position in an increasingly competitive job market. In addition, these same students at a later stage may improve their BTEC qualification from a certificate to a diploma by studying for and adding certain units. The Business and Technician Education Council is currently introducing a "top up" scheme so that part-time day-release students will be able to carry out this kind of process. The introduction of such a scheme will enable today's craft student to obtain a BTEC qualification in later years and thus develop his career.

Response and innovation

There are many ways in which catering education and training can therefore be both responsive and innovative; indeed it is important that all educational and training establishments should foster this approach.

Responsiveness can be cultivated by maintaining links with industry, at both local and national levels, by being alert to the industry's changing demands and by responding to them quickly and efficiently. We have seen the many ways that the industry is likely to change in the future in order to service an increasingly diverse range of customer demands. Accordingly, the various educational and training establishments will also have to change to satisfy the changing demands of industry.

Educational and training establishments also contain many individuals who are alert to the changes previously described and who, in addition, may be able to anticipate future trends. Such anticipation may lead to innovations such as the setting up of new educational and training schemes, e.g. distance learning and "open tech", or perhaps lesiure-orientated courses such as wine tasting and continental cuisine operated on a cost effective basis for the unemployed.

Such an approach, incorporating response and innovation, will ensure that hotel and catering education and training establishments will continue to satisfy the industry's demand for a skilled and qualified workforce as well as generate many new ideas and approaches that may lead the industry into a variety of new directions in the future.

SELF-ASSESSMENT QUESTIONS

1. Describe the way in which possible future trends may be predicted.

2. Define the "dependency ratio".

3. What is the significance of the "dependency ratio" to the hotel and catering industry?

4. Describe two advantages and two disadvantages of introducing automated systems into the hotel and catering industry.

5. Describe three significant changes in manpower that may occur in the hotel and catering industry.

6. Explain the possible effects of home-centred entertainment on the hotel and catering industry.

7. Give your own examples to illustrate the way in which educational and training establishments may (a) respond to changes occurring within the industry, and (b) innovate changes in the industry itself.

Index